Spirit Calling
Every Morning

LISTENING TO GOD WITHIN YOU

MICHAEL WUEHLER

Paperback: 978-1-969919-06-0
Hardcover: 978-1-969919-08-4
eBook: 978-1-969919-07-7
Library of Congress Control Number: 2025921388

This is a work of nonfiction.

Ordering Information:

Prime Seven Media
518 Landmann St.
Tomah City, WI 54660

Printed in the United States of America

To Megan and Melissa

I have been blessed and gifted by God beyond my expectations. The greatest gift I received was the gift of my two daughters, Megan and Melissa. They both continue to bring joy to my heart and delight to my soul. Thank you girls.

Lectio Divina

Does God talk to everyone? Yes, if we listen. God has not dropped the art of divine conversation; we tend not to listen as well as we could. Prayer is our opportunity to talk to God. My guess is many people talk to God daily through formal prayers and less formal passing thoughts.

When connecting to God, we tend to fall short in listening, meditation, or contemplation. Contemplation or meditation allows us to listen to what God says to us. While I use a variety of forms of meditation and contemplation, I use *Lectio Divina*, or Divine reading, when I write the Spirit Calling series.

You can quickly learn this ancient Christian spiritual practice from the monastic tradition. I have included the steps to encounter the Spirit of God in my writing and life. I encourage you to try Lectio Divina with the daily Bible verses you find in this book. Go ahead; God is waiting to talk to you if you listen.

1. Preparation
Begin by finding a quiet place where you can sit comfortably without distractions.
Take a few moments to relax and clear your mind. You might want to take a few deep breaths or pray briefly to prepare your heart and mind for this spiritual exercise.

2. Read (Lectio)
Choose a passage of scripture. This could be a few verses or a more extended passage. Many practitioners recommend starting with the Gospels or Psalms.
Read the passage slowly. Pay attention to each word and phrase. Read it multiple times if necessary, to let the words sink in.
As you read, notice any word or phrase that stands out to you. This could strike you as curious, comforting, challenging, or intriguing.

3. Meditate (Meditatio)
Reflect on the word or phrase that stood out to you. Mull it over in your mind.

Ask yourself what God might be saying through this word or phrase. Consider how it applies to your current life circumstances.
Allow this meditation to move from an intellectual exercise to a more personal dialogue with God.

4. Pray (Oratio)
Respond to the insights you've gained by talking to God in prayer. Express your thoughts, feelings, desires, and challenges to God as they relate to the passage.
This step involves forming a personal response to God's word and fostering a deeper relationship with God.

5. Contemplate (Contemplatio)
End with a period of contemplation, sitting quietly in God's presence. Unlike meditation, which involves active thought, contemplation is more about resting in God's love and peace. It's a time to be with God and allow God to work in you.
If your mind starts to wander, gently bring it back to focus on God's presence.

6. Resolution (Actio)
While not traditionally listed as one of the main steps, many modern practitioners include a resolution as a practical application of Lectio Divina.
Think of how to carry the insights or peace you have received into your everyday life. This could involve a specific action, a change in attitude, or an initiative to improve your spiritual practices.

7. Closure
Conclude your session with a prayer of thanksgiving for the insights you received and for the time you spent in communion with God.
If you're in a group, you might share your reflections to deepen the communal experience.

Lectio Divina is a flexible practice that can be adapted to your personal spiritual rhythm and the available time. It's not about achieving perfection in the steps but rather about growing closer to God through His Word.

Spirit Calling
Every Morning
A Daily Devotional

Michael Wuehler

JANUARY 1

*A*re you up, My sacred heart? I've been by your side all night, just watching you as you slumbered. I've prayed for you every moment through the inky darkness of the night. I did not utter spoken words, as you may imagine. My prayers are for sharing my spiritual essence and divine energy with My beloved children like you. You receive My best as your body sleeps, your mind slumbers and your soul rests. You may not feel or know it, but I am at work in your life every night.

I work throughout each night to prepare you for the next day. Yet, some people stay in bed and dream about what they might accomplish. Others rise from their beds and seek to fulfill their dreams. Which path to your dreams will you take today, My blessed child?

You are ready to accomplish much. I spent all night just getting you prepared for this glorious day. The rest is up to you. Let this be your first day of creating something unique.

Work like God and create something special today.

God called the light "day" and the darkness "night." And there was evening, and there was **morning**—the first day. (Genesis 1:5 NIV)

JANUARY 2

Can you see what power each morning has? The light of day allows you to see the accomplishments and achievements ahead. The red rays of the morning sun illuminate your workbench of life. No matter what you do, your handy work can be seen and enjoyed in the light of the day. Learn to enjoy your work and celebrate your accomplishments. Learn to say," It is good." Or even dare to boast that "It is very good."

Too many of My children sit out from the dance of Holy Celebration. Learning to dance to your creation's music will place you in step with your work and alignment with Me. The daylight shines so you can see what "Very good" looks like. "Very Good" is the glory of each sunrise, and "Very Good" is the majesty of every sunset. Learn to expect the "Very Good I have placed in each day, and you will soon recognize the "very Good in your daily living.

Make this a "Very Good" God Day.

God saw all that he had made, and it was very good. And there was evening, and there was **morning**—the sixth day. (Genesis 1:31 NIV)

JANUARY 3

*J*acob found the connection between heaven and earth in a dream. Moved and inspirited by the nocturnal encounter, Jacob raised a monument to the occasion. Remember, I am easily assessable, either day or night. Do not be disturbed or frightened by an encounter during your waking hours. I am ever-present and always available to you. Let prayer be your first call for help or your initial invitation to connect with Me. Remember that prayer is as much for your benefit as it is for Mine, My sacred heart.

The distance between heaven and earth can easily be traveled by spiritual means. Too many believe that connecting with Me is such a hard thing or a heavy burden. Jacob took an ordinary rock and turned it into a sacred stone. Is your imagination willing to treat this place and time as a holy encounter with Me? Open your eyes to the possibilities of what each day can bring. I just might be found in your very ordinary living. Don't hold yourself back from these sacred seconds; draw close to Me, for I am already with you.

You can encounter God at any time or in any place. Why not now and here?

Early the next **morning** Jacob took the stone he had placed under his head and set it up as a pillar and poured oil on top of it. (Genesis 28:18)

JANUARY 4

*W*hile Job's sacrifices were well-intended, he thought the worst of his children. Job focused on the possible sins of his children rather than on the potential good works they could do. I always send you out into the day, hoping you will do your best in My name. Sin surely awaits you but then so does success. Choose wisely between the two as if you were choosing life and death. I always leave the choice to you.

Let your daily custom become one of looking for the good in people. I bless each ray of sunlight with golden bliss and holy love. I hope that the sunlight will illuminate the inherent good each person has within them. I hope all my children will find a blessing in their hearts that will give cause for rejoicing and celebration. Come to Me early in the morning with the sacrifice of your love for Me, and your day will reveal its blessings to you.

Expect each day to bring its unique wealth of God's blessings.

When a period of feasting had run its course, Job would make arrangements for them to be purified. Early in the **morning,** he would sacrifice a burnt offering for each of them, thinking, "Perhaps my children have sinned and cursed God in their hearts." This was Job's regular custom. (Job 1:5 NIV)

JANUARY 5

I make My love fresh for you every mooring, My dear heart. Your sins of the past or former transgressions will not rise with you. My compassion is renewed in the gentle evening breeze and restored with the morning sun. I look only for the golden rays of sunlight that bring My forgiveness; I fail to see the night of sin. Let Me create a new life in you just as I recreate each day. Too many of my children sleep with shame and guilt as their blanket and pillow each night. Please know that the human emotions of shame and guilt are house guests of your selection; they are entirely unnecessary for your comfort.

This cycle of My faithful forgiving love is available to all who seek Me. Seek My compassion each night and receive My grace every morning. I do not hold back My love from anyone. My compassionate love adorns the stars, and My faithful forgiveness awakens with the morning sunlight. Rise each day with the assurance that something great and something new awaits you. I have planned it that way and created it to be so.

God's compassion can be found in every sunrise.

Because of the Lord's great love, we are not consumed, for his compassions never fail. They are new every **morning**; great is your faithfulness. (Lamentations 3:22-23 NIV)

January 6

*T*he men received instructions to dig in the dry stream bed. The result of their labors would reveal no wind, no rain, and no water. Yet, they dug just the same. They did not dig with hands and feet or shovels and tools. They excavated the dusty dry stream bed with faith. Faith prepared the way for what was about to happen; water would come forth. Do you have the confidence to labor throughout this day to receive tomorrow's riches? You hold no tools in your Hand; what you need is found in the heart, My sacred heart.

Not all my riches take the form of money or gold. The greatest blessings can take the shape of family or friends. I may ask you to dig where there is little chance of unearthing the hidden water for which your soul thirsts. Wait in faithful obedience, for the water will come to those who stand fast and trust in Me. Begin every day as a seeker equipped only with the tools of faith. Expect to find each day running over with My richness. I did not lead you this far only to take you this far; there is much more to come.

Faith can unearth the hidden treasures of God.

The next **morning**, about the time for offering the sacrifice, there it was—water flowing from the direction of Edom! And the land was filled with water. (2 Kings 3:20 NIV)

JANUARY 7

*M*y anger is present only at the moment you think it exists. You weep and cry throughout the night because you believe I am angry with you. Tears flood your pillow with droplets of fear as you contemplate My anger. The fear is your own. I have no offense or seek no revenge. I come to you with pardon and love. Why is forgiveness such a problematic notion for you to understand? Divine forgiveness naturally flows out of grace; both are products of My love.

Let the early morning light reveal a lifetime of love and favor I have toward you. Begin rejoicing now and let your fears slip into the darkness of the night.

Always be aware that any negative feelings you think I may have toward you are figments of your all too human imagination. I am composed of light and love; do not imagine Me in darkness and despair. I have heard your cries in the evening; I will dry your tears this very morning. If you must imagine anything about Me, consider that My love always outlasts your fear. As your fear that I won't forgive you passes in the night, the realization of My steadfast love awaits you with the kiss of the morning sun.

The morning sun has the power to reveal God's love toward you. Let every evening pass into a new day.

For his anger lasts only a moment, but his favor lasts a lifetime; weeping may stay for the night, but rejoicing comes in the **morning**. (Psalm 30:5 NIV)

January 8

*O*ne day can be a game-changer. Wake up tomorrow with the notion that I am with you, and your soul will sing a new tune. Your soul becomes satisfied knowing that My love is constant and is a lifelong gift. This knowledge will stir your soul and satisfy your hungry heart for the rest of your life. You will no longer dread the morning sun, thinking this will just be another useless day. I make morning sunrises to be spectacular and breathtaking. The morning bird sings tunes of glory at the first ray of golden sunlight. Only My children find dread in the morning rays and roll their meads back under their pillows.   Sadly, so many miss the miraculous minor miracle morning light show.

Learn to sing this song of the heart, and your soul will carry the tune of joy throughout the day. The world will not have changed, but the way you see the world will appear very different. Begin each day by seeing possibilities rather than obstacles; life will be different. Where there was lack, you will find abundance. Where you felt hate, you will encounter My unfailing love. Learn to see the world through My eyes, and you will genuinely behold the full beauty of My creation. Learn to search for My Love each morning, and then you will find a reason to sing like the Song Thrush.

The morning light changes nothing from the evening darkness.
Only your perception can alter your worldview.

Satisfy us in the **morning** with your unfailing love, that we may sing for joy and be glad all our days. (Psalm 90:14 NIV)

January 9

*D*on't let any day come and go and not cling to My side, My sacred heart. Your early morning devotions soon give way to the full light of the day. The words you read, the songs you sing, and the prayers you speak all have a way of letting the business of each day push them aside. Time spent with Me each morning should not disappear with the day's heat. The deeper we go, the longer our spiritual food will last. Let me touch your soul as deeply as your breakfast filled your stomach. Your soul thirsts for more when you are drained of your inner vitality. Just as the stomach growls and groans when empty, the spirit rumbles and roars, seeking essence as well.

Be mindful that when you encounter Me each morning, you take on a spiritual essence and energy to overcome any earthly distraction. The world pushes at your soul and will eagerly enter your life at any opportunity. Remain steadfast in Me rather than giving yourself over to worldly concerns. Believe in the devotions you read and the prayers you say, and the day will often turn into My blessing. Let your day begin and end in Me. I do not disappear or evaporate in with day's heat. When your body and soul have proper nutrition, it is impressive how far you can travel in one day.

Expect to meet and find what you prayed for at some time during the day.

"What can I do with you, Ephraim? What can I do with you, Judah? Your love is like the **morning** mist, like the early dew that disappears. (Hosea 6:4 NIV)

JANUARY 10

*T*he morning has a way of bringing everyone a fresh start and a new perspective on life. Each sunrise marks a new day and the promise of fresh possibilities. The memories of yesterday's problems can dissolve into the distant past. Be mindful of this cycle of letting go of the old and embracing the new with the dawn of each day. The process held on each new day reminds you that you, too, can become a new creation. Never forget this holy process of baptizing the soul of its sins. Your body was washed in the glory of the blood of the blessed Savior. You felt the three waves of water over you as you were claimed in the Trinity's divine name. You bear the sign and seal of holy baptism, and your sins are forgiven. Baptism is an outward sign of what I am doing inside of you. The darkness of sin is redeemed with the forgiveness that I give without hesitation. My redemption can be as deliberate as the sunrise. As assuredly as the sun will rise each morning to kiss the earth, my forgiveness will bless you like a holy kiss on the top of your head. Never stray far from Me, for I am your sustainer of life. Be assured that my work continues in you to cleanse the soul of all earthly impurities. Your sins are forgiven if you believe in your exterior washing through baptism and inner cleansing by spiritual sanctification. I did my work for you; all that is left is for you to believe it is so.

Each morning reminds us that God makes all things new in our lives.

I have swept away your offenses like a cloud, your sins like the **morning** mist. Return to me, for I have redeemed you." (Isiah 44:22 NIV)

January 11

*T*he clouds and morning sunlight join to give a warning for inclement weather. Your eyes have been trained over the years to recognize these weather patterns. Can your eyes also bear witness to the signs of the times? Hunger, starvation, poverty, sickness, injustice, and racism all lead to an interpretation that things need to change. These are all signs of human inception that point to the possible appearance of the need for drastic change.

These dramatic signs of a frightening future can all change. The change begins with you. Be assured that I do not blame you for these social ills, but all change begins with the individual.

   Each individual has the responsibility to exterminate all of these deadly signs from his or her life. Do not allow any of these social forces of destruction to take over your life.

Do all you can to reduce or eliminate them from your community. Every generation has to interpret the signs that lead to social decay. Every generation must do as much as possible to remove these signs. Will you help?

   The first step toward help and change is to see your neighbor through My eyes. Put on My love-colored glasses that see everyone as a blessed part of My creation. When your eyes see only love, the future will change.

The negative behaviors of society can point to a destructive future. Change your behavior, and you will change your future.

and in the **morning,** 'Today it will be stormy, for the sky is red and overcast.' You know how to interpret the appearance of the sky, but you cannot interpret the signs of the times. (Matthew 16:3 NIV)

JANUARY 12

$\mathscr{B}$e ready to hear my voice every morning. As my follower, I will instruct you in my daily plans. Do not worry; my instructions are simple, and My plan is focused. My teachings and goal for you today are to "Love with all your heart." To represent Me through your life, you must learn to love with genuine ferocity. Do not snicker or sneer that you are unworthy to serve Me. I call you as you are and will sanctify you into something more significant. A tax collector, fisherman, tent maker, and people who thought less of themselves than I did heard my call. I call men and women to be far more than they ever imagined. You are more than enough and rightly suited for the task at hand. I do not require perfection or greatness; all I need is a mustard seed of faith; let us begin there.

Let "I love you" become a typical phrase from your mouth. Let random acts of loving kindness become an unsuspecting blessing to friends and strangers alike. Let your love bring forth other emotions that can forever change your life and world. Love can bring forth joy, happiness, gratitude, compassion, and boundless hope for all my children. I know it may not appear to be such a grand plan, but person by person, My grand scheme can change the world. What began with the carpenter from Nazareth was revealed as a Messiah from Jerusalem and the Savior of the world. My plan starts with you today.

As you leave your home, remember that you are a chosen disciple of God. Do try to act like one.

When **morning** came, he called his disciples to him and chose twelve of them, whom he also designated apostles: (Luke 6:13 NIV)

January 13

*P*eople have been gathering in the mornings to hear My voice for centuries. It may be easier for you to listen to Me in the mornings before all the clatter of a busy day disrupts your life. The morning has not put a stranglehold on your day, and you are not required to fulfill your schedule somewhere. Use the freedom each morning can afford you to meet with Me. Listen to My voice whispers above the songbird's sound. Morning words have the power to set the tone for your entire day. Listen to My words rather than sitting in front of the TV every morning while you sip your coffee. Find a spare moment to inhale the freshness of each day I bring to you. You may look at the day as a series of appointments to connect. I see the day as an empty canvas to paint your life. Any place can be your temporary temple. You don't need anything fancy; locations become sacred because of My presence, not due to any decorations or religious icons. I am the Spirit of Life and can be found among the living. Gather with like-spirited people when you can, but know I am available to you anytime. Come and sit beside Me and listen to My words of hope for you. The temple was meant for many of My children to receive My words; this magnificent morning meeting is intended for your ears and heart. My children traveled far to the Temple to pray; I come to you to be closer to you than your hands or feet and more a part of you than life itself. This is our time, My sacred heart.

A few moments in the morning with God can change the rest of your day.

And all the people came early in the **morning** to hear him at the temple. (Luke 21:38 NIV)

January 14

*T*he ladies were looking for death on that first Easter morning. The small band of women must have encountered the need to prepare a dead body before because they came carrying spices to further care for it. Death would not be found lurking in its usual location in a tomb. Death had been conquered, and the need for burial spices was unnecessary. The ladies would soon learn that death is the first step in a resurrected life. Learn the lesson of the tomb, My sacred heart. The sun rose as usual on easter morning but so did the Son of God. Death cannot hold back the resurrected soul just as the night cannot push back the dawn of a new day. Both life after death and a daily sunrise are natural phenomena created by Me.
I do not give up on my children. I am always by your side from the moment you are born and throughout your life. Death does not alter our relationship. Death serves only to fulfill our eternal connection. I know the great grief you feel at losing a loved one. However, I know the other side of death, where your loved ones are taken from the tomb of death and dwell by My side forever. Let every early sunrise remind you that your loved one rose with the Son of God.   Do not look in an empty tomb; your loved ones are not there; they have risen.

Your eternal life with God has already begun.

On the first day of the week, the women took the spices they had prepared and went to the tomb very early in the morning. (Luke 24:1 NIV)

JANUARY 15

*L*ook closely when you are seeking to find Me, My searching child. The followers did not recognize their resurrected Rabbi because they were looking through the eyes of yesterday. They expected to see him as he was, but he was not what he once was. The Master did what he always did; however, he performed miracles and wonders. The Master told the disciples to fish, and they hauled in a large number of fish that day. You will never realize your complete human potential fishing on the banks of yesterday. No matter how great your achievements are, they are always shadows from the past. Learn to build upon your successes rather than resting on them.

Look for Me for what I do, not for how you think I should appear. What do I do, you ask? I love people. I empower them to exceed and excel far beyond what they ever imagined. I look like the helping hand reaching down to lift a fallen stranger. My image can be found in the free meals offered to the poor. I am the warm coat given to everyone who needs to keep them warm. I am your twin any time you care for someone I love. I appear in the image of every dollar spent to care for the needy. Love is a holy water that takes shape to form the need of the least, the lost, and the lonely. Always look for Me in the form of fluid-flowing love; I am love in action.

We look most like God when we act like God.

Early in the morning, Jesus stood on the shore, but the disciples did not realize that it was Jesus. (John 21:4 NIV)

JANUARY 16

Sometimes people may look at you and think unkind thoughts or say hurtful things about you. Some early followers were gifted with the ability to speak other languages. Some onlookers thought a spiritual blessing was the result of too much wine. You can never have too much of Me. Don't let the world tell you that you are too spiritual or religious. My gifts to you are for the service to others. Use my gifts to your benefit, the service of others, and for My glory. Compliments and congratulations *are not always byproducts of Christian service. On the contrary, many may think your love and kindness to be rather odd. I hold close to my heart what the world sees as weird or strange.

Be intentional in your service and generous in whom you minister. I freely spoke through the tongues of the apostles so that many would understand the message. I was generous so that all would receive My words. Do likewise with little concern about the random thoughts of bystanders. It is your mission to be in My service. Serve Me well, and understanding will naturally follow. Let the bystander scoff and laugh if they will, their outer utterances will undoubtedly change if your compassionate ministry turns toward them. Christian service is always the outpouring of My love; this can be understood in every language. Remember, love breaks down all barriers.

You can never go wrong in serving the needs of others.

These people are not drunk, as you suppose. It's only nine in the **morning**! (Acts 2:15 NIV)

JANUARY 17

*L*earn to take your time when you're witness to someone. Be clear in your message and patient in waiting for their response. Being My follower is a lifetime endeavor. Do not think people will understand you the moment you speak or in the twinkling of an eye. People will have the rest of their lives to process, grow, and walk with Me. It is your calling to tell My story and share My glory. It is up to the believer to receive My message and follow Me. Your witness plants a seed in the sunken soul of a person who has not encountered Me. You plant the seed, and I will help it grow. Tell the seeking soul about the kingdom of God and their place in it. Words alone are never enough, however. How you live your life is a witness to your faith and conviction. Words will instruct on what you believe; your behavior will testify to how fully devoted you are to your faith. So, from early morning until late evening, live out your faith in front of a world audience. Never be afraid of your witness, but be brash, bold, and brave in your speech and selective in your words. Let them hear the spiritual courage you have but let the words be gentle enough not to damage the soul. The world will see Me by watching you.

You confess your faith in words; you live your faith with actions.

They arranged to meet Paul on a certain day and came in even larger numbers to the place where he was staying. He witnessed to them from **morning** till evening, explaining about the kingdom of God, and from the Law of Moses and from the Prophets he tried to persuade them about Jesus. (Acts 28:23 NIV)

JANUARY 18

*Y*ou were once one of the many living in darkness and unaware of My love for you. You lived in darkness as a stranger to My light. But then, the spiritual sun rose in your life as you heard and received the testimony about My loving grace. A new day dawned on you that shines brightly today. You have become a bright morning star that illuminates the seeker's path and chases the darkness away. The more you share your faith with others, the brighter the morning star of salvation shines in you. Your life reflects my work in you to those seeking our relationship. The more open you are about your faith, the brighter I can shine.

Pay attention to your calling from Me. I need you to be diligent in your witness and shine brightly in the dark places of this earth. I created the sun and stars to give light to the outside world. I made you and all those like you and called you to brighten the inner world of My people. I need your living witness to reach shadowed, sin-sick souls sitting silently in the darkened corners of this world. My poor children are unaware of the blessings and love that await them; you are their first call for spiritual health. As the sun gives light to each day, you shall bring My spiritual light to a troubled soul or a hurting heart. Shine brightly today, My sacred heart.

God created you to share the inner light of your soul.

We also have the prophetic message as something completely reliable, and you will do well to pay attention to it, as to a light shining in a dark place, until the day dawns and the *morning* star rises in your hearts. (2 Peter 1:19 NIV)

JANUARY 19

I made you shine brightly, My child. Shine brighter than the stars in heaven so that the entire world knows that a new day is coming. I bless my children with many loving gifts but being a morning star that shines a light on My presence is a great gift. My children have this gift; only a few have realized how to employ it. Being a morning star is meant to be used for your benefit and My glory. Let your light shine on Me. Just as the North Star gives guidance and direction to travelers, you must shimmer and shine and constantly point toward Me. I do not want to deprive you of a personal life where your choices all revolve around Me. I give all of My children free choice. If you continually point to Me as your true spiritual north, then your tendencies in life will naturally gravitate to Me.

Use your gifts, personality, and charming wit to point to Me. You will then break the darkness with your light, making Me fully visible to all My children. I count on you and many others to brighten the gloomy dark days of people's lives. People sit in darkness because they cannot find Me. When they try to look beyond their life limitations, their lack of faith cannot penetrate the darkness that envelops them. Become My morning star on this day that brings light, hope, and joy to this earth. Many of My children fail to see Me standing before them; perhaps they can perceive My presence through you. Shine brightly, My child.

Do not hesitate to shine brightly to show you are part of God's creation. The stars in heaven shine in such fashion.

I will also give that one the **morning** star. (Revelation 2:28 NIV)

January 20

*M*y churches and places of worship are a beacon of faith and a light to the world. The congregations should be a bright morning star to a darkened world. Remember that the risen Savior has sent a messenger to bring his testimony to every congregation on this planet. As you sing your hymns, pray your prayers, and share your sermons pay attention to the angel among you. My angel guides you and points to My presence in My people. How do you see these angelic beings? They are easily recognizable. The celestial cherubs utter words that glorify the risen Savior. My angels preach sermons, sing hymns, pray prayers, and vacuum the floors of the holy gathering places. They may look like the person you dislike or sound like the stranger next to you.

Remember these words, for they are for every generation to hear. You are the "Bright Morning Star." Always act as if you are shining for the one who loves and saves you. The work you do, the love you share, and the ministry you perform all shine a light on who you are. You will be My Bright Morning Star when your works illuminate a lonely life, a troubled soul, or a searching spirit. Do not take too little of yourself to have angelic powers. The only power you need to fulfill your heavenly calling is to witness what the Root of David's offspring is doing in your life. I encourage you not to limit or hinder your witness to the inner sanctuary of your place of worship. The world needs to hear what you have to say.

Nothing shines brighter than the love you share.

"I, Jesus, have sent my angel to give you this testimony for the churches. I am the Root and the Offspring of David, and the bright **Morning** Star." (Revelation 22:16 NIV)

JANUARY 21

I will make everything possible as you do what I call you to do. Abraham became a great nation. You can find Abraham's name in the sacred writings of three major religions. His name is there because he was faithful and lived his life by trusting Me. Not only did I bless Abraham, but I also made him a blessing to others. Abraham's biological age told him being a blessing to many nations was not possible. His "faith age" told Abraham everything was possible. Old souls can inhabit young bodies; young souls can thrive in older people. The body's age is less impactful than the vitality of the soul inside. You allow your body to dictate who you are when you feel your age. You will enable Me to work through you when you activate your spiritual age.

I do not make shallow promises. My words are always trustworthy and true. I will bless you to the full extent of your faith and beyond what you ever imagined. Believe in My words and walk in faith as if you have already received My manifold blessings. Let your faith be the gateway to what you receive. Don't give up on yourself because My work in you is not complete. Abraham learned to wait for his blessing. Will you be patient and wait for what I have in store for you, My sacred heart?

God can bless us at any age. Perhaps the best is yet to come.

"I will make you into a great nation, and I will **bless** you; I will make your name great, and you will be a blessing. (Genesis 12:2 NIV)

JANUARY 22

*N*ot everyone wears the same-sized clothes. If you are tall, you must wear clothes fitting your size. Shorter people must select from the rack with their correct size. You can say the same thing about My blessings. My blessings are tailor-made to fit you perfectly. I choose my blessing for you according to your needs, your ability to handle My gifts, the urgency of your situation, and the requirements of those around you. A lot of thought goes into selecting My blessings from heaven that flow down to you. Nothing I make is mass-produced or from the rack; I measure every inch of your mind, body, and soul. My gifts are not just random acts of loving kindness flowing down from heaven. Blessings are meant to equip you and prepare you for what lies ahead.

Do not compare what you receive to the blessings that flow to another person. I have measured each blessing and spiritual gift and know precisely what will fit them perfectly. When you receive My blessing, be prepared to use it as a tool for the glory of My Kingdom. Each gift that flows your way may fill your human needs or desires but the larger picture is to empower you to glorify Me. You must remember, My sacred heart, that you are an extension of Me, I do My best work through you. Every blessing is a perfect gift from Me to you wrapped with My love and filled with hope for your future.

Every blessing from God has been tailor-made to suit your needs.

All these are the twelve tribes of Israel, and this is what their father said to them when he blessed them, giving each the **blessing** appropriate to him. (Genesis 49:28 NIV)

JANUARY 23

*Y*ou have the power to pronounce blessings on the life of another person. You cannot give spiritual gifts, but you do have the ability to request spiritual blessings. Certain people have had the charge of blessing others in My name. I listen to all requests for the blessing of another person. True love is giving yourself to another. I see the request for a blessing by one person on behalf of another as an act of love. Do not be shy or timid in your petition to call forth My holy gifts; be bold and brave and ask for the moon. After all, I created the moon, so it is undoubtedly mine to give. If you see a person in need of a soul in trouble, the formula is easy to remember; just say. "Bless this person," and it will be so.

What better request is there in life than to ask for My blessing? What better gift than asking Me to bless someone on your behalf? Feel free to request the bounty of My hand often. My blessing falls like the morning rain and floods the earth with My love. When you bless another person, you also send a part of your spiritual essence with the glorious gift. Requesting a blessing for another may be the greatest act of love you will ever perform.

Requesting a blessing for another person from God is an act of love.

At that time the Lord set apart the tribe of Levi to carry the ark of the covenant of the Lord, to stand before the Lord to minister and to pronounce **blessings** in his name, as they still do today. (Deuteronomy 10:8 NIV)

JANUARY 24

$\mathcal{S}$ome blessings are for a day or a predetermined period. These blessings sprout like a flower, bloom to serve their purpose, and then wither into the landscape. Their time may be short or long, but they are not an everlasting blessing. I am pleased to bless My children and even their households. Some blessings will come to you without restraint or boundaries. What was intended for you may spill over like a gushing fountain of overflowing water and cover anyone close to you. Some of My blessings are generational; they do not stop with the current person, family, or community. Generational blessings usually come in the form of a covenant or promise.

I am your everlasting, eternal blessing. From birth through your entire life, I am with you every day. You will continue to be in My holy presence from death to eternal glory. All blessings from the past may blow away like dust, but I am with you always. This is a promise and blessing I give to all My children. Do you understand the depth of this holy covenant? I cannot break My promise to you. I am tied to you with golden bonds of love from now into eternity. My words are more than utterances; they are what the very substance of creation is formed. I said, "Let there be Light," and light was created. I said I will always love you, and My sacred covenant will unite us forever.

Living in the presence of God is an eternal **blessing**.

Now be pleased to bless the house of your servant, that it may continue forever in your sight; for you, Sovereign Lord, have spoken, and with your blessing, the house of your servant will be **blessed** forever." (2 Samuel 7:29 NIV)

JANUARY 25

I seek to bring you joy and happiness; some of My greatest gifts bless you from the inside out. I hope My blessings bring you the joy and happiness you seek to have a wonderful day. The greatest gift I bring to you each day is the gift of Myself. I strive to be by your side from morning till night. If you feel My presence and see My activity in your life, then happiness has been found by each of us. Yes, I share in your happiness; I work so hard to be a source of joy for you.

Daily blessings of joy and happiness are no minor feat, yet I plan on being a source of joy to you for the rest of your life. Material blessings may come and go, but My love is eternal. Seek Me each morning, and I will bless your life with great joy. Together, we will find the happiness in life I alone can bring. Do not look so hard for happiness outside of you. True happiness is an inside job and will only have lasting effects when you find the true inner joy in your life.

  Too many of My children have wasted their lives trying to unearth the world's happiness. The world has no happiness; only you can find joy or satisfaction in what the world has to offer. Deep inner human emotions do not dangle from a tree like forbidden fruit. When you learn to unite My material blessings with your inner joy, you will find satisfaction and happiness in almost everything you do. Gratitude for the benefits you receive from Me is the internal trigger for connecting to the joy in your life. When the inner soul is happy, the heart will sing.

The greatest blessing is the realization that God is at work in your daily life.

Surely you have granted him unending **blessings** and made him glad about the joy of your presence. (Psalm 21:6 NIV)

JANUARY 26

*Y*ou will not work and labor all your life in vain. I will grant you provisions for your life's work and labor. You work to earn a living. You spend much of your life providing food, clothing, and shelter for yourself and your family. You also labor to care for the things you worked hard to earn. You must care for your property and maintain your belongings. You must share your love to ensure your family and friends feel supported and cherished. Your labors are endless and will last the rest of your days.

The hard work and dedication you show now will bear much fruit in the future. Look at each day as a fresh planting for further future blessings.

Enjoy what you have, for all you have is a blessing from Me. Enjoy your belongings, friends, and family as My blessed gifts.

Go beyond maintaining what you have and enjoy all I give you as the fruits of your labors and a holy blessing from Me. I will continue to bring prosperity into your life through My countless gifts of love. Great abundance and wealth do not usually blossom all at once; it may take several plantings before you realize your full yield.

Enjoy the fruit of your labor, and remember that your prosperity comes from God.

You will eat the fruit of your labor; **blessings** and prosperity will be yours. (Psalm 128:2 NIV)

JANUARY 27

*D*o not give up looking for My blessings. There may be dry periods when My blessings do not fall like the morning rain, or you fail to see the benefits you already have. I will quench your thirsty lands and fill your children with new hope. Come and drink from the stream of My goodness and sip from the waters of My loving blessings.

Be aware, My sacred heart, that you are both a stream and a well to receive all I give you. Blessings flow into your life daily like a stream flowing through the dry desert land. Drink to your fill from this rushing river of rich, robust blessings beside the stream that flows freely in your life. You are also a well-dug deep to hold calm, cool waters for others to drink. Your well is your heritage to your children from the blessings I bestow upon you. Plant yourself deeply between the river and the well to nurture your thirsty soul.

Do not wait any longer; I have made all things ready for you right now. Open your eyes to see what I am doing in your life, and your spiritual desert will overflow with blessings. The daily blessing will come from Me for you and your children alike. I know the dry dust taste in your soul, so drink now and be restored. Come and quench your thirsty spirit. Come and receive Me as an eternal blessing.

Drink often from the streams of God's **blessings**; your thirst will be quenched for the next generation.

For I will pour water on the thirsty land, and streams on the dry ground; I will pour out my Spirit on your offspring, and my blessing on your descendants. (Isaiah 44:3 MIV)

JANUARY 28

Look to the good earth as a source of My blessings. Your planet holds endless riches and untold benefits for you. The land is more than just a dwelling place; it is the source of your daily bread, building materials for your home, and clothing for your body. The seasons were created to restore and renew all the earthly comforts to make your life safe, secure, and satisfying.

All of creation was formed to sustain your life. The birds in the air, the fish in the sea, the animals that roam the earth, and the companions that coinhabit this planet are a source of blessing to you.

Do not disregard the beauty and glory of one tiny raindrop. Each droplet of water carries living, giving sustenance as a loving blessing from heaven. Sunlight, rains, and the seasons may seem trivial and an unimpressive routine in the earth's rotation, but they are more than seasonal cycles; they are life cycles. I tell you all this, My sacred heart, so you will know that a system is set in place to give you life and sustain it for your time on this earth. Do not overlook this blessing on which you live.

You must learn to care for this spectacular blue floating ball as it travels through the heavens. Do all you can to keep the air pure, the water unpolluted, and the land clean. I formed the planet by My hand to be a blessing to you. Do not destroy your constant source of life blessings. This is the only earth I created. I place you on this earth to be its caretaker and to return blessings to it.

Care for this earth as if it were a blessing from God.

I will make them and the places surrounding my hill a blessing. I will send down showers in season; there will be showers of **blessing**. (Ezekiel 34:26 NIV)

January 29

There is a vast difference between being a curse and living as a blessing. Curses are self-serving and live for their pleasure. Little thought or attention is given to the surroundings in which they live or to the people with whom they live. Curses exist for their gratification. People are used to meeting the ends of their desire for self-serving gratification. Cursed people have adopted the life of a parasite that attaches to a host and drains it of its life force.

A person who is a blessing realizes the great value of the place in which they live and the people with whom they live. Rather than constantly taking from their host, they have learned to return their blessings with kindness and love. Blessed people become a source of strength to those around them. They enhance the lives of those around them rather than subtract from their existence. People who live a life of blessed people are fearless in their generosity to others.

I give freely to the cursed or lost soul and to the person who is aware of who they are in Me. The difference is a person who lives as a curse to others has not seen the great value in sharing the blessings they receive. I do not curse My children; some live in a closet of closed and self-contained spiritual separation. Persons who stopped the flow of divine blessings from Me to them and those around them self-sabotage their spiritual health. The world sees the self-centered soul as cursed because no blessings or love seems to flow from it. All of My children must choose between being a blessing or a curse; I ask that you select a blessing, My child.

Blessings flow from God's heart to our hands.

Just as you, Judah and Israel, have been a curse among the nations so that I will save you, and you will be a **blessing.** Do not be afraid, but let your hands be strong." (Zechariah 8:13 NIV)

January 30

*P*eace may be the greatest blessing you can bestow on another person's life. Peace comes from the assurance that I love the world. Peace comes from the confidence that I am with you always. Peace comes from the inside. My indwelling in you creates a field of peace that flows from the inside out. If you know Me, then you know My great love for you. Peace comes when you rest in My love. Share My blessing of peace often, for My indwelling changes the world from the inside out. Fear gives way to sacred security and holy comfort. Internal comfort and assurance make their way to the collective outer world. One good word, one small gesture of My blessing of peace, can change the world. Peace creates a familiar blanket of trust that cannot exist apart from Me. Always depart someone's presence with a blessing of peace and send them into a troubled world that awaits their blessings.

Peace or Shalom is always sent as a commandment, or that you should find peace within you. When you find My holy inner peace, you will also encounter Me. When you send someone off with a blessing of peace, you send them with Me because I am the power behind your blessing. Do not take this blessing of peace lightly, whether you are giving it or receiving it. My peace is as real as a dove carrying an olive branch to you: or with you. You cannot separate My peace from Me.

One blessing of peace can flower the planet with God's love.

After spending some time there, they were sent off by the believers with the **blessing** of peace to return to those who had sent them. (Acts 15:33 NIV)

JANUARY 31

*T*he gospel does indeed proclaim a myriad of blessings to my believers. The promise for the forgiveness of sin sits lovingly on the throne of mercy. All you need do is confess your transgressions, and I will forgive all your sins. Come to me with a repentant heart, and you will be washed whiter than snow and cleansed from your former sins. Forgiveness is a blessing for your benefit; open your hands and receive it like mana from heaven.

You also receive the resurrection and everlasting life in My holy presence. My love for you cannot be conquered or diminished. My love does not fade or die with the finality of your mortality. The promise of the gospel is revealed with the resurrection into eternal glory. Receive the promise of the gospel as a gift from Me to you. My promise is a blessing that will live beyond your expectations.

I left My promises and your hope in the bound blessing of the Bible. The words written in My book contain My power and essence. The words themselves are resurrected from the pages of the Bible to inspire your soul today. The Gospels are more than good news; they bring you new life in Me. Inhale each word you witness as My loving movement in your life. You will not only relive ancient stories; you will inherit their promises. I gave the Good News to all of My children for all time to come. The promises and gifts of the Bible are yours as well, My sacred heart.

The Gospel is more than just "Good News"; it holds God's eternal promises.

I do all this for the sake of the gospel, that I may share in its **blessings**. (1 Corinthians 9:23 NIV)

FEBRUARY 1

Do not let unholy words drag you into a pit of evil actions. I created you much better than that. Love does not repay evil with evil. True love repays evil with loving kindness and a blessing. The moment you react with sin, you have stepped over the line into the land of the lost. You have forgotten our holy union and abandoned your life in Me. Evil and sin have such great power that they can extract the goodness right out of your soul.

Learn to respond to all evil attacks with the open arms of love. Your open arms will bring the words and actions of the wicked person straight into My presence. Evil will then melt like dripping snow on a spring day. Repay evil with a holy blessing; My blessing will rescue your assailant from the evil pit into My loving light. My blessings will wash all sin from them. Rather than vanquishing the enemy, you have learned how to love a lost soul.

No mystical secret or magical spell is involved in this dynamic alteration of evil into good. You are merely altering the intent of the spoken word. Words have power, but the word can be refined and reshaped from evil intention to a holy blessing. The curse thrown your way can boomerang back to the sender as a blessing. Always remember your calling, My child. You are called to reflect on Me at all times. I do not curse; I bless.

Repay all evil with good. Let love be your first line of defense.

Do not repay evil with evil or insult with insult. On the contrary, repay evil with blessing, because to this you were called so that you may inherit a **blessing**. (1 Peter 3:9 NIV)

FEBRUARY 2

*P*lant yourself deeply in My love. Do not hesitate to draw close to Me and receive the goodness of My daily blessing of love. Once planted in My house, trust in Me always and fear nothing or no one. My love never fails. You may feel vanquished and beaten down by the world at times, My sacred heart, but those are the times to draw even closer to Me. Always remember that you are like an olive tree living in My holy house. All that you will ever need is at your disposal.

Learn to branch out and include others in My love. My branches should extend as deep as the roots of My love for you. You do not bear fruit for yourself, but you produce a harvest meant for the hungry nations—a harvest of unfailing love and everlasting grace. Flourish in My house and bear witness to My love as you produce great fruit. The yield of your spiritual fruit is not dependent on the seasons or good weather fortune.

Your harvest is the result of the depth of your planting in Me. You will only produce fruit in proportion to the depth of your roots. Your faith must root deeply in Me and cling tightly to Me. You are placed and planted in My house as a glorious source of blooming and blossoming spiritual fruit. The fruit you bear and the harvest you produce will show the world of My work in you. Plant yourself deeply, My child, and bloom abundantly.

Plant yourself deep in the house of God, and you will bear a bounty of God's unfailing love.

But I am like an olive tree flourishing in the house of God; I trust in God's unfailing **love** forever and ever. (Psalm 52:8 NIV)

FEBRUARY 3

*O*ur relationship began long before you were born, My sacred
heart. Before I moved across the waters of the deep, I had you
in mind. Long before I breathed the breath of life into Adam, I had
the first inkling of your life. Even before your parents, grandparents,
and ancient ancestors walked this earth, a vision of you came to Me.
At the very first thought of you, I wrapped you in My love and carried
the image of what you would be close to My heart. Because My
divine love created you, you existed in My love before you were born.
I was by your side from the very time of your inception.   I watched
as cells divided and grew. I watched in awe as birth gave way to
life and you entered this world. I walked alongside you with anxious
anticipation as you took your first steps. With every step and every
breath, I surrounded you with My love. My arms were wide open as I
held them out to receive you at the end of your first toddler walk.
My love for you continues to grow as you mature and age. Now
that you can walk alone, I charge you with the mission of caring for
my good news with the hurting world. Now that you can speak, I
encourage you to share the message of My loving grace in a thirsty
land. You have been nurtured to be a walking and talking symbol of
My love on this earth. Walk like Me, talk like Me, and love everyone
as I do. You were born and raised to be My holy image on earth.

Always walk in God's steps and speak of God's love.

God's Love for Israel "When Israel was a child, I **loved** him, and out
of Egypt I called my son. (Hosea 11:1 NIV)

February 4

*A*lways remember My sacred heart; one constant in your life is My love. My love for you and all my children is endless, ceaseless, and limitless. Count on My love just as you relied on the sun to rise to wake you this morning. Constantly cling to the love I offer you; it is your life preserver for times of trouble and your source for celebration on the good days. Nothing can replace My love for you; the cosmic glue holds all life together. It is the strength of our spiritual relationship.

This world can offer you much that looks like a substitute for My love. Money, power, status, and wealth are just a few of the modern-day idols that will call your name. They will promise you everything but give you very little. These idols only glitter and glow from the outside because they are hollow and void of any natural substance on the inside. They will give you a sense of false comfort for a short time, but they will never offer you the love that I can provide you. Lasting love can only come from an eternal source.

My Love is more than an emotional feeling or spiritual connection. Genuine blessings flow from Me to you. My blessings of health, relationships, wealth, food, and shelter manifest my love for you. Be careful not to limit yourself to any of My physical gifts; my love for you is far greater than the gifts I bestow upon you. Idols are false phantoms of your wants and desires. My love is visible in fulfilling your needs and hopes. I give you everything out of love with no expectations or any return.

Don't be fooled by false idols; they know how to call your name, but they will never love you.

"Those who cling to worthless idols turn away from God's **love** for them. (Jonah 2:8 NIV)

FEBRUARY 5

I am pure love. I am the Spirit of love called Holy that moves in you, lives in you, and gives you purpose for living. I bring passion, and I am love. I am the constant source of divine love that dwells in your heart so that I can speak to you through every heartbeat. Your heart pumps blood through your veins, but I carry your life source. Without Me, you would have human life but not know divine love.

This, then, is your hope that My love is closer to you than hands and feet and more a part of you than life itself. Never be ashamed or discouraged because of Me because My love will lift you beyond human comprehension. Many will ask, "How can God love you?" Answer them quickly and clearly, "Because that is what God does, and God loves you as well." Show them the gift they can have by letting My love shine from you.

I am the gift of love freely given to all of My children. I do not limit Myself to the holy or self-righteous person. I place and plant myself to work in you from the inside out. Holiness is not something you achieve; it is something I do in you. I am poured into the hearts of all who seek Me and even some who do not know Me. Do not struggle and strain in life to improve your spiritual connection. Begin your spiritual journey by looking within your heart. I am always found comforting and loving you with every heartbeat.

The Holy Spirit is God's living gift of love.

And hope does not put us to shame because God's **love** has been poured out into our hearts through the Holy Spirit, who has been given to us. (Romans 5:5 NIV)

FEBRUARY 6

*Y*our faith will open the door to unlimited love. People will no longer appear as human objects; they will take on the color and hue of divine light. People never seem as they are. You interpret who they are through the eyes of your life lens. You may see their size, shape, color, and hue, but whether you like or dislike a particular person or group depends on your interpretation. Remember, this is your interpretation and not My reality. Let your faith open your eyes to see what I see.

I see people with beautiful outer shells but are hurting and riddled with pain inside. I see people who appear happy and carefree on the outside but fits of depression and despair torment their inward souls. Your faith in Me will allow you to see an outer human vessel overflowing with My divine love. Nothing will change you more drastically than seeing people as I see them. Yet, a more challenging quest awaits you, my sacred heart.

You must not only begin to see people as I see them, but you must also try to love them even as I love them. Each person has value and worth far beyond any precious stone this earth may produce. I planted their special sacred spiritual stone deep in their souls on the day they were born. When you struggle to find inner beauty in someone, ask yourself, "Why does God love them?" When you can answer this question, you have found the lens of love from which to view all life.

No matter how people appear on the outside, they still hold the beauty of God's love.

For this reason, ever since I heard about your faith in the Lord Jesus and your **love** for all God's people (Ephesians 1:15 NIV)

FEBRUARY 7

I will lead you in the example of My love as one of My beloved children. I will embrace you with arms of love and surround you with bonds of My grace. My connection to you comes out of My love for you. My love for you grants grace and forgiveness for all your transgressions. Only pure divine love can work to let go of past sins while expecting future faithfulness completely. Love is who I am. Loving completely is what I do.

Can you learn to follow My example for living My sacred heart? Loving completely will change the entire world. Hatred, greed, selfishness, racism, war, poverty, bigotry, and injustice are a few examples of a world deprived of My love. If you treat My dearly loved children as I do, these antilove expressions will soon disappear. Start every day to act as if every person you meet is one of My dearly loved children because they are.

I do not place an impossible life pattern before you, My child. Loving is as much a part of letting go of negative thoughts as it is of welcoming positive images to take control of your mind and soul. I am free of all negative influences, ideas, or limiting beliefs. When you release yourself from the power and influence of destructive and harmful thoughts, you will make more room for love to grow in your mind, body, and soul. This mindset is a simple example of addition by subtraction. Limit your negative thoughts, and you will flourish in positive spiritual growth.

Every person you meet today is loved by the same God that loves you.

Follow God's example, therefore, as dearly **loved** children. (Ephesians 5:1 NIV)

February 8

*F*aith is just a catch-all term unless you express it outwardly. To believe means that you have surrendered the struggle of seeking the external truth. You have given yourself over to the truth that I alone speak to your spirit. Giving yourself over to the My truth does not mean you give up seeking the truth. It means you accept My truth through inward spiritual means. You find the truth in Me and rely less on the material evidence from the world around you. Once you surrender to My spiritual truth through your belief in Me, you will find my hidden treasure of love waiting as your prize. Once you accept My love through your faith, your life course is eternally altered and changed. You are now called to live in the love I offer to all people who believe in Me. In turn, you must learn to love My children so that My divine love in You is evident to the people around you. This, then, is faith in action, loving people in such a way that you give evidence of My love. Begin this day caring, My compassion in your words, and My love in your actions.

Let your faith be so strong that if you were arrested for being a Christian, you would have enough evidence to convict yourself. Faith with no visible evidence of love in action is nothing more than a dead or dormant belief dried up and decaying in the soul. Lively, vibrant love must find a way to express itself in the lives of those around it. When you connect yourself to divine Agape love, you adhere yourself to Me. Once you become My companion, My love will naturally flow from you into the world around you; it has no other choice.

Be the evidence of God's love in your life by loving God's people.

Because we have heard of your faith in Christ Jesus and of the **love** you have for all God's people. (Colossians 1:4 NIV)

FEBRUARY 9

*A*fter you brush your teeth and comb that unruly hair, and before you get dressed for the day, put on Me. You will need your business suit or your work uniform. A standard dress code is still required of you. But put Me on for the rest of the day. Clothe yourself in the Godly garments of compassion and kindness. Accessorize yourself with humility and gentleness. Top your head with a stylish adornment of patience. These spiritual garments must be your fashion for every day.

Make no mistake, My sacred heart, your outer spiritual wear is a clear sign of My work in you. Compassion and kindness must be clearly visible, just as your fashionable tie is evident. Kindness and humility make a spiritual fashion statement as much as your Louis Vuitton dress. Display My patience and gentleness as if you are walking down a fashion runway. Let My Love become your fashion statement and chosen lifestyle.

My chosen people dress in the fashion and style of the One who first loved them. These are garments of holiness that define your actions for the day and your calling for life. Wear these items daily and see what an incredible difference they will make in your world. Dressing in spiritual holiness is always in fashion and will never go out of style because My love for you is always relevant. Dress for success, but also clothe yourself in My garments of love.

Let each day begin by dressing yourself in the holy garments of God's active love.

Therefore, as God's chosen people, holy and dearly **loved**, clothe yourselves with compassion, kindness, humility, gentleness, and patience. (Colossians 3:12 NIV)

FEBRUARY 10

*N*ot everyone will believe as you do or have the faith you do. The world has many people who will not acknowledge Me. These nonbelievers may insult you, make fun of you, or even cause you some harm. Don't give up on your faith; I will not give up on the nonbeliever. A nonbeliever is just one of My children who has not met Me face to face. Pray that the nonbeliever will take an opportunity to encounter My love and grace I freely give to all people.

In the meantime, take heart and persevere over any difficulties and challenges to your faith.

The faith you show in Me amid life's strives may be the sign and wonder a nonbeliever needs to find Me. You already have the love many people seek in their unfulfilled lives. Let the faith in your heart direct all people to My love.

Be keenly aware that the nonbelievers you encounter in life may be of My selection. I did not place them in your path as a stumbling block to you; instead, I put them in front of you so they could see what faith is. Witness powerfully My child and persevere in their presence of the love we share. The testimony of a strong faith usually quiets the chirps of non-believers to the point that their insults may turn into curiosity. Curiosity is the first step toward accepting Me. Be brash, bold, and beautiful in your faith, and I will direct nonbelievers into a life of faith.

Start each day believing that you may be the sign and wonder if someone needs to find God's love.

May the Lord direct your hearts into God's **love** and Christ's perseverance. (2 Thessalonians 3:5 NIV)

FEBRUARY 11

*T*rue love, perfect love, comes from Me. You must be bold enough to express your love for Me, My child. Love from Me must be displayed every day of your life. Love for another person must be given as freely as the air around you. Let the sunrise remind you of your mission of love and to love every morning. You are invaluable in spreading My love to each corner of this earth. The ripple effect of divine love begins with you. The love you create will find its way like one wave chasing another wave across a pond.

You were born again into the spiritual world when you received My love. You will be perfected in My love when you learn to share your love in the same selfless manner I share. You know Me by My love; others will come to know Me by the love you show them. Do not make love such a tricky thing; just let Me work through you as an envoy of My love. Just take care to leave behind signs of My love in the hearts of the people you meet today.

Too many of My beloved children look for concrete evidence of My existence. Biblical archeology will never dig up the evidence they seek. I do not exist in ancient artifacts or buried deep underground. A cardiologist may better serve to find the evidence for the existence of God. I am found in the heart and soul of every person on earth. I do not have to be extracted or exhumed; all you have to do is share Me. The reality of My existence will become self-evident when you share My love, My sacred heart.

Being loved by God is your birthright; loving others is your mission.

Dear friends, let us love one another, for love comes from God. Everyone who **loves** has been born of God and knows God. (1 John 4:7 NIV)

FEBRUARY 12

*C*ome to Me each morning in sincere prayer. Perhaps you will find other like-minded believers joining your morning prayer vigils. These morning prayer sessions will help build your faith and strengthen your spiritual perseverance. Gather in My name and pray in the center of My love. Let your prayers flow outward from the center of My love into a spiritually hurting and starving world. Let your prayers reach outward to touch the lives of the people who seek My mercy but have not found My love.

Keep yourself in the center of My love and draw your circle of love more enormous daily. Include the unfaithful in your prayers, asking that they might find My love to fill their empty hearts. Your prayer could be the game-changer someone has been looking for but cannot see. Receive others into our circle of love and wait patiently for the blessing of My eternal mercy. My mercy will always find those who seek to live faithfully in the center of My love.

Your world of prayer has no limits, My child. Use Zoom, Messenger, and any other internet apparatus to expand your prayer circle constantly. Reach across the globe to find people of kindred spirit to unite with you in your mission of prayer and spiritual devotion. Creating a worldwide prayer blanket will surround the earth with a spiritual magnetic field of hope. One small prayer rappelling across the spiritual field could alter the course of human behavior and the global future. Prayer can move mountains and change the world. Keep praying, My sacred heart.

May your circle of love constantly expand.

Keep yourselves in God's **love** as you wait for the mercy of our Lord Jesus Christ to bring you to eternal life. (Jude 1:21 NIV)

February 13

I am so very proud of your growth and maturity. I see you put your faith into action by doing good deeds and loving your neighbor just as you love Me. You share My love any time you care for another person. You put your faith into action by giving to the poor and helping this world's lonely and forgotten souls. Even during difficult times, you persevere and move forward through personal adversity to be My faithful servant.

What? Do you say you have accomplished none of these acts of faithful service? Perhaps I am looking at you through my eyes of your potential. I see the reality of the possibilities of serving Me in the future, and I mark them as complete today. Perhaps you can start today by helping Me more than you did yesterday. After all: good deeds, love, and faith all walk hand in hand.

Faith is just the starting point of your Christian spiritual journey, My child. Faith must blossom and bloom into Christian service. Devils and demons believe in me, yet they remain desperate spirits. When you put your faith into action and serve your neighbor, you are transformed into my hands and feet. This transformation does not happen through mysterious magic; love will bring divine light to even the darkest heart. Ministry is your faith putting My love into action. I encourage all of My children to engage in this spiritual practice.

God knows our good deeds.

I know your deeds, love and faith, service and perseverance, and that you are now doing more than you did at first. (Revelation 2:19 NIV)

FEBRUARY 14

*L*earn to sing and dance to My tune of thanksgiving. Rise this morning with the song of thanksgiving in your heart and the music of gratitude in your soul. Sing happy words to fill your day with positive expectations of My movement in your life. As you practice giving thanks to Me for My blessings, daily grace, and My everlasting love, your eyes will adjust to seeing Me more often. I am always before you, but an ungrateful heart and a soul that does not give thanks will never see Me.

Don't mistake the ordinary for the extraordinary, My child. You have a job, home, car, income, family, and friends. These blessings of My love create the core of your life. Food, shelter, companionship, and other daily activities are minor sprinklings of My love upon the foundation of your life. I hide all of My gifts of love to you in plain sight; you must distinguish between an earthly delight and a heavenly blessing. I do not mean to offend you, but most of My children believe their daily gifts exist because of their hard work. You did the work, but I blessed you with the ability to do the job.

The act of giving thanks to Me trains your heart and soul to see more of My movement in your life and all of the love I so freely give to you. I do not permanently hide My blessings from you; you must learn to see My blessings and appreciate them for what they are. My blessings are gifts to you from Me. Before you leave your home each day, practice giving thanks for five things for which you are grateful. Then look for five new blessings in the day ahead. You will be amazed at what you see, My sacred heart.

Seeing God in your daily living comes from recognizing God's blessings and giving thanks.

Enter his gates with **thanksgiving** and his courts with praise; give thanks to him and praise his name. (Psalm 100:4 NIV)

FEBRUARY 15

I require the sacrifice of your heart for the repentance of sin and transgression. Come to Me with your prayers and petitions and make a holy living sacrifice of the sorrow in your heart for the wrongs you have committed. Place before Me the names of those you have wronged and those who have harmed you. Your prayers should seek their forgiveness so that peace between my children will exist. Let no thought, word, or deed separate you from My children. Replace any transgressions with thoughts and words of holy peace. When you restore peace between you and another person, you have strengthened the bonds of love between the three of us. Whatever you do to one of My children on this earth, you do to Me. Learn to live and love in peace with your neighbor; peace and love will fall on you like the morning rain.

I insist on your heart's dedication and your soul's commitment. I will know that you make the self-sacrifice I require when you join your neighbor in a holy meal. You do not have to dine with the people who offended you, but you must love them. Hate and resentment cannot hide under the light of divine love. Divine love will expose any ill feelings you have toward one of My children; take care of how you set the table for the day. Let love always be at the center of the table of fellowship. I will always be present when the table of fellowship is adorned with My love.

Fellowship offering of thanksgiving exists when you join your neighbor in peace.

The meat of their fellowship offering of **thanksgiving** must be eaten on the day it is offered; they must leave none of it till morning. (Leviticus 7:15 NIV)

FEBRUARY 16

*L*ay a foundation of thanksgiving in your life. A thankful heart will dramatically change your life. Audibly giving thanks for My daily blessing will allow you to hear what I have done in your life as your voice carries your gratitude. Seeing, hearing, and praising My gifts is a formula for a successful life. Raising your hands skyward and singing My praises energizes your soul with My divine spiritual life force.

Let your acts of praise and thanksgiving become your morning ritual for the foundation of each day. Say to yourself, "God is good to me, and God's love toward me endures forever." Sing this happy tune every morning. Repeat these words of praise out loud many times so the ear will train the heart to believe them. I will build other blessings on your foundation of praise throughout the day. Giving thanks to Me in the morning will prepare your soul to see even more gifts throughout the day.

I encourage these daily activities of praise and thanksgiving, My sacred heart, so you will align your heart, soul, body, and mind with Me. Connecting to Me through Thanksgiving celebrations creates a pathway for spiritual revelation. You will only celebrate what you see. You will only sing songs of sacred celebration after seeing signs and wonders of My movement in your life. The foundation of your spiritual life is laid when you see Me, hear Me, and feel Me in your life. I am always with you.

God's love endures forever; God is good to me.

With praise and **thanksgiving**, they sang to the Lord: "He is good; his love toward Israel endures forever." And all the people gave a great shout of praise to the Lord because the foundation of the house of the Lord was laid. (Ezra 3:11 NIV)

FEBRUARY 17

*G*iving thanks can be a generational celebration, My sacred heart. Mothers and fathers, sons and daughters, parents and grandparents can give thanks for My blessings—each generation giving thanks and lifting prayers for My gifts that flowed into their lives. Together your family will make a divine connection to My movement through each generation and in every life of your family. Many of My heavenly blessings can be handed down from generation to generation as an earthly inheritance.

By giving thanks generation by generation, you will learn to see how I work throughout the years to build blessings that will outlast your lifetime. You will see that many of My gifts are long-lasting and continue beyond the life of the initial recipient. Take time this morning to give thanks to your ancestors; they carry My DNA of spiritual blessings. Which of My gifts can you pass along to your descendants?

Let your prayers of thanksgiving for My heavenly gifts become a list of descendants and recipients of My blessings. Abraham could not imagine how far-reaching the blessing I bestowed upon him would branch out. Yet thousands of years later, the world's major religions still reach back in history to their spiritual father Abraham. Do not sell yourself or My work through you too short, My child. The blessings you receive today may be as limitless as tomorrow's sunsets.

Receiving your generational blessings from God.

Mattaniah, son of Mika, the son of Zabdi, the son of Asaph, the director who led in **thanksgiving** and prayer; Bakuchiol, second among his associates; and Abda son of Shammua, the son of Galal, the son of Jeduthun. (Nehemiah 11:17 NIV)

FEBRUARY 18

*N*ever start your day on an empty soul. Learn to feed your soul before you leave your home. Perhaps cymbals, harps, and lyres are a bit much for you first thing in the morning. Find a softer approach to feeding an empty soul each morning. If you need help, look to devotional writings, sacred music, holy scripture, or the gentle sound of My voice. If you are not a morning person, perhaps just sitting quietly contemplating Me is an excellent start to your day. This day awaits you as a glorious time of celebration. Seek out the good Godly blessings that I will provide. Do not hesitate to draw others into the glory of this day. My gifts can often be shared, and there is always a bounty of My love for all to enjoy. Begin each day with the expectation of what can be and end each day with a Thanksgiving celebration of what was. Give thanks to My blessings in your daily songs of praise.

I do not encourage you to join in morning celebrations as a passive participant. Actively look for things for which to give thanks. Your spirit will feel quenched when you find that I have already placed low-hanging fruit before you. Another day on this earth is a blessing. The ability to work is a God send. Friends and family that love you are a daily blessing from Me. You need not look too hard or long for things to celebrate; I place most of My blessings in plain sight., My child.

Never start your day on an empty soul; partake freely of the blessings around you in feeding the spirit.

At the dedication of the wall of Jerusalem, the Levites were sought out from where they lived and were brought to Jerusalem to celebrate. (Nehemiah 12:27 NIV)

FEBRUARY 19

I am grateful for the praise and thanksgiving you offered me this morning. Giving thanks to Me shows that you are open to seeing My movement in your life. You have seen what I have done in the past, and you responded to My blessings with a thankful heart. Let your songs of praise flow from your heart and fill the air every morning as you recount My blessings given to you. What an excellent way to begin each day as you glorify Me with your words. Giving thanks does more than just help you realize how much I have done in your life. Being thankful fills your heart with good feelings of completeness and fulfillment. These feelings of being grateful for the blessings I have given you often lead to acts of gratitude. Gratitude is putting your thankful feelings into action. When you feel the warmth of My gifts, go into your world and give others a reason to be grateful. This will become your song of thanksgiving.

Living a grateful life will improve your spiritual connection to Me and those around you faster than any other spiritual act or discipline. When you recognize my movement in your life and are openly thankful for My blessings, your life will change. Celebrating past blessings will prepare the soul to receive future gifts. The hands of your heart are open to receive whatever blessings I send. Your soul will be grateful, and you will soon see the people around you as a source of My blessings. Practicing gratitude naturally leads to living a grateful life.

Living a Grateful life comes from. Practicing gratitude.

I will praise God's name in song and glorify him with **thanksgiving**. (Psalm 69:30 NIV)

FEBRUARY 20

*H*ow I rejoice when My children come to Me with hands lifted, hearts open, and their spirits singing My praise. Music is an expression of the human spirit calling out to Me. Have you found your spirit song? A spirited song is a piece of music that opens your heart and soul to a deeper connection between you and Me. I often speak through the movement of music.

Do you ever feel compelled to clap your hands or stomp your feet when you hear good music?   Do some songs inspire you to sing without restraint or concern? Do you ever feel your body swinging and swaying with the tune as it floats through the air?   When these things happen, you join me in that music's glory. Do not be shy or self-conscious; just jump right in and sing, dance, and clap along with the music and song. You will often find Me doing similar movements to the music, My child.

It is no accident that my sanctuaries are filled with music. It is not just a random chance that the church's music stirs your soul to sing and dance My praises. Music is one of the primary languages that I speak to people of all countries in every generation. Through the music, you will hear My voice, feel My love, and learn to draw closer to Me. Find your spirit song and play it every morning.

Praising God in song and music is one of the languages spoken by the Spirit of God.

Let us come before him with **thanksgiving** and extol him with music and song. (Psalm 95:2 NIV)

FEBRUARY 21

The greenest valley can soon seem like a desert of dry ground. The lushest gardens soon lose their color and splendor and wither to a patch of weeds. The bluest waters seem to become covered with a dark cloudy mist. Your world will soon turn into a wasteland when you deprive yourself of giving thanks to Me. Spiritual perception sees your world through the eyes of what I can bring to you and not through the eyes of human lack.

Is your world all that bad, or do you have a cloudy perception of how you think life is? Too many of My precious children miss the reality of what I am doing in their lives because they place their hope in what they want. You will never be satisfied or spiritually fulfilled unless you learn to rejoice in what you already have. Treasures are accumulated over time. Do not expect worldly riches and heavenly blessings to plop down before you. Patience is a virtue that prepares the heart and soul for what is to come; practice it daily, My child.

If you lack the spiritual eyes of a thankful soul, all that you see will soon appear as ruins. I move to you out of compassion and love. Respond to My movement with songs of thanksgiving and praise. A Rembrandt can occur as a paint-by-numbers portrait of an unthankful heart. I have the power to replenish the earth; you must have the spiritual vision to see it. Be thankful for what I am doing in your life today.

Turn Sadness into Joy by Giving Thanks for what God is Doing.

The Lord will surely comfort Zion and will look with compassion on all her ruins; he will make her deserts like Eden, her wastelands like the garden of the Lord. Joy and gladness will be found in her, **thanksgiving** and the sound of singing. (Isaiah 5:13 NIV)

I hope you were refreshed today, my friend. I think gardening and spiritual growth are very similar. You must prepare the soul for the Spirit of God to grow and blossom within you. How do you prepare your soul for growth? By doing spiritual things like praying, reading scripture, worshiping, and being diligent in your daily devotionals. All of the aforementioned spiritual

FEBRUARY 22

*R*ejoicing is a joyous and cheerful act of praise you should seek every morning. The rejoicing that comes to you through songs and prayers of thanksgiving not only brings honor to Me but also blesses you in the same way. There is much to fear and even more to worry about in your world. Find time every morning to set your mood on the positive things that could occur in your life and not on the adverse events that may not even happen.

The world has often found itself in difficult times throughout history. I did not forsake My children then, and I will not abandon you now. You have a choice in every situation in your life. You can let life overtake you or learn to overcome difficult times with your faith. Your faith will give you a reason to rejoice. A lack of confidence turns a blind eye to the good things that may happen in your life. Learn to rejoice and celebrate all life.

Too many of My children seek shelter in silent sheds of shielded fear. There is no shelter from fear; it creates a prison of false security. I called My children out of exile by promising a vision of what it means to give thanks to Me and not be afraid. Fear will leave your presence when surrounded by voices of praise and thanksgiving. In every situation, you have a choice, fear, or faith. Choose faith, My child.

Turn fear into faith and draw a joyous crowd for rejoicing.

From them will come songs of **thanksgiving** and the sound of rejoicing. I will add to their numbers, and they will not be decreased; I will bring them honor, and they will not be disdained. (Jeremiah 30:19)

FEBRUARY 23

The people around you are a gift from Me to you. Let them know how thankful you are for their help and support in your life. I provide spiritual helpmates to everyone. Not everyone accepts My gift of love through the lives of their helpers. Be grateful for these people because they are My earthly angels providing heavenly care for your daily existence. They are not your servants, but they are your spiritual helpmates. I called them to walk alongside you in your life journey.

There are no casual helpmates; all of them are intentional in their assistance, from your first-grade teacher who provided instruction and guidance daily to the person who held the door open for you for just one fleeting moment. All of these short and long-term helpmates were in your life to help you achieve your goals and lead a righteous life in Me. Thank these helpers often, and look for more along the way.

These ordinary and extraordinary people are a blessing to show you what a grace-filled life can look like. Their behavior may not always reveal My grace, but you must learn to see signs of My revelation in who they are and what they do. Some stars shine brighter than others, yet they all have the same cosmic energy. Some of My children portray My love and grace more openly, yet they are gifts from Me to be your spiritual companions in this earthly life. Rejoice in these people always, My sacred heart.

Give thanks to people who are your spiritual helpmates; they are a gift from God.

I always **thank** my God for you because of his grace given to you in Christ Jesus. (1 Corinthians 1:4 NIV)

FEBRUARY 24

*T*he Communion Table is more than just a cup of remembrance of the Last Supper. The word "Eucharist" means Thanksgiving. The Eucharist is the holy table where sinners and saints gather to encounter the blessed Savior. Your Savior is present as you give thanks and drink from the cup of blessing and partake from the bread of life. These elements are visible gifts for a holy event that is occurring in your life. You are communing or becoming "One" in Me. You are made one by remembering this blessed event at the Last Supper on the night of the Savior's butyral. On that night of betrayal, the Savior gave thanks as he broke the bread and sipped from the cup. Realize that you enter a sacred circle and stand on holy ground when you share in the Eucharist of Thanksgiving. The visible signs of salvation are manifest in the Eucharist, which gives thanks for this sacred encounter.

There is more, My child. All food and drink that enters your body will chemically change you. That morning cup of coffee you so desperately seek will alter your heartbeat after the first good morning gulp. The bread of life and cup of blessing have an even more powerful influence on you, My sacred heart. Sharing in the Eucharist will alter your soul. You will be transported to the holy night of betrayal in a flash and the twinkling of an eye. You will stand in the presence of the sacred Savior who first broke the bread and raised the cup to his lips. Make no mistake; you are at one or in communion with your savior. You are changed.

Spiritual transformation happens when we give thanks for the Cup of Christ and the Bread of Life.

Is not the cup of **thanksgiving** for which we give thanks a participation in the blood of Christ? And is not the bread that we break a participation in the body of Christ? (1 Corinthians 10:16 NIV)

FEBRUARY 25

*N*ot all people will understand your morning ritual of prayer and praise. Some may find the spiritual things you do foreign and completely irrational. Do your morning ritual anyway. Giving Me thanks for what I have done in your life may awaken an understanding in the nonbelieving observer that I am authentic. At this point in their lives, they lack the intellectual and spiritual insight to comprehend who I am. Your prayers may help enliven their minds and kindle their spirits.

Not even like-spirited people may know what you are saying when you speak to Me in words and songs of prayer. Be sure that your spiritual encounter with Me can be translated into an understood language of mind and spirit. My words are meant for you, but other people may benefit from their meaning. Let your human language and spiritual words be discernable so that they may believe in My work in you.

Always remember that I am the essence of the Hebrew word Ruah, or Spirit or life force. I am the breath within you, the inspiration around you, and the divine spiritual power in all prayers. You may feel and know who I am, but you bless the other worshippers when they can interact with us. I exist in all of My children; I use blessed people like you to connect everyone together. The connection happens when you all realize I was empowering and emboldening your prayers. Let the amen be the crescendo to your holy prayer.

The power in prayer is revealed when people see God's work in you.

Otherwise, when you are praising God in the Spirit, how can someone else, who is now put in the position of an inquirer, say "Amen" to your **thanksgiving**, since they do not know what you are saying? (1 Corinthians 14:16)

FEBRUARY 26

*N*othing on this earth can contain My boundless grace. Nothing can measure the depth of My love, the breadth of My forgiveness, or the height of My grace. Trying to hold My grace is like placing a cup at the bottom of a stream. The cup soon fills, and the water continues to flow past the brimming cup. Do not hold back from sharing My constantly flowing grace. Your prayers and praise of thanksgiving give glory to Me and inform those who hear you. Your prayers will carry My grace into their hearts.
Give thanks for My stream of overflowing grace; it will create great reasons for celebration in your community and bring glory to Me. My blessings will fall like the morning rain and create an even larger stream of ever-flowing grace. One small prayer of thanksgiving will generate a river of overflowing blessings. Once set into motion, this spiritual stream cannot be stopped.

When you place your cup in the stream of God's grace, it will always overflow.

All this is for your benefit, so that the grace that is reaching more and more people may cause **thanksgiving** to overflow to the glory of God. (2 Corinthians 4:15 NIV)

FEBRUARY 27

*D*o not sow sparingly with the gifts I give you, My sacred heart. My abundance overflows in your life with a very intentional purpose. You receive in abundance so that you can share even more. This is a spiritual model for tremendous success. Learn to give freely of what you have received from Me, and I will bless you with endless bounty. The clouds give countless raindrops; they do not worry about the next immeasurable cloud burst. The next rain will come from Me.

I will provide opportunities to be generous with your giving on every occasion, knowing I will replenish what you have shared. This flow of My divine spiritual energy will cause a healthy spring of thanksgiving to bubble up all around you. Your generosity will always glorify Me because I am the originator of all your gifts. Never stop this flow of divine blessings; you are only part of the ever-flowing stream, not the dam at the end.

Raindrops have no specific target; they flutter and float through the air indiscriminately, landing on whatever enters their path. Likewise, blessings can slash and sprinkle beyond their intended recipient. Whatever you ask in prayer may come your way, but there may be more than enough that I can bless those around you. Believe that every blessing you receive is the beginning of a grand echo that will reverberate throughout the land with thanksgiving and praise.

Your generosity will result in thanksgiving to God.

You will be enriched in every way so that you can be generous on every occasion, and through us, your generosity will result in **thanksgiving** to God. (2 Corinthians 9:11 NIV)

February 28

*Y*our outward actions must always reveal My movement in your life. Your words will always tell the story of who I am in your life. A rude gesture or a thoughtless sentence from you will point people away from Me. People will look at you like I was never even part of your life. Do not display a spiritual vacancy sign on your life. I am always at home in your life, and you must live in such a way that people will see My ongoing residency.

Rather than causing people to cringe at you, inspire them to give thanks to Me. Encouraging people to give thanks to Me is your mission in life. Put out the welcome mat of love that invites people into your life so they can see My movement in everything you do and speak. I equipped you to show My glory and sing songs of My generous grace. Obscenity is not a language I chose to speak. Let kind and loving words flow from your mouth; it is a language I understand very well.

When you talk to someone, be an encourager. Let your words tell them that God loves them and that you are a living representative of God's love. You will know that you fulfilled your mission as an encouraging ambassador when you finish a conversation and the person gives thanks for being with you. Remember, I created everything by just speaking it into existence. Let your words create as much good as possible. Speak good into existence, My child.

God doesn't talk like that, so use language that sounds more like God.

Nor should there be obscenity, foolish talk, or coarse joking, which are out of place, but rather **thanksgiving.** (Ephesians 5:4 NIV)

MARCH 1

*A*nxiety is the result of the soul being drained of faith. If you are anxious, the vision of My movement in your future has been blocked or diminished. Your soul becomes anxious when you do not spend time with Me in prayer or petition. Lack of a spiritual connection with Me darkens the deeds I have already accomplished in your life. When you fail to see what I have done for you, thanksgiving will not occur in your life. Lack of thanksgiving causes death to the soul.

Come to Me believing that what you ask for will be manifest in your life as a reality. Let your prayer carry the tone of thanksgiving even before the event occurs. This process of giving thanks will restore your soul, enliven your faith, and open the door to the future you. Learn to celebrate what I have already given you and anticipate with thanksgiving what is yet to come.

Anxiety is always future-oriented. The problem arises because anxiety shields the soul from any vision of what I can do. When you are thankful for what you've already done and grateful for what you will do, there is no room left in your life for anxiety. Your soul is immediately centered in the seat of hope, and hope opens the door to the future. Whenever your heart is grateful, your soul will find its way to me, My child.

Be grateful for everything and anxious about nothing.

Do not be anxious about anything, but in every situation, by prayer and petition, with **thanksgiving,** present your requests to God. (Philippians 4:6 NIV)

MARCH 2

I love to hear thankful prayers about the people in your life. Your prayers mean that they are doing the job I have given them to accomplish in your life. You are not on this earth alone. Earthly angels surround you every day. Seek them out, use their gifts, and allow them to improve your life. The earthly angels are here to give you their best so you can do your best in life. These earthly angels may wear the face of a parent, child, or neighbor, but they are in your life to be your spirit mate; use them often.

Pray for your earthly angels often. Lift them up to Me in prayers of thanksgiving so that I will know you see the work they are doing in your life. Prayers of thanksgiving compel and propel My earthly angels in their daily work to support you. Never stop praying for My angels; they will never stop serving you. Prayers of thanksgiving without ceasing are always welcome and in order.

Remain keenly aware that I did not place you on this earth to be alone. You were formed and shaped in My holy image; you must continue to do what reflects Me in your life. The holy office of living the Christian life is a lifelong affair. Remember, you are only a part of the body of Christ. You need the other members to complete you and your Christian community. Draw from the depth of spirit that abides in your God gathering. When you give thanks to your earthly angels, it tells me that you are aware of My gifts of spiritual support and direction.

Giving thanks to angels, they are a gift from God.

We always **thank** God for all of you and continually mention you in our prayers. (1 Thessalonians 1:2 NIV)

MARCH 3

*A*ll people are worthy of praise, and every person deserves to be thanked for what they do for you. "Thank you for all you do." should be a deliberate and daily phrase from your lips to their ears. The diversity of this world makes your life complete and the world more enjoyable. Praying for those in your physical world soon draws them into your everyday spiritual world. It is this world of the spirit where you will all encounter Me face to face.

Let your time of prayer with Me include all people in this world. After all, these are the people with whom you share your life. These are the people with whom you share the planet. These are the people with whom we share our common spiritual ground. As you share your prayers of thanksgiving with Me, you open up a sacred space where everyone can live together in peace.

Be very particular and specific in your prayers of intercession. Intercessions to Me on behalf of another person make a huge spiritual shift in the world. You create the holy trinity of prayer when you draw in yourself, Me, and another person into the sacred circle. An unseen spiritual force connects us with cords of My holy love. You create a portal of prayer as you come to Me with petitions of intercession. Praying for the needs of another is a great blessing of your Christian love, My child.

Your prayers of thanksgiving for all people will create an everyday spiritual world of peace.

I urge, then, first of all, that petitions, prayers, intercession, and **thanksgiving** be made for all people. (1 Timothy 2:1 NIV)

March 4

*E*verything in My creation is good. You are part of a long line of humanity that I deem to be very good. Only people can look upon My creation and see it as not good. The intrinsic value I have placed in all good things remains no matter how people view it. Learn to find what is excellent and helpful to you. All items are good, but not everything is going to be beneficial to you. All foods are good, yet some bodies have an allergy to certain foods, and those foods are not helpful to that person. Yet the food remains good. Learn to give thanks for all of the gifts that are a part of my creation. Certain things may not be helpful to you, but they are useful to someone else. Give thanks for everything, and you will soon learn to appreciate all things. Thanksgiving is your gateway to seeing the goodness in My creation and My in people.

Do not let your tastebuds challenge your appetite for giving thanks for My work in you and the world. Each person has the right to discriminate taste, yet their disdain for a part of My creation does not diminish its glory for another person. Learn to see the hand of the Creator in all things; then, you will give thanks for everything. Only misuse and abuse of My creation can alter or diminish the perception of its glory. Your physical beauty may diminish with time, but you still reflect My holy glory within you, My child.

The glory of God's creation is worthy of your praise and thanks; you are part of it.

They forbid people to marry and order them to abstain from certain foods, which God created to be received with **thanksgiving** by those who believe and who know the truth. (1 Timothy 4:3 NIV)

MARCH 5

*D*id you rise this morning with thanksgiving in your heart? There is a lot to be thankful for in life. I have draped My creation with beauty and covered all life with My blessings. My creation is not just a play that you casually watch. My creation requires your complete attention and full participation. My creation comes to you on this day and every day as a gift from My hand. Receive my gift with thanksgiving and gratitude.

It is important for you to understand and give in to the fact that you are part of and participate in My creation. You cannot separate yourself from what I have done. You must totally buy into this spiritual premise because the minute you separate yourself from creation, you cease to be Mine. When you feel the hand of God upon your mind, body, and soul, you will look at yourself with the same awe and wonder in which I created you.

I have painted a golden sunrise to give light to your morning. I hope you enjoy it. The grass, trees, and birds are a living part of My creation gift to you. Give thanks for the scenery you barely notice as you drive by. I will paint the heavens with stars and planets that watch over you this evening. Enjoy their brilliance. Receive My daily gifts with the love that I give them. Give thanks.

You are God's caretaker and part of God's creation.

For everything God created is good, and nothing is to be rejected if it is received with **thanksgiving** (1 Timothy 4:4 NIV)

MARCH 6

*M*y creation is built on the formula of abundance. The rain falls to the earth to water the plants. The plants give life for food and oxygen for breathing. Heaven and earth work together to bring life to every living thing on this planet. I do not miscalculate My abundance; it is never meant to run short. Abundance means that" There is more than enough." More than enough to feed the animals, more than enough to feed the fish, and more than enough to feed all My children.

I encourage you to find new ways to share in My generous abundance. My abundance turns into human lack when the earth's riches are not fairly distributed. I do not blame you, but I do encourage you to help share My blessing, so the earth's resources fall to all My children. Hunger and want are not meant to be part of My ecosystem of abundant blessings. Feed the world; I have created more than enough to go around.

Not all abundant blessings will come in the form of cash, coins, or credit cards My sacred heart. Heavenly manna comes to you in the form of daily blessings. These timely blessings are what you need to exist, grow, and thrive in your life. Food, shelter, work, companionship, and love all are necessary manna that falls to earth from Me. I know what you have earned, but I blessed you and gifted you with the ability to earn a living. Through you, I turn My heavenly dew into your earthly riches.

God's abundant life means there will always be more than enough.

May God give you heaven's dew and earth's richness— an abundance of grain and new wine. (Genesis 27:28 NIV)

MARCH 7

*T*here is an excellent cycle to life and the abundance that flows to you. The seven years of abundance created enough to cover the seven years of famine. I do not withhold My blessings of abundance; I bless a thousandfold so there will be plenty even when the rains fail to fall. Be diligent as you store up the abundance of this earth and the blessings from heaven. You may not need your grain storehouse, but your neighbors may need your help as they experience personal famine.

Do not forget how My hand has blessed you. Your earthly riches represent My heavenly blessings. Do not be afraid to be generous with your silo of stored blessings. Famines come and go, and I will continually replenish your store in the good times so you will have abundance in the bad times. Remember that I am always with you; my presence will always create abundant life.

Abundance means that you will receive more than enough. I bless with more than enough for the times when there doesn't seem to be enough. All of My blessings are meant to spill over from you to those around you. Be generous and helpful when there is a lack and want in your land. You share the bounty of abundance with other people every day. Food, clothing, gas, and heat are all examples of abundance that flows from another source. Yes, you have to pay for their abundance, but you would have nothing if they did not have excess. Try to share your storehouse of plenty in time of need.

Receiving personal abundance from God may require us to share it as well.

Seven years of great abundance are coming throughout the land of Egypt, but seven years of famine will follow them. Then all the **abundance** in Egypt will be forgotten, and the famine will ravage the land. (Genesis 41:29-30 NIV)

MARCH 8

*R*eap without hesitation and with little concern during times of abundance. The rains will fall, the sun will shine, the crops will rise, and the harvest will be plentiful. Harvest is the time to store up today's abundance so that tomorrow will never be filled with lack. I am not asking you to hoard your wealth or withhold the blessings flowing to you. Prepare yourself for the shifts and cycles that naturally happen in life.

I have shown my children how to ride out these phases and emerge as winners. Let today's healthy harvest prepare you for tomorrow's fragile famine. Tend to your soul in the same manner; you tend to your fields or your bank account. Reap from the harvest of plenty that comes by walking with Me. The yield of plenty will give you collateral for future famines when you fail to find Me. Prepare for the times when you think you will not need Me, but realize that I am always with you.

You may not realize it, but whatever you do for your mind, you do for your soul. Whatever you do for your body, you do for your spirit. Take time every day to take in everything you need to build an abundance for your personal well-being. The soul becomes as hungry or thirsty as an unfed body. Your spirit will live in a similar fog as an ill-informed mind. Feed your soul with My abundance daily; the human spirit is always the last part of you to give in.

God gives daily bread and blessings for tomorrow.

During the seven years of **abundance,** the land produced plentifully. (Genesis 41:47 NIV)

MARCH 9

*L*et the wisdom of Joseph be your teaching for today. My servant did not act on his behalf; he followed My prompting for the good of an entire nation. Joseph's decisive action created a storehouse so that all would be fed and none would starve from lack of sustenance. When your faith is future-focused, you will do the same and even more than Joseph.

When food, water, and clothing are plentiful in your community, share your excess with thankful generosity with all who are short-changed by life situations. This is a spiritual approach to solving a physical problem. Listen to Me, follow Me, and I will lead you to the storehouses where My abundant blessings can be found. None of My precious children need to suffer if you act out of faith and love.

I lift up leaders in every generation to care for My people. I called Joseph thirty-five hundred years ago in Egypt. May I call you today, My child? You don't have to save a nation; just make a noticeable difference where you live. A warm coat for a cold body. One good meal for a starving soul. One kind word to a troubled mind. I know you can do these things; I gifted and blessed you to do more. By giving one small portion of your abundance, you will change your life and alter your world.

What you do today will change your tomorrow.

Joseph collected all the food produced in those seven years of **abundance** in Egypt and stored it in the cities. In each city, he put the food grown in the fields surrounding it. (Genesis 41:48 NIV)

MARCH 10

*A*s you rise this morning, prepare to seek the blessings of this day. I do not try to hide My blessings from you; you just fail to see what is placed in plain sight. Blessing flows to you directly from My hand and manifests through the earth's abundance. Some of My blessings come from My children who are around you. Some blessings may appear hidden in the shallow sands, but they are just waiting to burst into the very things you need.

Sometimes My children carry My blessings directly to you. The friendly smile on a gloomy day comes from Me. The courteous driver who allows you to pull in front of him or her is a gift from Me when you are running late. The coworker who shares an affirming word or gentle kindness bears My blessing. Pay attention to what I do for you every day. Many of My gifts a subtle but blessings are not the same.

You must have two things to receive My blessings. You must have faith enough to believe that you are always on My mind. No second of any day goes by without Me thinking of you, My sacred heart. Believe your blessings are coming. You must also have patience. While some blessings are obvious and readily available, others are delayed, and you must shift through the sans of time with a patient hand. Just know that everything you have comes from Me.

Feasting on God's blessings and receiving the hidden treasures of abundance in due time. Wait for the sands to shift.

They will summon peoples to the mountain and there offer the sacrifices of the righteous; they will feast on the **abundance** of the seas, on the treasures hidden in the sand." (Deuteronomy 33:19 NIV)

MARCH 11

I do not take from you to build My churches, sanctuaries of houses of worship. The resources for temples that carry My moniker are created by My abundance given to you. Each stone. Board and brick carry My name. I have blessed you so that you will have more than enough to sustain your life and honor My life in you.

Come to My temple for worship, prayer, and celebrations. My temple was built as a dwelling place for Me, where you can encounter My love and grace. Fill My sacred space with holy music, fervent prayers, and acclimations of worship. Give freely of yourself in My presence, and I will return your efforts with divine blessings. Come to me as a gathered crowd and worship Me in spirit. My sanctuaries were not just built to honor Me; they exist to welcome you.

You must remember that all of My places of worship and prayer are built from the abundance that I gave you. No one had a lack or want because of their generosity in building My houses of worship. Overflowing abundance built My dwelling places as a sign of My physical presence whenever you enter My home. I can manifest many major miracles in your life if you remain open to Me. My churches are just the beginning of what we can do.

God built heavenly dwelling places in earthly locations. Visit the temples of God often.

Lord our God, all this **abundance** that we have provided for building you a temple for your Holy Name comes from your hand, and all of it belongs to you. (1 Chronicles 29:16 NIV)

MARCH 12

A fantastic event occurs when My people come together to worship Me. Their individual and personal feelings of lack quickly change to create a collective celebration of abundance. What was deemed too little suddenly transformed into more than enough. The fellowship of the heart filled the shortcomings of the hands. Minor miracles seem to occur on these occasions that should not go unnoticed.

Do you see what happens to you when you come to My house and worship Me? Do not let My minor miracles go unnoticed by your untrained human eye. Dedicate yourself to serving My holy temple with your best efforts of worship and praise. I always honor those who find the time to honor Me by sacrificing their souls and worshiping with their hearts.

  You will find that your participation in worship has the potential to transform your life. Any time you make an offering to me through the sacrifice of your worship, you create sacred space for Me in your life. The holy ground of your worship is the threshing floor for reaping an abundant harvest in your life. Make no mistake, My sacred heart; worship is the divine portal to Me.

God blesses our worship and will multiply our offerings.

There were burnt offerings in abundance, together with the fat of the fellowship offerings and the drink offerings that accompanied the burnt offerings. So the service of the temple of the Lord was reestablished. (2 Chronicles 29:25 NIV)

MARCH 13

*M*y abundance and grace are offered to all the people of this earth. I do not restrict My love and charity to one region or another area of this earth. My blessings pour out from heaven to give life and abundance to all of the lands of this glorious blue planet. I share freely with everyone, from the desert sands to the snowy mountain tops.

Rise from your slumber this morning, knowing that you live in a heavenly realm in an earthly location. The place where you live and the spot where you sleep are all part of My glorious world. It was by My hand that the lands were created, and it is through My love that they will be blessed. Go into My world and encounter My blessing everywhere. My creation exists for your use; enjoy it daily.

I must be clear in stating that the entire earth is covered with enough food to sustain all life on this holy planet. Any lack or want by the people of earth is a human manifestation of the improper allotment of My blessings. I do not intend to point a guilty finger at leaders or nations; I only want to open caring hearts so the world will join together in feeding those who hunger needlessly. I provide the blessings; humanity must determine a loving allocation. Please choose wisely, My children.

God covers the earth with countless blessings.

This is the way he governs the nations and provides food in **abundance**. (Job 36:31 NIV)

MARCH 14

*R*ise each morning and wash in the river of delights. In this river, you will be cleansed of all transgressions and will be ready to receive My daily blessings. Such a state of spiritual readiness to receive My blessings can only come from worshipping Me. Worship is more than just a specified service at a specific time and within a particular place. Worship is also placing your spirit before Me and giving all that you are to Me.

This state of spiritual openness and adoration of Me places you in the river of delights. Delight in My presence and begin each day ready to receive My blessings as you give yourself to Me in worship. Come and feast on the abundance of this day and drink from the goodness of My love.

How will you know you are in the River of Delights, you ask My child? You will feel joy. Joy is a spiritual fruit and feeling that comes from spending time with Me. Unfortunately, joy is rarely felt by My children today. It is so very sad because I bless all of My children with the spiritual fruit of joy just by coming close to Me. Do not look so hard for the things in life to make you happy when I can bring you joy anytime just by being with Me.

Joy is a spiritual fruit found in the River of Delights.

They feast on the **abundance** of your house; you give them drink from your river of delights. (Psalm 36:8 NIV)

MARCH 15

I created each season to give you its abundance and blessing. Sometimes there will be an overflowing abundance of a spiritual crop. These are the times in your life when things go well and your life is easy. Look back upon the year with satisfaction, knowing that I walked with you each step of every day in your journey through life. I do not abandon you in the lean years; I walk even closer to you than you can imagine.

Gleam for yourself a bounty of spiritual blessings. Fill your cart until it overflows with My goodness. Feel free to take from Me as much as you need or desire. My blessings will last for this day and provide for the days ahead. Do not worry about the lean times in your life; I will always bless you with more than enough to carry you through the dry seasons of life. Seasons are just what they are; no season lasts forever. Learn to be patient in the lean years and rejoice in the abundant harvest.

I encourage you to follow abundance with a cart of gratitude. You will have a great physical and spiritual harvest when you recognize My work in your life and are grateful for My blessings. When you lack gratitude, you have nothing to place your blessings in. An ungrateful heart cannot see the blessings I place before you. Your morning manna will dissolve before you can collect it. Let gratitude become your spiritual eyes so you can clearly see all my abundant blessings, My child.

Be grateful for today's blessings; they will provide more than you will need.

You crown the year with your bounty, and your carts overflow with abundance. (Psalm 65:11 NIV)

MARCH 16

*D*o not fret over the behaviors of the unjust. All My children are welcome to drink from my waters of abundance. I give freely to everyone, but not everyone sees what they have as a blessing from Me.   They do not see that their daily bread is buttered with the glory of creation itself. My gifts are nothing more than physical items removed from the shopping list of this planet.

Take note of those who are wronged and treated unjustly. These are the people you must assist in life. The poor, the needy, and the forgotten have been offered the waters of My blessings of abundance, but society has short-changed their fair share. Care for these thirsty souls who stand mid-stream hip-deep in My blessings but cannot get enough. Begin your mornings with a prayer for all who are offered blessings but have been pushed aside from the waters of life.

You have journeyed with Me for some time, My child; I hope you are gaining insight into the spiritual workings of this world and your life. My guidance gives you the quickest, most certain way to success. Success is never yours alone; you can only be successful when none of My beloved children are left behind. Many great competitors have crossed the finish line first and alone. In life, there are no winners unless everyone finishes the race. Abundance means that there is more than enough for everyone.

Drink from abundant water.

Therefore, their people turn to them and drink water in abundance. (Psalm 73:10 NIV)

MARCH 17

*T*he world can offer you much to make you wealthy and create a life of abundance. Minerals, jewels, and ores are just part of My creation to beautify the world. You place more excellent material value on them than they were intended to have. To Me, a diamond is just a beautiful rock; you see it as a priceless jewel. Rubies were created to give beauty to My earth; you deemed them to have great value. I am delighted that you think so highly of the ordinary stones of creation, but you give them far more importance than intended. You hold the most excellent value on this earth. Rocks and stones cannot carry My wisdom or harbor Me. You can outshine the most brilliant jewel by sharing My understanding and love. You are worth far more than gold or silver when you testify to the daily blessings you receive from Me. Set yourself as the crown jewel of the world and radiate My love.

You can produce more abundance than any diamond mine, My sacred heart. Speak to others about Me. Tell your neighbors about your life with Me, and how you come to Me in prayer. Give your friends an insight into our spiritual relationship, and how I guide you through life. When you share your knowledge about Me, you unearth the greatest treasure in the world, My child.

Speaking knowledge is better than gold.

Gold there is, and rubies in abundance, but lips that speak knowledge are a rare jewel. (Proverbs 20:15)

MARCH 18

The only way to cleanse your soul is by sacrificing your heart. I live in the heart of the penetrant person who has come to Me through the work of the Savior. No soap can purify the soul, and no sanitizer can remove the stains created by sin. My saving grace alone makes the perfect room for My indwelling in your life. I do not coexist with sin.

As you clean the outer person this morning through your daily ritual, give thanks for the cleansing of the inner person by My grace. My grace is the most abundant gift on this earth. I have created enough for every person in every period of time. Even though I cleanse you whiter than snow you must do one thing to complete this spiritual cleaning process, my child. Do not hang onto the sins that I forgave.

Too many of My beloved children cling to their sins or even their parent's sins. Guilt is always an option of your choosing, I always let go of the sins of the past. My grace washes all sins completely from your soul, you must release the memory of them from your mind. The only past sins or generational sins that exist are the ones you dig up from the past. Do not let your guilt chain your soul to sins that were cleaned and erased from your life. Rather than choosing guilt, select My Love and Grace, they are a healthier option.

Living free from guilt through God's grace.

Although you wash yourself with soap and use an abundance of cleansing powder, the stain of your guilt is still before me," declares the Sovereign Lord. (Jeremiah 2:22 NIV)

March 19

*Y*ou will betray yourself through your own words. Your words can never hide the desires of the heart. It is tough to do good in the world when your heart demands evil deeds from you. Ask yourself these simple questions, "Does God talk like that, and does God act like that?" If you answer "Yes," then you are walking with Me. If "No," then you are not with Me; you walk alone.

Evil cannot exist in a purified heart. The life span of sin is short-lived when I dwell in your heart. Seek Me every morning through fervent prayer. Prayer will plant Me deep in your heart, and sin will have no place in your life to dwell. The difference between an evil person and a good person has Me in your heart and soul. Make a good choice every morning.

Godly actions only happen through a holy heart and a sincere soul. You cannot live a life in Me when your heart and soul belong to this world. A true disciple follows the teaching of the master. When your mind thinks like Me and your heart feels what I do, you will soon act as I would act. You are given free will in all matters, My sacred heart. When you give your life over to Me you will be freed from the traps and poor choices of this world. Faith is always the first step to walking by My side.

Acting like Jesus will only happen when our hearts are sincere and open to God.

You brood of vipers, how can you who are evil say anything good? For the mouth speaks what the heart is full of. (Matthew 12:34 NIV)

MARCH 20

*A*bundance is a live organism. Abundance is not just a collection of things or material wealth. True abundance is My blessings that come to you from My hands. Do not treat your abundant blessings from Me as inanimate nonliving things. If you treat them as a gathered hoard of your possessions, they will wither and die. Abundance is an ingathering of a spiritual harvest.

Learn to honor My gifts by keeping them alive and growing. Abundance naturally regenerates when it is shared. Sharing creates multiplication, not subtraction. The more you give to help others, the more I will bless you to restore your treasures. Do not worry, My child; I will provide you with even more than you can imagine.

Think of yourself as a hen caring for a nest of eggs about to hatch. Abundance is not what you have but the potential of what it can become. If you set on a nest of accumulated wealth, be ready to hatch, food, clothing, medical supplies, and homes for the poor. Your brood of chicks will grow and prosper and do likewise in My name. The spiritual law of abundance is simple, "What you have is more than enough and it will become even greater when you share it. Remember, you are the only restriction to your abundance, My child.

The more you have, the more will be given and the greater the expectation.

Whoever has will be given more, and they will have an abundance. Whoever does not have, even what they have will be taken from them. (Matthew 13:12 NIV)

MARCH 21

*Y*ou may have earthly riches, but do you have heavenly abundance? I have placed My blessings in your life for your most competent care. Do your best to care for what I have given you; there is an accounting for what you have and what you will gain. Some will store up all My gifts for their glory and gratification. Store up what you need for the day and some for times of famine. But learn to multiply what you have been given from Me.

This is not a harsh statement; it is your divine calling from Me. My heavenly reign is tied to your earthly life. I choose to speak through you, work wonders through you, and make Myself known through you. The more you share Me through you, the more I will bless you with Me in your life. I am the abundance you seek, manifesting through My blessings and love.

I cannot be untied from the blessings I give to you, My sacred heart. I am the pure energy of love incarnate, or love made real. I showed all of My children this wonderful sign of My divine love through the blessed Savior. All physical gifts are spiritual manifestations of My love for all of My children. The sun, stars, and moon are all perfect gifts of My love for you. I do not take from My children; unfortunately, they fail to realize what blessings they have.

God works through faith; believe it, and you will see it.

Whoever has will be given more, and they will have an abundance. Whoever does not have, even what they have will be taken from them. (Matthew 25:29 NIV)

MARCH 22

*H*onor what you have but learn to live without the things you do not need. Earthly wealth can be a deadly demon that always requires more. The problem is, you will never have enough to feed it more constantly. It will whine and whimper at your feet, and your ego will want to feed its starving carcass, but if you feed this greedy beast, it will only want more. You will never have enough to fill the bottomless pit of need and greed.

You are better than that. You have learned to distinguish between a blessing that fulfills your life and a possession that will only drain you of your spiritual energy. My blessings and gifts are for your comfort. Blessings are to enhance your life and are not meant to be the focus of life. Let your possessions serve you, and your blessings employed to serve Me.

I give you this warning, My child. You were created to belong to Me. You are one of My blessed children. If your heart strays or your soul wanders, a wide array of things in this world would love to own you. At first, these shiny toys seem to be made just for you, but they only want to consume you. All of these worldly treasures look different, but they all carry the same surname of Greed. Remember, your name is Christian.

A warning against greed. There is a fine line between possessing things and things possessing us.

Then he said to them, "Watch out! Be on your guard against all kinds of greed; life does not consist in an **abundance** of possessions." (Luke 12:15 NIV)

MARCH 23

I make things holy. I turn the ordinary into the extraordinary and sacred. I created Adam out of the red dust of the earth. I gave Adam life as I blew My holy breath into him. Because of the sin that originated with Adam, I must move in your life to bring the cleansing power of the Blood of Salvation. You are made holy through the forgiveness of your sins by this sacred offering of Salvation Blood on your behalf. As I gave life to Adam, I redeemed life through the Savior.

This sanctifying will bring holy peace through grace to your life. This peace will continue to flow to you with unique and everlasting abundance. My sanctifying act will bring you the only peace you will need because you know you belong to Me, and I am a part of your life. Revitalize your soul in Me every morning, for you are now My holy child. You are well-loved.

There are no mistakes here, My sacred heart. I chose you and called you from your mother's womb. My work began in you before you gasped your first breath of air. You are my living representative on this earth. You must learn to show loving-kindness, grace-filled compassion, and a loving heart to everyone around you. Whenever you face times of trouble or doubt, just look at your hands as a reminder that you were formed and fashioned by My holy hands. My fingerprints are on your soul.

We are created by God, forgiven by God, and sanctified by God in holiness.

Who have been chosen according to the foreknowledge of God the Father, through the sanctifying work of the Spirit, to be obedient to Jesus Christ and sprinkled with his blood: Grace and peace be yours in **abundance**. (1 Peter 1:2 NIV)

MARCH 24

*M*ercy, peace, and love are the gifts that you should look for every morning. Start each day seeking My mercies, centered in My peace and knowing how much you are loved. Dip into this well each morning and draw your fill of My gifts. Drink deeply from the waters of peace and carry My love into your world so that all will receive My divine mercy. Offer peace to those you encounter today. I give My peace to you from an abundant and bottomless well, so share it freely.

My love comes to you with endless abundance as well. Give freely of My gifts because your kindness to another person may be their only encounter with My mercy, love, and peace all day. My understanding, love, and peace are given in heaping portions so they will spill out from you into the lives of others. My mercy withholds judgment which creates peace centered in My love. My gifts work together to create the life you seek.

  Do not look so hard to find My mercy, peace, and love, My child. I planted all three to grow abundantly across the earth. Mercy, peace, and love are in all of My children. Mercy occurs when you forgive another person of their sins. Peace occurs when there is no animosity between My children. When you grant mercy and find peace you will uncover the glory of My love. My love is always present, but it is easily covered by an unforgiving and troubled heart.

Finding God's mercy and love in abundant blessings.

Mercy, peace, and love be yours in **abundance**. (Jude 1:2 NIV)

MARCH 25

*L*et these words of Scripture be your song to Me each morning as you rise from your slumber. My love has led all of My people to My offering for redemption from sin. I offer redemption without hesitation or question. Redemption is provided because it flows from My love of My children from generation to generation. It is My divine and holy nature to offer My love so freely. My love is My morning offering to you. Open your heart to receive My love as your first gift of the day.

Take My gift of love, which will guide you throughout your day. You will find Me in My holy dwelling of divine love. I choose to dwell wherever My love abides. I am located in temples, worship centers, and churches worldwide. I reside in the hearts of men, women, and children in every corner of this planet. Let My love lead you to wherever I dwell, all places, and every person is made holy by My presence.

Remember this, My child. You are the greatest achievement of my holy temple church. I choose to dwell in you just as I chose the Temple in Jerusalem, the Cathedral of Notre Dame, or the little brow church in the dale. I made you holy so I could dwell in you, and you could become a holy temple to Me. I will guide nonbelievers to you so that they can see my work in you. Because of your splendor and majesty, their faith will be ignited, and their lives will be changed.

God's holy temple church is one place to find God.

In your unfailing love, you will lead the people you have redeemed. In your strength, you will guide them to your **holy** dwelling. (Exodus 15:13 NIV)

MARCH 26

*T*here are boundaries between the sacred, secular, holy, and profane. Without Me, you remain in a world with no spiritual foundation. You put limits on yourself if you do not seek a sacred and holy life with Me. I am sacred, and I am holy. Once you receive Me, you will stand in My divine presence and hear My sacred words of comfort and peace. You will continue to live and work and have your life in the secular world, but I will be the center of your life and the foundation for living.

Moses brought My holy commandments to My people. You will carry My divine presence to your place of work and your family setting. You will cross over between both the secular and sacred through Me. You will live in both worlds. Rise from your holy rest each morning and move into the material world as you take My power with you.

I will not limit your access to the world or to My holy presence. You must be mindful, however, that not all things in this world can share the holy ground you stand on. Everything in this world is My glorious creation. However, My children have created combinations and concoctions that are deadly. These combinations of curiosities stain and profane the sacred ground you stand upon. Holy means "set apart," so do not stain the sacred with the secular.

The sacred power of God is meant to be carried into the secular world.

Moses said to the Lord, "The people cannot come up Mount Sinai, because you yourself warned us, 'Put limits around the mountain and set it apart as **holy**.'" (Exodus 19:23 NIV)

MARCH 27

I created a holy day of rest for you. You must try your best to find rest for your sacred soul in Me on this Sabbath day. Without this day, you will diminish your spiritual power if I do not renew the soul and restore the body. Without our time together, it will soon feel like you have died spiritually. If you cannot take the time to be with Me on the Sabbath for countless reasons, try to find just one easy way to make your Sabbath happen. You will thank Me for the time together later when your daily grind oppresses you.

On the Sabbath day, you will find the rest in Me you so desperately seek. I will make everything new in you on this holy day and restore your soul for the week ahead. You work hard all week trying to keep up your worldly life. Seek the time to refresh, renew, and improve your heavenly spirit and your life with Me. Come to Me, and I will give you holy spiritual rest.

Sabbath means, "To rest." When you find the sacred space of rest in Me, your rest will be holy. Sabbath does not have to be a specific day; it just needs to be a time dedicated to honoring Me in My holy presence. You can find rest for your body or mind in relaxing leisure, but you only find the sacred holy rest in Me through your Sabbath time. I am not making a demand on your time, My child. I invite you to receive restoration, relaxation, and renewal for a weary spirit that consumes all of My children. Come to Me now.

Finding rest for your spirit comes from spending time with God.

'Observe the Sabbath, because it is **holy** to you. (Exodus 31:14 NIV)

'Observe the Sabbath, because it is **holy** to you. Anyone who desecrates it is to be put to death; those who do any work on that day must be cut off from their people. (Exodus 31:14 NIV)

MARCH 28

*Y*ou are the priceless treasure of My heart, My sacred child. I searched the world over to select you as one of My holy people. I chose you and called you to join others in forming a holy nation and a sacred people. I claimed you with My divine love and blessed you with My everlasting grace. You are mine forever, and now, share your life with like-spirited people across this planet.

I did not call you to remain My hidden possession or treasured trophy sitting motionless on a shelf. I called you and sent forth to be My holy blessing to this world. Others are looking to become your sacred spiritual sibling in Me. Show them the way to Me and give them My holy name. There are too many people who do not see their priceless spiritual value. Show them what it means to be one of My sacred jewels. Help Me Create a jeweled crown of glory with a place for everyone in the setting.

You must see your value and worth in everything, My sacred heart. You are the crown jewel of My glorious creation. You were perfected and placed on top of all that came before you. I stopped creating everything after you, My child because you were as close to Me as I could make. Treat yourself with due respect and awe, and treat your neighbor likewise. My children are all My priced possessions and glorious creations.

God's holy possessions are glorious treasures and priceless people.

For you are a people **holy** to the Lord your God. The Lord your God has chosen you out of all the peoples on the face of the earth to be his people, his treasured possession. (Deuteronomy 7:6 NIV)

MARCH 29

I will look down upon you every morning as you rise from the night's sleep. While you have been resting your body and restoring your soul, I have been busy. I have been busy fulfilling My promise given to your spiritual ancestors so many years ago. Through a spoken sacred oath, I promised to make your land flow with the wealth and blessings of milk and honey.

I honor My promises; I keep My sacred oaths. My blessings will come to you new each morning in countless, never-ending ways. Heaven and earth will embrace you as your land takes on heavenly beauty. Life will appear the same to the untrained eye, but you will see the vast difference through the eyes of your spirit. You will see how I move and live among My people. You will witness the transformation of your land into My holy dwelling place. I will genuinely bless the area in which I dwell.

You have survived and thrived on the land because of the blessings from My holy hand. I am the same Spirit that moved over the deep and parted the waters of creation. I continue to create and do signs and wonders in your life today. Never take the world or what you have for granted, My child; I am active in your life more than you can imagine. I fulfill what I promised to your ancestors out of love for you. My blessing is more than shallow memories; they are gifts of love to you, My sacred heart.

God's promise to bless us with the land of milk and homey when we recognize God's work in our lives.

Look down from heaven, your **holy** dwelling place, and bless your people Israel, and the land you have given us as you promised on oath to our ancestors, a land flowing with milk and honey." (Deuteronomy 25:16 NIV)

MARCH 30

I am holy and want all of My people to live in holiness. I dwell in the religious and sacred ground of infinite love and divine forgiveness. Do not bother yourself by seeking Me in your worldly wonder or earthy experiences. I cannot live amongst the dark lands of human greed, envy, hatred, poverty, war, or self-destruction. These are lands of your creation and worlds where you dwell on your own limited devices. All of these aforementioned things are against My nature to love and forgive all humans.

Come to Me now, My child. The land of holiness is wide open to all believers who dare to follow Me. Drop all sinful habits and pick up holy, healthy living centered in Me. If you place your life in My care, you will always be in the center of My divine love. This holy land is adorned with love, forgiveness, compassion, and blessings. Arise this morning and dwell with Me in this.

The blessed Savior gave you a model for holy living. Jesus ate with the sinner, but he did not sin. The loving Savior cared for those who broke the Law, yet he fulfilled it. Make no mistake, My child; you are My modern-day holy vessel. In the same way, the Ark of the Covenant and the Savior carried My holy presence, so do you today. Whenever you fail to walk the road of holiness, My grace is available for you.

How to live in holiness when sinners surround you.

And the people of Beth Shemesh asked, "Who can stand in the presence of the Lord, this **holy?**
God? To whom will the ark go up from here?" (1 Samuel 6:20 NIV)

MARCH 31

I have empowered My people to go beyond their human limitations for generations. The meek have found the spiritual strength to speak to kings and queens. The smallest have seen the physical strength to stand up to the greatest giants and most terrifying foes. People of little consequence have significantly impacted the world and changed lives forever. I have empowered the lame to outrun the wicked and finish the race ahead of them.

What is your Goliath? Your inner fear causes you to see the most diminutive creature as your most significant threat in life. My spiritual power gives you the ability to see things as they are. Do not cloud your life with fear and trembling; rise each day knowing I am with you. Wash away all the fear you have created in your life and let it swirl down the drain with your morning shower, knowing that I will fill you with the power and spiritual strength you need for this day. Faith and fear do not mix well together; choose one over the other.

I am the greatest spiritual force on the earth. Meek, mild men became super spiritual slayers because they carried my power within their frail frames. Weary, worn women transformed into dynamic damsels destined for greatness. You have the greatest power in the universe dwelling inside of you, My child. First, you must trust Me to use you in ways that you never imagined.

Destroy your demons with spiritual strength from God.

Then Peter, filled with the **Holy Spirit**, said to them: "Rulers and elders of the people! (Acts 4:8 NIV)

APRIL 1

*D*o not try to out-think or outwit Me. I am here to help you in life and bless you every day. Yet, history is dotted with foolish attempts to outshine the sun and cast shadows on the stars. I give My servants the spiritual ability to share My message with power and hope. Nothing can hinder My movement or soften My words. So, do not be afraid of any obstacle in your way; I will give you the strength to overcome and outshine any feeble human attempt to impede your progress.

The world saw My servant David as a small Shepheard boy too tiny and too young to benefit Me or change the world. I saw David as a king and ruler of a great nation. I gave David the spiritual power to live up to My expectations for him. You have the same opportunities David had, My child. Do not hesitate to step before your Goliath; challenges are My specialty. Overwhelming odds are My forte.

You carry My voice into a world that too often seeks an unholy life path. Let Me speak words of wisdom through you as you stand firm and say, "No more!" No more senseless crimes. Stop killing each other with random acts of hatred. No more starvation when the planet produces abundance. Let My children hear My words of comfort and love when they hear desperate utterances of destruction and hate. Help the world say, "I love you to each other, My sacred heart.

The Holy Spirit will speak against evil plans.

APRIL 2

*D*o not resist Me as many did in years past. Do not rise in the morning with your neck stiff and stuck looking in one direction. Let your neck be subtle with the ability to sway back and forth so you can follow Me throughout your day. If you remain spiritually stiff-necked in the mornings, you will lose the day's focus. Open your heart to feel My love, and open your ears to hear the sweet whisper of My voice as your day begins.

With your neck mobile, your heart open, and your ears attentive, you will see the miracles of this day that I will bring you. Each day brings the possibility of a holy encounter with Me. The meeting may happen on your way to work. You may feel My presence in the aisle of the grocery store. Or the warmth of My spiritual hug may bring you comfort as you enjoy a meal with your family. Remain open to My presence in any and every setting of your day.

Age is not a contributing factor to a spiritual stiff neck. Your body will align with the direction you want it to go. If you no longer listen to me or follow me, your neck will look elsewhere for direction. A subtle neck indicates an active spirit. Learn to follow Me with heart, mind, and soul. That way, you will not become stuck facing in just one direction.

You must remain spiritually flexible to follow the moment of God in your daily life.

"You stiff-necked people! Your hearts and ears are still uncircumcised. You are just like your ancestors: You always resist the **Holy Spirit**! (Acts 7:51 NIV)

APRIL 3

*Y*our life will be filled with encounters with My holy messengers to give you direction, help you find your voice, and give you courage in difficult times. These divine encounters will encourage your spirit to stir and follow My direction and lead. How often have you heard someone say, "God was true to Me when that happened?" This is more than just a casual comment; it recognizes a dramatic spiritual event.

The next time you are in the middle of a difficult life situation, pray for My help. When you are burdened with the oppressive weight of daily anxiety, seek My support. When you feel alone, unwanted, and unloved, come and sit by My side and feel the warmth of My divine love. Whenever you pray, ask, or seek. Look for My messengers to come to your aid; My messengers are here to serve you.

Angelic holy beings are not always celestial cherubs. Oftentimes, terrestrial beings who live next door can bear My message. It is not so much the messenger but the message that will need your immediate attention. I will select the vessel that will carry My message with the greatest care. Your only role is to listen, My child.

Angels still carry messages from God. Remain open to their presence in your life.

The men replied, "We have come from Cornelius the centurion. He is a righteous and God-fearing man, who is respected by all the Jewish people. A **holy** angel told him to ask you to come to his house so that he could hear what you have to say." (Acts 10:22 NIV)

APRIL 4

*P*eople will always flock to witness the presence of the unexpected and unknown. Fear gives way to curiosity, and people will place themselves in the middle of harm's way to just get a glimpse of something extraordinary and unusual. Your life doesn't have to be a sideshow attraction to gather people to see what I am doing in your life. Show them how the ordinary act of living each day can be enhanced and blessed through Me.

Show them how I can quiet your soul amid a whirling out-of-control daily schedule. Be like a sideshow barker who draws attention to My divine work by openly giving thanks for My blessing in your life. Let your faith become the main attraction in your life as it shines a spotlight on Me. The curious will come to you, but the faithful will remain in Me.

Let God be the main attraction in your life, and the world will gather to see the show.

He was a good man, full of the **Holy Spirit** and faith, and a great number of people were brought to the Lord. (Acts 11:24 NIV)

APRIL 5

I called all of My beloved children to be My holy people. You are made righteous through your association with Me. My indwelling in you in your life creates a sacred bond of spiritual energy through My divine grace. Learn to live a life that honors all the people of My holy family. Rise each morning, knowing that your spiritual brothers and sisters walk by your side, work next to you, and shop in the same stores where you shop.

Seeing people as My holy gathering on this earth will change how you live. You share My name; you participate in My calling to serve all humankind, and you are all loved by Me. There are no strangers in your community, only the same spirit-minded people you have yet to meet. Walk with My holy people and share in My grace and peace. I created you to be one big glorious family, not a smattering of groups around the earth.

We are all the holy people of God; welcome to the family.

To all in Rome who are loved by God and called to be his **holy** people: Grace and peace to you from God our Father and from the Lord Jesus Christ. (Romans 1:7 NIV)

APRIL 6

I will open the eyes of your heart so you can see the blessings I bring to all My holy people. My blessings will come to you as a glorious inheritance from Me. I want to bless you in mind, body, and spirit so you will lack nothing as My holy child who lives among My sacred people. I will provide food for the body, enlightenment for the mind, and inspiration for the soul.

The greatest gift I will give to you is My gift of hope. Use hope when it seems to be lost. Hope will reopen the eyes of your heart when fear covers them in desperate times. Hope is the one thing you must hang onto when everything else seems to be failing. Even if the world is plagued with a deadly pandemic, grasp onto My hope. You engage hope when you put your faith into action. Faith allows faith to fill the emptiness of the future.

When all seems to be lost, open the door to hope. You will find God there.

I pray that the eyes of your heart may be enlightened in order that you may know the hope to which he has called you, the riches of his glorious inheritance in his **holy** people, (Ephesians 1:8 NIV)

APRIL 7

*M*y love for you and all of My children is immeasurable because My love encapsulates all of My glorious creations. I formed the sun and moon, the stars and the glorious heavens out of love. I created a basin with My hands to hold the ocean's waters, and My love supports the sky above you. The very air you breathe contains My passion. The water you drink is two parts hydrogen, one part oxygen, and includes all of My love. My love can be found in every place and everything in heaven and on this earth.

The great height of the enormous mountains will never measure up to the divine love I bring to My holy people. The ever-expanding universe will always chase the breadth of My love in vain; it will never measure up. Together, My sacred people have an untied spiritual power that outshines the stars in the heavens. Never underestimate what My love brings to you. My passion comes to you without measure.

The universe cannot contain all of God's love.

May have power, together with all the Lord's **holy** people, to grasp how wide and long and high and deep is the love of Christ, (Ephesians 3:18 NIV)

APRIL 8

*Y*our faith has placed you among My holy people. You heard the words of faith spoken to you, and you responded. Testimony about My divine presence in your daily living has the power to change lives forever. The words you share about how I empower your life will indeed find their way into the hearts of those who do not believe in Me at this time. Your testimony about My presence in your life will encourage a struggling soul.

The holy chain of faith begins with hearing My living word, you believe, and you testify to another person. The chain of religious belief is only broken when believers fail to testify about Me. Make sure you are a strong link in this vital chain of trust. If you do not share your faith through your testimony, believers may be excluded from My holy people. I place My future in your capable hands. Help all believers marvel in My divine presence. Tell everyone of My generous love.

Does your life give enough testimony to convict you of being a child of God?

On the day he comes to be glorified in his **holy** people and to be marveled at among all those who have believed. This includes you because you believed our testimony to you. (2 Thessalonians 1:10 NIV)

APRIL 9

*Y*ou are My beloved child, My sacred heart. The moment you accepted My calling to become a child of the blessed Savior, I brought you into the family of My holy people. Being part of My family is no small matter but should be considered a significant milestone in your life. I awakened your spirit to My movement in your life. Without the quickening of your soul, you would still be dead in your body and unaware of My activity in your life.

You now carry the invisible marks of salvation on the outside and My indwelling in you on the inside. We form a holy spiritual union with others like spirit-minded people who also believe in Me. Do not take this union of divine nature for granted. I am what unites the dissimilar and unique peoples of this earth into a holy unified family. Always live your life to bring honor to Me and your brothers and sisters in our spiritual family.

You live in a holy family sanctified by God.

Both the one who makes people holy and those who are made **holy** are of the same family. So Jesus is not ashamed to call them brothers and sisters. (Hebrews 2:11 NIV)

APRIL 10

*T*he soul cannot see My glory under the dim light of nonbelief. Only by believing in Me will you come to accept My calling to serve Me. I called you to be a royal priesthood of faithful believers. Yes, I have chosen you to be a vital part of this priesthood of believers who honor Me with their lips and lives. As you rise from the dark cover of the night, open your eyes to the glorious light I bring to you every morning. Jesus rose from the grave alone but immediately went to be with his followers. Easter was a fulcrum for peoples and nations to unite and join in Christian companionship. In My glorious light, your spirit will naturally want to gravitate toward people of similar faith. Go to them, together you make a holy nation whose sole purpose in life is to serve Me. Step into the dawn's early light and sing My praises and say your sacred prayers to Me. Remember that I called you out of darkness into My glorious light with each sunrise. While the body may want to sit silently in silence to slowly sip coffee, let the soul be free to gravitate toward active faith with other people of kindred faith.

You do have a purpose on this earth, My child of faith. To find your purpose in life, you must first deny yourself in the fashion of the blessed Savior. This does not mean that you think little of yourself or throw your life away. You are a vital part of the living body of Christ. Your purpose lies within the body and as part of the royal priesthood. If you ask yourself how you can best serve Me and build up the body of Christ, you will find your life path and your spiritual direction. I formed you and created you to be your own unique person who represents Me on earth. You are My hands and feet; I have no purpose without you.

God has chosen you to live in the light of the priesthood of all true believers.

But you are a chosen people, a royal priesthood, a **holy** nation, God's special possession, that you may declare the praises of him who called you out of darkness into his wonderful light. (1 Peter 2:9 NIV)

APRIL 11

*P*ractice dressing your world in fine linen every morning when you rise from your sleep. Fine linen will brighten your day as you see how My holy people honor Me through their righteous living. My followers' righteous acts are present daily in the world; you just fail to see them. Do not restrict your vision to observing only humans' selfish and shameful acts. The evening news shows too much negative unholy behavior.

Instead, see the people of this world for what they can be and for the good deeds they have already performed. I see the poor clothed, the hungry fed, and the thirsty blessed with water. Become a part of the world that dresses in My finest linens and does not sustain the stains of shameful sins. Righteousness is always fashionable.

You must put on the new person, or clothe yourself in the blessed Savior. You must adorn your soul to be radiant and glorious from the inside out. Practice, compassion, kindness, humility, gentleness, and patience as a way of life, and you will Sparkle like the sun. You must learn to be as forgiving of others as the Savior is of you. Forgiveness and compassion will make your soul the Lois Vuitton envy of everyone who sees you. If you were the actions of Jesus on the inside, you would appear as the Christian Pierre Cardin on the outside.

Cloth your world with the fantastic fashion of righteous living.

Fine linen, bright and clean, was given her to wear." (Fine linen stands for the righteous acts of God's **holy** people.). (Revelation 9:18 NIV)

APRIL 12

*R*emember where you came from, My child. You are the result of earthly human creation with a divine spiritual origin. Honor your father and mother for the gift of life they gave to you. Carry their names proudly into the world as a part of your human heritage. But always remember that you carry My divine name as well. Be thankful and proud of your starting point in life, and anticipate that the best is yet to come.

Honoring your father and mother keeps you connected to your earthly extended family and support system. This temporal connection will improve your life throughout your days. Honor My holy people and Me, and peace will thrive in the land in which you live. Recognizing and honoring your earthly heritage and spiritual blessings will fill your days with peace and love. You honor your parents and Me when you live up to our hopes for your life.

   When you honor your parents and celebrate Me, you connect yourself to the power of creation. I created the first humans. I also created the process by which humans are formed. I am not a passive bystander in the life chain of human creation. My power, fingerprint, and holy breath exist in each living soul. Honoring your parents begins with gratitude, My child. Being grateful for the gift of life your parents gave you is the first step in honoring them as a cocreator of you with Me. The next step in honoring your parents is to love them even as you love Me.

   There is power in Honoring your parents and celebrating God.

"Honor your father and your mother, so that you may live long in the land the Lord your God is **giving** you. (Exodus 20:12 NIV)

*Y*our home or apartment is the earthly nest where you can find rest for your weary human body. Tend to your refuge lovingly; it is the sacred space where you will encounter Me. Your home is not the only space where you can connect with Me, but it can become our sacred space. Do not make your home a hostel for unhealthy human practices; otherwise, peace will elude your earthly sanctuary. The demons of disaster and despair tend to nest in the hollow of unholy habits.

Place a sign above the doorposts of your home that reads, "God lives here." The sign will remind you and invite others that I offer peace and rest to everyone who enters your home. When I abide with you, your home becomes more than just a physical structure. Your home becomes a spiritual bastion of peace in a hurting, struggling world. Enter each room of your home as if I were already present.

The same rules apply to your life as to your home. Your home is where you live; your body is where I abide. Just as I gave your ancestors the land, I blessed you with a physical body. Your body is the physical structure that houses your soul and Me. When you keep your body and mind free from earthly contaminates and destructive pleasures, you make room for Me. The more room you make for Me, the more peace you will find in your life. You will surely find peace in the land when you create sacred space for the soul.

Your physical house is where you live. It becomes your spiritual home when you find God there.

"Remember the command that Moses the servant of the Lord **gave** you after he said, 'The Lord your God will **give** you rest by giving you this land.' (Joshua 1:13 NIV)

APRIL 14

*D*arkness will seem to overwhelm you until the morning light kisses your eyes. People can say the same thing about your relationship with Me, My sacred heart. You will not see the brightness of a spiritual day until you open your eyes to the spiritual light. You are not a dualistic being living separate physical and spiritual lives. You are a complete being, comprised of a spiritual life force dwelling in a physical body. Do not separate the two; learn to unite them. You must understand how the body informs the spirit and how the soul influences the body.

I give you the light from the sun so you will see your way in the world. I bless you with the spiritual light from My presence so you will recognize My work in your life. I have placed you in this world to have a physical life; I put you in My sanctuary for spiritual life. Begin each day with a brief moment with Me in sacred solitude. In your morning prayer and meditation, you will find My holy presence.

Many of My lovely children have realized the strength and depth of resolve the soul has in the most desperate of times. When placed in bondage, My children found that I could open the eyes of their hearts so that they could see things their physical eyes could not perceive. Do not let troubled times steal your vision like a thief. Call to Me in prayer and look beyond your turmoil. I will help you overcome the darkness of any day, by illuminating your soul with hope and enlivening your life with My presence. Trouble is always defeated at the hands of faith., My child.

The sun brightens our day, and God's Spirit illuminates our lives.

But now, for a brief moment, the Lord our God has been gracious in leaving us a remnant and **giving** us a firm place in his sanctuary, and so our God gives light to our eyes and a little relief in our bondage. (Ezra 9:8 NIV)

APRIL 15

*L*et My light beam forth from your life. Let your heart shine with the beauty of My instruction and guidance. Begin each day in My holy word so that the Scripture will give you spiritual guidance and inspiration each day. Be inspired as the pages of the Bible touch your heart and fill you with joy that will bring happiness to you throughout the day. Remember that behind each word in the Bible is an inspired hand that wrote them. Contemplate that within each page, is a life that encountered Me in a holy embrace. The Bible is filled with stories that reflect a life shared and loved by Me.
I remain hidden from you until your eyes become wide open to My holy presence. The sacred stories of days gone by retelling the enlightened encounters of your Biblical ancestors are show stoppers. Do not just read the pages as ancient stories. I continue to encounter people today if they can see Me spiritually. Ancient spiritual encounters with Me are repeated daily in many lives. Do not be surprised if your eyes are opened to My radiant light this very morning.
  Perhaps the best question you can ask yourself is, "How will God love me today?" Will I be loved like Moses, who carried the Lord's Commandments to the people? Will I be loved like Mary, who was blessed beyond all people? Or will I be loved like Jesus, who carried divine love to the cross and beyond? Be mindful that each Bible story represents what once happened and reflects what could happen in your life today, My child.

 Read the Bible, and it will bring joy to the heart and light to the eyes.

The precepts of the Lord are right, giving joy to the heart. The commands of the Lord are radiant, giving light to the eyes. (Psalm 19:8 NIV)

APRIL 16

*L*et your morning song be one of praise and thanksgiving to Me. Even in your grumbly, scratchy, morning voice, practice giving Me thanks with a joyous heart. It is not the quality of your singing voice that I listen to; it is the sincerity of your heart giving thanks to Me that pleases Me. Find a reason to be filled with joy every morning. The reasons are out there if you can find them. I have placed blessings for you to find throughout your day. You will have enough food, clothing to cover your body, and friends to support your day. These are not hidden treasures that need a lost map to find. I place My blessings where I am certain that you will find them. Practice being grateful for what you are about to receive, and My blessing will be even easier for you to find. This is not some sort of Easter egg hunt. My blessings are usually hidden in plain sight. Use the echolocation of praise and thanksgiving to find your blessings. Gratitude is a spiritual eye-opener. When you give thanks for my blessings, you open the spiritual eyes of your soul, and seeing even more blessings coming your way will become much easier. When you shout to Me in the morning, the rest of the day will align with your acclamations and expectations. The blessings are present in your life. Revelation occurs when you base past performance on future expectations and hopes. When you recognize My past blessings, revelations today, and expectations for tomorrow are much easier to see. Your spirit will train your body to see what I am doing, and blessings will appear in your life, My child.

Be grateful for what you will receive and shout for joy with great expectation.

A psalm. For giving grateful praise. Shout for joy to the Lord, all the earth. (Psalm 100:1 NIV)

APRIL 17

*Y*ou will receive countless blessings as one of My chosen children. Rise this morning looking for the many gifts of love I shall give to you throughout this day. I will bless your family so that they will be strong and as healthy as possible to surround you with their love and care. I will give you work to have a lifetime career and a steady income. I will bless you in mind, body, and spirit so that you will sparkle and shine as one of My chosen children.

You will also receive countless gracious gifts from Me as part of your holy inheritance. Praise Me for your earthly prosperity and spiritual wealth when you receive My gifts. All things in life are a gift from My hand. As you practice praising Me for My gifts of the past, your eyes will be opened to see the blessings of the future. I will never stop blessing you; find it in your heart to always praise Me for My loving gifts to you.

I have spent much time talking to you about joy, blessings, and giving thanks. I did this because these are pathways for communicating with Me. I feel your joyous celebration. I rejoice when you give thanks for the blessings I give to you. You must realize that you are not only communicating with Me, but you are also claiming your spiritual authority when you give thanks to Me. You have the power and authority to move mountains and part seas, learn to appreciate what I give you, and more will be coming. I chose you and selected you out of love. You have the birthmark of my love on your soul.

God's blessing is your birthright, and praising God is your inheritance.

That I may enjoy the prosperity of your chosen ones, that I may share in the joy of your nation and join your inheritance in giving praise. (Psalm 106:5 NIV)

APRIL 18

*D*o you think you have too little to give a lot? Giving is not restricted to money flowing from one source to another. Giving comes in various forms and can be accomplished in myriad ways. Let kind words flow freely from your mouth from an endless stream of compliments, affirmations, and regards to the people I have placed in your life. Your physical and spiritual support system is clearly a gracious gift from Me, but each individual's care, feeding, and growth is in your hands, My child. A gesture of kindness will feed the soul for days.

Kind words and loving replies can come back to you and bring joy to them. If you want to feel good inside, fill your family members with affirming words first. If you want to feel appreciated, compliment the service person who brings you your meal. Do not hesitate if it is your desire to feel on top of the world today. Find someone living at the bottom of the world to lift up in praise with glowing comments. Fill every encounter with joy with the kind words you share.

I created everything that exists by merely speaking. Grow to appreciate and understand your awesome power in harnessing the spoken word. Let there be kind, loving, affirming words flowing from your mouth to create a supportive environment around you. When your affirmations come from your heart, they can touch and change the recipient's soul. An affirmed life creates a wonderful world in which to live. Speak your world into existence, My sacred heart.

You will find joy in each kind word you share with another person.

A person finds joy in giving an apt reply— and how good is a timely word! (Proverbs 15:23 NIV)

APRIL 19

I appreciate every dollar you give, every kind word you share, and all the loving gestures of Christian kindness. I am the only one you have to impress in life. Writing a generous check to your favorite nonprofit comes with its own reward. The reward is My gratitude from Me. Thank you so much for your generosity. I hope you realize that I make your generosity possible. What flows from your hand passes directly from me as a gift.

Practice praising Me for blessing you with the resources you can so freely share with worthy causes and people in desperate need. I see what you do. Have you seen what I have done? I have blessed you generously with wealth beyond your need. Use your excess to bless others and come to Me with a grateful heart. The world will notice your generosity by the changes you make and not by the bragging you do.

I always watch the activity of the heart and soul, not just the hand and checkbook. Some of My beloved children can write checks of staggering amounts, but they have little impact on the giver's heart. Giving is a spiritual act that allows Me to pass from the giver to the recipient. Be as generous as possible when you give Me away, My child. Giving money, kind gestures, and supportive words are not just acts of physical generosity but dynamic spiritual forces.

The silence of your secret gift is always heard in heaven.

So that your giving may be in secret. Then your Father, who sees what is done in secret, will reward you. (Matthew 6:4 NIV)

APRIL 20

*D*o not become so set in your ways that you forget that I hold your future in My hands. The people of Noah's time thought everything would move according to their plans and schedule. This would not be the case. Their world changed in the twinkling of My eye. Do not fear; a flood is not coming to the earth, for I have set My rainbow in the sky as a reminder to keep the peace. But change happens.

Remain open to My movement in your life to show you an excellent way to live. I long to grant you the gift of your future. Everyone who follows Me has a future, a purpose, and a reason for being alive. Have you found your purpose in life? You will never find your life's purpose by looking at the world around you. Seek Me, and I will give you the keys to your spiritual purpose and future on this earth.

  I placed a passion inside of you; feel it. You have a desire and drive that cannot be quenched; follow it. You have gifts and abilities that will serve your life purpose, employ them. Everything you need I gave you, do not look any further, My precious child. Too many of my children do what is easiest to obtain. The problem is if it is not their passion, they will feel trapped or like they are merely going through the steps in life. Live each day as if there is no tomorrow because you do not hold the keys to the future. Live with gusto and let your passion drive your life; let Me care for your tomorrows.

God will help you find more passion and purpose in life.

For in the days before the flood, people were eating and drinking, marrying and giving in marriage, up to the day Noah entered the ark; (Matthew 24:38 TLB)

APRIL 21

*P*ain is often a travel companion on the road of life. It need not be that way. Struggles and problems will always be a part of the human condition. I do not create these problems to make your life hard; an unattended soul has the ability to attract its own issues. You must learn to find the joy that awaits you on the other side of pain. Bad situations can bear good fruit if you remain centered in My life.

You will find the joy that comes from difficulty by looking inward for your answers and support. Learn to pray often and meditate even more. Bring your prayers to Me every morning as the sun streams in your window. Take heed and listen for My words of discernment. Your answer does not come in your questioning prayers. I will answer your prayers as you sit quietly in sincere meditation listening for My voice. I will give you the joy you seek. Learn to find your joy hidden in the pain, my child.

I am not trying to relieve you of all of your pain. Sometimes the pain is trying to tell the body something; pay attention, my child. I want you to know that life does not have to succumb to physical, emotional, or spiritual pain. Pain is often a good teacher but seldom a good friend. See the pain in life like dark clouds, they will part, and the sun will once again shine. It may be difficult to remain hopeful in the midst of pain, but this, too, will pass. My child.

Our problems are often the birthplace of God's gift of joy.

A woman giving birth to a child has pain because her time has come; but when her baby is born, she forgets the anguish because of her joy that a child is born into the world. (John 16:21 NIV)

APRIL 22

I am no accident or chance occurrence. I am the divine and holy gift that every person longs to receive. Did you think the same hand that created heaven and earth would neglect you as if you were an abandoned puppy? Or do you believe I am so busy that I am off in some distant corner of the universe, unaware and unconcerned about your life this morning? You are completely wrong in your false assumptions of Me.

I know the inner hope of the heart just as I know the way to the other side of the universe. I understand the groanings of your spirit just as easily as I hear the songs of the Humpback whale. I love to hear your prayers and psalms of thanksgiving, but I feel them before you can think or utter them to Me. I am the spiritual force behind every prayer.

I am your divine gift that will never leave your side or miss hearing even one of your breaths in life. My very presence in your life shows the depth of My love for you. I was very intentional in creating you, my child. You have My breath of life in you. You carry My blueprint, My fingerprint, My DNA; there is nothing closer to you in life than Me. I know your heart because I am the spiritual power that enables your heart to beat.

You were created by the hand of God and given the Spirit of God to show the love of God.

God, who knows the heart, showed that he accepted them by giving the Holy Spirit to them, just as he did to us. (Acts 15:8 NIV)

APRIL 23

$\mathcal{E}$verything I give to you is to serve a purpose in your life. I give to you out of My abundant ever ever-flowing generosity. You must learn to imitate Me as I bestow gifts upon you and all My children. My gifts are meant to enhance your life, mark you as My servant, and flow through you as a vital spiritual energy that comes from Me. The moment you stop sharing My gifts, it will clog the flow of divine energy to those who need it.

You are a precious conduit, not a stopping point for divine energy. Money is earthly energy used to purchase worldly items. The blessing of earning money comes as a gift from Me. Let money pass through you, and I will widen the financial flow of spiritual energy to you. You must learn to trust Me that there will always be more than enough for you and for those in need around you. You are the beginning of a line of My blessings; never let yourself be the end.

I caution you not to be frivolous with your money. Just throwing money at material things that do not serve you or help others is not what I am all about. Use your financial resources to buy your daily bread and share some with your neighbor. Be thankful for what you receive; I will send you even more. My spiritual and material blessings can never flow evenly to everyone. I rely on special people like you to share the wealth of my love and blessings.

Give as generously to others as God gives to you.

If it is to encourage, then give encouragement; if it is giving, then give generously; if it is to lead, do it diligently; if it is to show mercy, do it cheerfully. (Romans 12:8 NIV)

APRIL 24

*T*he purpose of worship is to bring Me honor. During your times of worship, bring your prayers of thanksgiving before Me in recognition of what I have done in your lives. Sing hymns and songs of glory to Me and lift your spirits through sacred music. Read and hear My words as they come to you in holy scripture. All these acts of worship honor Me and bring instruction to the worshippers.

Do try to be on the same page as a worshipping community. Leave no one aside as you gather for song, praise, prayers, and witness to Me. Your language should be so that everyone can understand clearly so all will be edified and guided by your worship. Inspiration is the language of the soul, but it must be understood by the mind if everyone is to have a common meaning. Leave nothing to chance or interpretation in your worship of Me.

Worship represents the holy triangle of corporate praise. You worship Me, but you connect to those around you. Your prayers may help instruct, inspire, and bless the person next to you. The song that flows from your heart through your lips honoring Me may be what the troubled soul next to you needs to hear. When you sing and shout, "Great is the Lord," in your worship and praise, the energy the words carry from you will bless everyone around you. Let your worship of Me bless and inspire those around you, My child.

Let your acts of worshipping God be clear words of instruction to the believer.

You are giving thanks well enough, but no one else is edified. (1 Corinthians 14:17 NIV)

APRIL 25

*Y*ou were created in My image, but you look nothing like Me. The divine image is one of purpose and action, not a solid reflection of My being. I blew life into My creation Adam, but he sometimes fell short of living the life of the spirit. Adam was created from the dust of the earth; you are a recreated spirit of heaven. Adam brought forth the physical child and the blessed Savior raised the spiritual being. Adam was the father of physical life, and Jesus was the father of life everlasting.

You are an earthly person empowered by a living spirit. The physical body will decay and die, but the spirit will always remain by My side. Learn to act as I act, and you will soon discover your spiritual life. Your spiritual life is the heavenly life you live in your earthly body. You will resemble Me in my actions when you learn to live and act in the spirit. If you want to experience the power of eternal life, try to live as close to My image as possible.

You carry the best combination of both worlds and each creation. Your physical body is an ongoing developing model of Adam. Your Physical body may be perfectly formed, but you are prone to sin. Your spirit or soul carries the DNA of Christ and the power of Me. You were born to die in your physical body; you were born again to everlasting life in. your spiritual soul. Remember, My child, you have the life print of both Adam and Jesus, but you also have the Life force that only I can provide. My Bible study partner may be correct, we look more like Adam, but we must try to act more like Jesus.

The world will best recognize us by our heavenly spiritual actions.

So it is written: "The first man Adam became a living being"; the last Adam, a life-giving spirit. (1 Corinthians 15:45 NIV)

APRIL 26

*Y*ou must remember to give thanks to the people in your life. Rise this morning with the expectation that your friends and family will be present to support and love you in various ways. Rise with their names on your heart, sharing prayers of thanksgiving for their lives as they continue to bless you. Prayers of thanksgiving have a multifold purpose. Prayers of thanksgiving open your heart to experience gratitude, a powerful emotion. Thanksgiving prayers tell Me that you recognize My work in your life. The prayer also makes a spiritual connection between you and the person you pray for.

Recount each person by name. If you are out for your morning stroll or healthy run, let their names exhale from your body and float into the air. This will push your thanksgiving prayer out of your body and back toward them. Your thanksgiving prayer to Me for what they have done will make a vital spiritual connection and help you realize all the support that we give to you. You are never alone in building the life that you so desire. Give thanks for your many helpers.

Prayers are more than mere words flowing from your lips. Prayers are golden spiritual links between us and those we pray for. Yes, My child, I am involved in your prayers as well. I touch the hearts and souls of the people with a silent tap of divine love. I carry the spiritual sentiments you share with Me to those you thank in your prayers. A chemical spiritual reaction occurs through your prayers that ignite a holy flame of love.

Never stop giving thanks to the people around you. They helped make you who you are.

I have not stopped giving thanks to you and remembering you in my prayers. (Ephesians 1:6 NIV)

APRIL 27

*T*he morning sun ushers forth the kingdom of light each day. Try not to miss the majesty that each sunrise brings to you. The sun is more than just a stagnant star floating at a distance in outer space. The sun is My calling card to begin another day as My child of light. Being a child of divine spiritual light is your inheritance. Do not squander your daily birthright by hiding behind your curtains. Get up and move out into the kingdom that awaits you.

There is a Godly world that coexists with the earthly world. You will find one amongst the others. Look for My holy people as you go about your day. Give thanks to those who have found their way into the divine light and brightened this earth with their presence. Give ample reason for others to give prayers of thanksgiving for what you have done in their lives. You are all children of the light.

You are a child of the light from the inside out. Everything you eat is the product of sunlight. All plants, animals, and fish were raised on foods grown in the sunlight. You consume the sunlight through them. You also have the light of Me shining from within you. Most of My beloved children cannot see the holy spectrum of spiritual light that fills the body. To help My children see the tremendous physical and spiritual power of light within them, you must act like Me. Love puts light into action.

The sun can never outshine the children of God's divine light.

And giving joyful thanks to the Father, who has qualified you to share in the inheritance of his holy people in the kingdom of light. (Colossians 1:12 NIV)

APRIL 28

*Y*our life represents more than just who you are and what you say on this earth. You represent your divine calling, so be very aware of what you do or say in life. If you follow Me, people will interpret your words as My words. I don't want to be misinterpreted. As My child, people will assume you are working on My behalf. I don't want you to leave the wrong impression. As My living embodiment, I don't want people to mistake you for someone else. Ensure that everyone understands you are a living representative of the risen Savior. You carry his glorious name as your calling card. Your actions must be those of a loving, caring, and healing gentle soul. Your words must carry the divine power of healing, forgiveness, and love. You carry the hallmark of Jesus' name. Let your words and deeds match their source.

   Lose yourself in Me, My sacred heart. Do not be afraid of a complete surrender to who I am. I will not take over your life to control you; I will empower you spiritually to help and guide you. When you give yourself over to Me, you will enhance the dormant spiritual side of yourself. If all of My children would learn to walk in the Spirit, you would instantly see Me in each other. This is an earth-shaking and life-changing spiritual shift, My child.

Give the world a reason to thank you for your kind words and loving deeds.

And whatever you do, whether in word or deed, do it all in the name of the Lord Jesus, giving thanks to God the Father through him. (Colossians 3:17 NIV)

APRIL 29

*P*repare yourself for each day's unexpected, unplanned, and unknown events, My child. You do not know what door this morning will open for you to enter. Begin each day with Me, and you can walk with assurance and confidence that all will end well. Each day crawls closer to the fulfillment of time for you, a reality all humans must live with. Live each day without fear. Each day I give to you is a gift and not a life sentence. Learn to appreciate the gift of life, and you will find the joy you seek.

Surround yourself with like-spirited souls who will meet with you regularly for worship, prayer, and encouraging each other in holy habits in your shared love for Me. Never lose sight of the fact that you are mortal and a child of the dust of the earth. Remember that you are also an eternal spirit filled with God's holy power. In the end, you will meet Me face to face. In the meantime, learn to see My holy presence in the sacred circle of similar souls who follow the spiritual path of life.

Your time on earth is to fulfill your purpose in life. Each soul enters the physical world with a spiritual purpose. Your primary purpose is to love each other. This calling of divine love can only be fulfilled when you gather in My name to seek My presence. During this time, build each other up in the Christian faith, and pray for each other with fervent petitions. Sing sacred hymns to fill the air with my glory and preach the Word. These holy habits will enhance your life and prepare you for everlasting life. to come

God has numbered our days on earth but count on the countless days eternal life brings.

Not giving up meeting together, as some are in the habit of doing, but encouraging one another—and all the more as you see the Day approaching. (Hebrews 10:25 NIV)

APRIL 30

*H*ope is the last thing you should ever give up. Hope itself has no power, yet hope in Me is limitless. Learn to see the world of shadows through the bright eyes of My hope. Without My hope, this earth will make you feel like an unknown and unwanted stranger. When you surround yourself with My hope, you will always feel welcome as I call you by your name. Hope is tailor-made with a custom fit just for you and your circumstances.

Hope holds the door open for faith. Faith shows you the possibilities that lay ahead of you. Without My hope, all doors remain closed, and faith cannot bring divine light to the darkness of despair. Hope comes as your spiritual companion as you learn to follow Me. Begin this morning with hope next to you and Me within your heart. Hope can reach beyond the inking blackness of the morning and capture the first ray of divine gold sunlight.

Your faith will inform you that I have the power to do things for you; hope sets the expectation that they will happen. Faith carried the people of Israel through the wilderness, but hope led them into the promised land. Believe that I am with you in your life journey, My child, and have hope I will lead you into your promised land. Place your faith in Me, and I will bless you with the future you hoped for.

Hope opens closed doors so faith can enter your life.

We are foreigners and strangers in your sight, as were all our ancestors. Our days on earth are like a shadow without hope. (1 Chronicle 29:15 MIV)

MAY 1

*Y*our piety is the life you live in Me. Piety is the display of your faith in Me as you go through your day. Live your spiritual life with confidence and hope in My work in your life. A life free from the shackles of sin will lead you to a life of boundless hope. You are the main thing holding yourself back from having complete hope and trust in Me. If you believe your outward piety is not worthy of any hope in Me, then change how you live, and your perception will also be altered.

Follow Me with complete faith and do away with the unholy habits that cause shame in your life. A life without blame and shame is a clear path to My hope. Rather than beating yourself up for what you have done, focus on what you will do. Being future-focused in faith brings you hope. You will never be perfected in holiness in this life, but a sincere, pious attempt at righteous living will bring you hope. I bring hope to the hopeless, but you must seek My blessings. Blessings are always heaven-sent, so do not place your heavenly hope in earthly vessels.

The more you practice listening to Me and walking humbly with Me, the closer I will be to you, My child. I do not expect you to live a blameless, holy life alone. The blessed Savior died to purge your soul of sin, and I was sent to comfort and influence your journey through life. I will always feel spiritually aloof unless you turn your life over to Me. I hold the hope of the future in My hand; you will only see the revelation of your hopes and dreams when you practice spending time with Me.

Live a life that honors God, and you will be blessed with holy hope.

Should not your piety be your confidence and your blameless ways your hope? (Job 4:6 NIV)

MAY 2

*T*he scales of justice are held in My hands. I am not blind to what goes on in the lives of My blessed children. My ears are open to the cries of the poor. My eyes see the blight of the downtrodden. My heart goes out to all suffering from an unjust overlord. My eyes can see, My ears are attentive, and My heart is open to the plight of all who struggle. I feel the depth of human pain and suffering deep within their souls. I am aware of the smallest of injustices in this world.

The way to balance injustice is through your hope in Me. Allow Me to work in your life so you can be the last ounce that tips the scale in favor of the poor. Your support for the needy will quiet the mockingbird of injustice that taunts the helpless. The love in your heart will open even the most closed and hardened hearts so the struggling souls of this world will live in justice, you must show them My hope, and you must become their active hope in Me.

How can you do all of this, My child? Is it possible to make a major shift in your world? Start small and let the spiritual shift come from your heart and soul. If you model the blessed Savior's love and compassion, injustice will not be able to grow beyond you. Injustice cannot speak if your Christ-centered life halts it. No miracles need to occur; all you need do is follow the Savior and stay close to Me.

God's justice is never blind; hope is used to tip the scales to care for the suffering.

So the poor have hope, and injustice shuts its mouth. (Job 5:16 NIV)

MAY 3

*C*ome to Me without fear and free from indigent requests. I answer prayers; I never respond to demands. Prayers come from the heart through the spiritual channel of the soul. Demands are nothing but barking egos wanting to be fed. Once fed, the egos are quiet for a while until the next wave of desperate hunger demands even more than the last request did. Let go of demanding the moment's needs and pray for the comforts of tomorrow.

I know your needs before you request them. I see your struggles sneaking up on you like a silent shadow. I will fully grant what you hope for when you learn to hope for what I alone can grant. I do not just feed growling stomachs; I fulfill empty lives. I divinely inspire most hopes and dreams. I hear the inner groanings of your spirit talking to Me, and I convert them to inspiration and desire. You align yourself with Me when you listen to your heart and soul and pronounce your hopes into prayers.

You must know, My sacred heart, that you have influential spiritual power. The blessed savior told you to persist in your petitions, and I would feel and hear your inner groanings. I feel the innocence of your heart and soul; I know what you want before you pray for it. When you do not give up or give in on your hopes, your prayers carry a higher spiritual frequency. As I answer your prayers, you will find hope at this higher spiritual level.

Let your prayers become the voice of what you hope for.

"Oh, that I might have my request, that God would grant what I hope for, (Job 6:8 NIV)

MAY 4

*L*earn to look beyond the bifocals sitting on the end of your nose. You are looking for short-sighted answers that need long-term solutions. Hope held too close has a small vision range. Hope held at a distance can see greater possibilities even in the most desperate situations. Hope in Me empowers your faith to see My blessings and to avoid your obstacles. Do not line the road to the future with obstacles that I intended to be prospects and blessings. Your spiritual strength comes from your faith in Me. It is through your spiritual strength in Me that you will find hope. Once found. Hope through faith in Me will allow you to see the future as I envision it. You see a foggy land of desperate dark shadows. I see a land of milk and honey. Where would you rather live? I always prepare the best possible place for your life. Trust that I am working ahead of you and will lead you into green pastures.

Hope is just an ordinary name for Me. Hope is not a. place or thing. Hope has no power or ability to move mountains. Honestly, My child, you are powerless and, therefore, hopeless. You may make it through this life without me, but I am what you hoped for. Humans were created with limitations. Your limitations leave off where I begin. I intentionally created the spiritual connection so that you would find My strength in your weakness. In the same way, you will find your hope in Me.

Never let go of hope. It is your first step to the future.

"What strength do I have, that I should still hope? What prospects, I should be patient with? (Job 6:11 NIV)

MAY 5

*H*ope stands between the believer and death. Death of the body may occur; death of the mind may happen, but most assuredly, the desperate death of the soul will totally consume you. Hope is the indomitable part of the human spirit I have placed in my children. Hope stands firm when the body crumbles. Hope will talk the mind into facing unmeasurable odds. Hope lifts the human spirit when the world smashes it underfoot.

I have placed My divine hope in the deepest center of your mind, body, and spirit. Hope is the tiniest fragment of your DNA. My hope is always present lest you forget it. No one should struggle with the belief of whether or not I exist. I exist; therefore, you exist. Your destiny is marked with the hope I have given you. Do not fear the future.

Just as your life is a gift, your future is a blessing from Me. Do not fear the unknown or uncertain. When My children fail to find Me, they will also fall short of their future hope. I cannot impress upon you the reality that I bear the name of "Hope." The Savior knew this far before he entered the tomb of death. When you remember Me in your prayers and worship Me with your heart and soul, you will always have hope. The day you forget about Me and no longer honor Me in your heart is the day you will lose all hope.

Hope does not exist without God. You cannot exist without God's hope.

Such is the destiny of all who forget God; so perishes the hope of the godless. (Job 8:13 NIV)

MAY 6

*A*rise each morning knowing that you are in the secure safety of My loving arms. You may not feel me, but I am here and always present in your life. You will fail to feel My holy presence when you let human emotions overshadow you. Fear, frustration, hatred, loathing, and other negative emotions strangle your spirit and choke out any hope for the future. Just breathe and let these feelings pass through you; there will be plenty of hope for the future when you let air and light into the soul.

Hope and faith grow on the same branches. I am the tree of life from which hope and faith receive spiritual nutrition. You do not feel secure because you do not believe. You see no hope for the future because you do not see Me there. Let the heart of your faith talk to the hope in your soul. Together they will help you find the secure rest you seek. The lack of faith will dim your hope. A dim hope will drain the soul of vital spiritual energy, leaving you with a sudden, shallow, and sad spirit. Have faith, and you will also have hope.

I do not mean to speak harshly to you, My sacred heart. I am trying to narrow your spiritual focus and widen your hope for the future. I did not allow you to see into the future, but I did bless you with the gifts of hope, dreaming, and inspiration. Hang on tight to your gits when all seems to be lost. When all seems lost, My child, you are not looking in the right direction. Look inward with prayer, and you will find Me. I never really left you, and I never will.

When all hope seems lost, turn to faith.

You will be secure because there is hope; you will look about you and take your rest in safety. (Job 11:8 NIV)

MAY 7

*H*ave you been cut down at the knees? Has life chipped away at your soul like a beaver gnawing a tree? Many things in life will eat at your heart and soul, leaving you lifeless and discarded. There is always hope for these major meltdowns in life. Life does not end at the first tragedy or catastrophe. There may be even more difficult moments awaiting you in life. Rejoice if trouble does not find you, but be prepared if it does.

It may not be easy to believe, but great things can grow from a major mess. What you lose in one moment may bear fruit in another season. You will never know the outcome ahead of time. Still, hope will allow you to look beyond any temporary destruction and anticipate My holy presence in, threw, and on the other side of the most difficult situations. Faithful patience in Me will bear the fruit of hope.

You cannot plant the sprouts of future hope in the dead dust of the past. The bad memories from the past are the rain clouds that never lose their cargo of life-giving water. The past rain clouds hover above and darken the sky but never give you anything. The easiest way to let go of the past is to turn your attention toward Me. When you place your faith in Me, your life will become future-focused and hopeful. Driving a car by only looking at the review mirror is impossible. When you look for Me on the horizon of life, you will also see hope.

Hope gives up the hurts of the past for the new future sprouts.

"At least there is hope for a tree: If it is cut down, it will sprout again, and its new shoots will not fail. (Job 14:7 NIV)

MAY 8

*I*f you are looking for your home, you must look toward Me. I give hope to the hopeless, love to the brokenhearted, and peace to the downtrodden. I've been giving eternal optimistic hope to lost and lonely souls for generations. Take My Servant Job. He lost all visions of any hope. Job threw himself on the junk heap of life and gave up. To Job, a shallow faith in Me created the inky illusion of a hopeless future. It was not to be so. While my suffering servant sat hopelessly on a dung heap, I was placing hope on the horizon of his life.

Don't let life run you over and knock you down. Most miseries are short-lived and moved aside by incoming hope creating new possibilities. I can see your hope for you. I can bring blessings even in the most difficult dilemmas. Job received the blessing of hope manifest in his life. Will you wait for the same blessings?

Where is your hope? When you tie your hope to the material world, you will sit and sulk on a dung heap like Job. The problem is that you are looking from the outside in. You were not created to be your own source of hope. I did not place you in this world so that it would be your source of hope, either. Look from the inside out to find hope. I am the same spark of life that brings eternal hope. Begin with Me before you look any further.

Only God can see the hope that awaits you.

Where then is my hope— who can see any hope for me? (Job 17:15 NIV)

MAY 9

*D*o not look for the living among the dead. Do not seek good in the land of evil. An unlit candle will never shine in the darkness. Hope for the good that I alone can bring. I am never found in the land of evil, so search the land of milk and honey. The darkest night must give way to the first evening star. Looking for hope in a hopeless world. All of these sayings lead to the fact that you cannot find what you seek if you look in the opposite place where it is. These are not just pithy sayings; they are maxims of the divine hope I grant all My children. If you have no hope, then look where hope will be found. You will find hope in Me, and I give life. Seek the goodness that flows from My hand, and I know no evil. I am the shimmering, shining essence of golden light that causes the night to run and hide. If you are looking for hope, look again and find Me.

I am your Spirit guide messenger. I bring you the divine light that will bring you hope. Do not worry about your future; place all of your trust in Me. If you are looking for hope in a hopeless world, look no further. The world was not created with hope as one of its virtues. You were not formed to fashion hope like a glass blower. Hope is always future tense and does not yet exist in your hopeless world. Always look beyond your hopeless world and struggling life to see Me holding your hope. My child.

You can only lose hope if you look in the wrong places.

Yet when I hoped for good, evil came; when I looked for light, then came darkness. (Job 30:26 NIV)

MAY 10

*W*hatever life brings you; I will always be by your side. Life has a way of overwhelming you at times. Do not let the difficulties of life wash away any or all hope. Hope does not depend on your state of mind, nor is it limited to a simple single feeling. True hope is not dependent upon you at all, My child. I am hope incarnate. I am the hope you need in troubled times. All you need to do to have hope is to trust and believe in Me. It is that simple, don't overthink it. Refrain from conjuring up hope from within. Hope cannot be tapped like an adrenaline rush of sudden strength. Hope is what flows from Me to you through your faith in Me. Personal hope soon diminishes or is forgotten. I will never forget you or let My hope for you fade. Like My love, My hope never dies. If you feel lost and struggle to find hope in life again, turn to Me. I am always here to help you get what you still need to get.

I am not trying to give you some inner strength motivation like a life coach or motivational guru. The truth is that hope does not reside in you. The needy or afflicted soul has no power; all they hope for resides in Me. I am sorry if I am using strong language to impress this concept upon you, My sacred heart, but hope has nothing to do with you; it is present only in Me. I am your hope always.

Finding hope in troubled times with God's help.

But God will never forget the needy; the hope of the afflicted will never perish. (Psalm 9:18 NIV)

MAY 11

*L*ook for My hope as you rise each day. Look hard and long for the hope I have placed in the hearts and souls of My children. Sometimes My hope is hidden among the poor and impoverished who do not have enough to eat or even the most basic shelter. Hope can be found in the single parent working multiple jobs trying to offer the best to their children. Hope is found in the prayers of the person whose spouse is severely sick and seeks My healing touch.
My hope has the power to lift its head up above the human struggles in life and find a better way. My hope will guide the lost, lonely, and left behind to gravitate toward My side m for comfort and support. My hope can grow in the most difficult of situations and flourish in the darkest of days. My hope is always found in the last place you would think of looking for it, begin there.

God's hope can grow in the harshest of human conditions, including yours.

Guide me in your truth and teach me, for you are God my Savior, and my hope is in you all day long. (Psalm 25:5 NIV)

MAY 12

*U*se that deep-down inner strength that comes from the source of abiding faith in Me that resides in your soul. Never give up, never give in, and never ever lay down as a vanquished soul in defeat from overwhelming circumstances. Your strength will come from your hope in Me. Do not take this statement as a shallow promise but receive this as a blessing from Me. Take heart and have faith; when you fall, I will pick you up.

I will not leave you alone to face the dark and stormy nights of uncertain times, My child. I am closer than you can imagine and will give you the strength you need to persevere. All of life will appear to be hopeless and without purpose if you do not see life through the lens of My hope. You were not placed here to roam the earth; you were given life to flourish and receive My abundant blessings.

When you find your spiritual strength, you will become a conqueror, not a victim. Be strong in the Lord, and never give up as the Scriptures say; place your hope in God as your money says. I place these sayings in your heart so they will touch your soul. The inspiration you receive today can become your motivation and strength tomorrow when you are faced with life challenges. I am not speaking shallow and hollow words to you, My child; I am planting seeds of hope.

How to find your spiritual strength, and trust in the Lord.

Be strong and take heart, all you who hope in the Lord. (Psalm 31:24 NIV)

MAY 13

*D*id you notice I watched you as you rose from bed this morning? I watched you throughout the night as you slept. I counted each beat of your heart and listened to each breath from your lungs. Nothing passed before My eyes without My notice. I am always watching over you and caring for you. These actions come from My unfailing love for you, My child. Place your hope in My unfailing love. My love is the source and spark that ignited the creation of the universe.

Go into this day knowing that I am always watching over you. Base your hope on this fact, center your life on this knowledge, and place all hope on My unfailing love for you. There are no shortcuts in life, but hope in Me will outlast even the most difficult times. You have been told to fear God; I assure you I am not a source of fear. Whenever you see the words, Fear God," replace them with Awesome God of hope."

The trembling My children feel is not fear when they come close to Me; it is only Me moving in the body. I stretch and move My children in new and uncomfortable directions. You cannot ask Me to find a new way to achieve your future hope by letting you remain in the same comfortable position. Your glorious future is out there, but you must get up, get moving, and get going in the direction I will lead you. Your need for comfort is what got you stuck in the first place. Take My hand, and I will stretch you to new limits and boundaries.

God's Hope is Found Here.

But the eyes of the Lord are on those who fear him, on those whose hope is in his unfailing love, (Psalm 33:18 NIV)

MAY 14

*T*he psalmist sang sacred songs in the sanctuary about having hope in Me. Let your mornings begin with a cup of My blessings as I fill your life with new possibilities in My hope. As you open the door to your home, an optimistic invitation opens the door to hope. No day will be lost; no problem is too big when hope walks before you. If you are looking to find a better world, it must start with you. Walk with the assurance knowing that faith is key to surrounding yourself with the protection and shield of My hope. Hope is far more than just wishing for a better future. Faith-based hope casts away fear and will allow you to tread where fear may hold you back. Begin each day in My hope, knowing I am with you.

You may not realize it, My sacred heart, but we are co-creators. I created the world you live in by saying, "Let there be." You must create your world by proclaiming, "Let there be." as well. If you want a better world, start by creating it in your mind when you rise. Continue to create peace as you live out each moment of the day in a peaceful manner yourself. I am your help and shield, but only if you create a world where I am also your God.

Finding a better world.

We wait in hope for the Lord; he is our help and our shield. (Psalm 33:20 NIV)

MAY 15

A troubled heart has difficulty seeing any future. A downcast soul seiches for hope in vain like a blindfolded person looking for a door. Prayer helps to remove the blindfold that covers the spiritual life. Begin each morning in prayer asking Me to guide you on your daily path. It is easy for Me to lead you through the thorny obstacles of life, it is far more difficult for you to follow.

This is the day I have made, rejoice in the hope this day will bring you. I have lifted you from the shadows of sin into the life of My shimmering and shining grace. Morning prayer will allow you to see what I have in store for you each day. Hope becomes reality when you lift up your downcast soul in prayer. Pray often.

The secret to finding God's hope begins with prayer.

Why, my soul, are you downcast? Why so disturbed within me? Put your hope in God, for I will yet praise him, my Savior and my God. (Psalm 42:5 NIV)

MAY 16

*S*peak often of the hope you have found in Me. It is easier to have hope for the future if you hear the stories of hope fulfilled from the past. Giving praise to Me reminds My faithful children that there is reason to have hope at all times. Freely attach My name to all the good events that have happened in your life so people will associate goodness with Me.

I don't want all the credit for the good that happens in your life. I want people to see what having hope in Me can bring to their lives. Past blessings can provide a road map for future hope. Knowing that I was there yesterday will allow people to have the hope that I will be here today and again tomorrow.

Over the centuries, people have called out my holy name, hoping I will respond. I gave Moses the name Yahweh, but the children of Israel feared to speak my name. The blessed Savior bore the name of Jesus, which is above all names. What name do you wish to place upon me, My Sacred Heart? Select a name that speaks to your heart and will ignite your soul whenever you utter it from your lips or feel it in your heart. I am Who I am, no matter what you call me.

Learn to associate God with all good things, for all good things come from God.

For what you have done I will always praise you in the presence of your faithful people. And I will hope in your name, for your name is good. (Psalm 52:5 NIV)

MAY 17

*H*ope does bring you the rest of your soul that you seek. Peace is that feeling you get when all is well, and you know your world is in harmonious balance. Peace brings knowledge that your life is going as planned and expected. Your hopes and dreams are coming to fruition. Rest comes to your soul when your faith leads you down the path I called you to follow. The hope that I gave you is now fully realized in your life on this day.

My hope creates a state of perfect peace for mind, body, and soul. Hope unfulfilled brings chaos and unrest. Place all your hopes in Me, and you will find rest for your soul. Do you understand how this works, My child? Your fears and anxiety are removed when you place your hope in Me. Rather than dwelling in the land of chaos and fear, your soul rests in Me, free from the uncertainty of the future.

Hope is not a wishing well for earthly material objects and desired delights. Hope is a nest for your spirit to ease away from the concerns of this world, knowing that your future is in My hands. Hope is the spiritual mindset that keeps you grounded today because you have hope for all your tomorrows. When you view hope through the spiritual lens of your soul, you will not be able to unravel the difference between hope and Me. Hope, and I are synonymous.

Place your hope in God, and you will find rest for your soul.

Yes, my soul, find rest in God; my hope comes from him. (Psalm 62:5 NIV)

MAY 18

*B*e very careful where you place the hope of your heart. Living a life that yearns daily for more and more material possessions will lead you to a life without any end. More and more requires and longs for even more. Riches alone can never fulfill the desires of your heart. Your heart is only fulfilled when your hopes are realized. A material-driven life will fill your bank account but rob you of your spiritual riches.

Misplaced hope is a magnet for all sorts of evil desires and shallow hopes. The secret to a fulfilled spiritual life is to have all your hopes fulfilled by Me. I have counted the hairs on your head and numbered the freckles on your face. I know how to fulfill your hope, complete your life, and bring you peace. I am not telling you not to strive for financial freedom, riches, or great wealth. Many of your spiritual ancestors were richly blessed by Me.

Try to remember that money goes in a bank and should never be stored in the soul. Intermingling finances and faith is only healthy when you see the spiritual power of your wealth. Money only has spiritual power when it is used to serve Me and you. If you reverse this formula, you will create a shallow sea of false hope that you will soon drown in. When you use the spiritual power of money, you can dare to go into the deep end.

Do not let your spiritual blessings drown in a shallow sea of hope.

Do not trust in extortion or put vain hope in stolen goods; though your riches increase, do not set your heart on them. (Psalm 62:10 NIV)

MAY 19

Stretch out your arms. How far do they stretch? Not nearly far enough. You fall short in measuring the breadth of the hope I offer all My children. Imagine the depth of the oceans. Your imagination can only lead you to the water's edge. It will never bring you to the ocean's depth. Imagine the mountain's heights if you dare. Once again, you fail to measure up to the mountain's splendor. Don't worry, my child; you were never intended to reach such heights.

Have I not been your hope in the past? Have I not shown you a perfect way and fulfilled your hidden human hopes? Let your faith inform you where your mind cannot stretch. Wrap your faith around My hope and expect even more than you ever hoped for. Begin each morning knowing that I lead the way into an endless bounty of hope fulfilled.

While past performances do not guarantee future hope, My past promises are always fulfilled in My children. I brought awesome and righteous deeds to help My children in ages past. I have not given up on performing sacred blessings in your modern world. The times have changed, but My love and desire to serve My children will never cease. Why should you count on Me in the future, My sacred heart? Because I have been there in the past and will always be here.

God's awesome deeds of the past give us hope for the future.

You answer us with awesome and righteous deeds, God our Savior, the hope of all the ends of the earth and of the farthest seas, (Psalm 65:5 NIV)

MAY 20

I was present to witness the wonders of your birth. I anxiously await each morning as you greet a new day and rise from your slumber. As you grew and matured, I watched you develop in mind, body, and spirit. I lifted you up when you felt. I held you close when you cried. I rejoiced when you achieved your goals in life. I have always been with you from sunrise to sunset as each year passed by. Remain steadfast in your faith and confidence in your hope for My continued movement in your life. Confidence comes from understanding your strength; hope comes from realizing My commitment to you. Keep your child-like hope and believe I am always with you, helping you grow and preparing you for what lies ahead.

Your hope and confidence in Me are intended to last a lifetime. Unfortunately, too many of My children fail to thrive in their spiritual development and lose sight of Me amidst the clutter of worldly living. In short, their bodies and minds outgrow their souls. When the spiritual part of you remains, underdeveloped, impoverished, and neglected, hope dies along with your spiritual confidence. I am the Spirit Lifeforce that will feed your soul; drink from Me often, My child.

Never outgrow your hope for the future; God is still working in your life.

For you have been my hope, Sovereign Lord, my confidence since my youth. (Psalm 71:5 NIV)

MAY 21

*L*earn to walk in My holy ways and live by My divine truth. My laws and commandments were not meant to imprison you in a life that traps you without any freedom. I placed My laws before you to keep you safe and help you grow in your relationship with all the people you encounter through life and Me. Living a righteous life does not set up a roadblock to personal freedom but creates a doorway for hope.

The Law was given to Moses as a gift for my children to help guide them in life. My children were wanderers in the desert land and needed stability, direction, and spiritual guidance. You no longer are desert dwellers but still need My direction to help guide you. If you strive to live by the Law and love through My grace, you will create a marvelous world.

As you live a life that honors Me and guides you, you will find that My ways create possibilities, not restrictions. The most important law to follow is to love Me, your neighbor, and yourself.

Loving Me, neighbor, and self creates a triangle of constant support and endless hope for the future. Rise this morning knowing that I have prepared this day for you. Enjoy it.

Living a righteous life creates endless possibilities for hope.

Never take your word of truth from my mouth, for I have put my hope in your laws. (Psalm 119:43 NIV)

MAY 22

*H*ave heard your morning cry and listened to your early day's prayer. I listen with a heart open to help you in any way possible. I never forget the righteous prayers of My beloved children. Go into your day knowing I am with you and preparing the way for you. Do not let the individual struggles of the day compile into an enormous battle. You will only defeat yourself if you do such a thing.

Walk this day in the light of My hope. Troubles will not go away, but they will appear to be their actual size. This will help you see the solutions to your problems and keep them from becoming undefeatable giants. Living in My Hope makes all life challenges manageable and conquerable. Never ransom your tomorrows to the problems of today.

Living in My Hope allows you to see past your nose stuck in today's process. You will never see tomorrow's hope by fixating on today's problems. Come to Me in prayer and listen for the sound of My still, small voice. I will talk you down from your ledge of despair into a land of living hope. When you are facing your greatest challenges, you will need My most powerful hope to defeat them. My hope can move your mountains.

Facing your greatest challenge with hope.

Remember your word to your servant, for you have given me hope. (Psalm 119:49 NIV)

MAY 23

*Y*our hope for eternal life must be placed in Me. All you have worked for and everything you have strived for will wither and die with you. You can keep no promises, save any treasures, or bring anything from this world with you into your eternal life with Me. That is why you must place all of your hope in Me if you want to live out what you have hoped for.

Hope placed in Me will never die because I am an eternal Spirit who gives everlasting hope. I am the only hope you can have that will outlive itself. Only I have the power to give you this eternal hope; receive this promise with My love. Trust in Me, place your hope in Me, and live forever in My love. My hope never dies.
  You need to look further than the life you are living. Your physical life is like being a spiritual embryo. You are growing and developing, but you are waiting for something beyond what you are ow. Your physical life is a journey that prepares the soul for the great life span of eternity. When you understand this, you will realize you can out-live your life. You will pass on from this life on earth like a caterpillar morphing into a butterfly.

Only God can offer eternal hope for you.

Hopes placed in mortals die with them; all the promise of their power comes to nothing.

MAY 24

I speak to you each morning about hope, My beloved child. I hope you are listening to My words. Aside from My love, hope is the most cherished gift I can give you. Without My hope, your heart will sicken at the loss of the comforting feeling hope brings. Without my hope, the soul withers and shrinks at the thought of an empty future. Hope is the only way out of the past and into the future. Receive My hope today.

I come to you each morning with My comforting words about hope because I know hope's great value in all life. Root yourself deeply in My hope each morning. My hope carries fulfillment from the roots through the branches and to the leaves of the tree of life. Nothing grows without hope. Hope is the only thing you have when all else is lost.

While My love and hope are eternal gifts from Me, your faith has human limits. Usually, when you fail to thrive in My Love hope seems distant, diminished, and dead. Your faith is waning. Hope heals your heart and restores your soul if you have the mustard seed faith to allow it to come into your life. Practicing spiritual disciplines like Bible reading, prayer, Christian conferencing, worship, and meditation are all vital links to keeping your faith healthy and alive. You will be amazed at how much hope and love there is in the world when you view them through a faithful heart and soul.

Hope heals the heart and restores the spirit.

Hope deferred makes the heart sick, but a longing fulfilled is a tree of life. Proverbs 13:12 NIV)

MAY 25

I come to you each morning to inform your mind and instruct the soul. Understanding My hope in your life will sweeten every day. Hope will help guide you out of trouble and distress when the dark days of your life appear. Having this knowledge is vital to living a life of fulfillment through Hope Me. Without hope, the soul darkens and dries into despair.

Having hope in Me also enlivens your soul. Knowledge of My hope informs the mind, but living in the fulfillment of My hope gives life to the soul. The soul can see what the mind cannot understand. I teach you about My hope so your soul will receive its future destiny. Your destiny is to be with Me forever.

You may. Never know or even feel it, but I whisper to you in sweet hushed tones from Spirit to soul. The spiritual language is as much feeling and intuition as it is words or talking. My children tend to talk with their minds and listen less to their hearts or souls. I listen to your words as you pray, but I reach out to feel your heart and the inner groanings of your soul. When you practice closing your mouth and opening your heart and soul, you will gain greater knowledge and experience the depth of Me.

Your soul will know the hope your mind will never understand.

Know also that wisdom is like honey for you: If you find it, there is a future hope for you, and your hope will not be cut off. (Proverbs 24:14 NIV)

MAY 26

I instruct each morning because I want you to have My hope.
Many try to understand this world through their own limited
philosophical systems or cognitive adaptations of current reality. I
hope to be excommunicated from their systems because they failed
to account for Me. Hope is just a human word trying to describe a
future reality. If I am not present in the definition of hope, then the
future can hold no reality.

Let your faith inform your spirit about the hope I hold for all My children. The mind has severe human limitations in what it can comprehend. The spirit is boundless in what it can imagine. Hope is always
the next step beyond the limits of the mind. Hope is the first step
of faith. Do not fear the world branding you as a fool; it means you
have placed your best foot forward into the future.

Many of My beloved children think they are a delight to the world
and a joy to behold. Unfortunately, not many around them share the
same interpretation of who they are. Each of My beloved children
has great divine value and worth. You are all priceless in My eyes.
Self-deception occurs when you overrate your own worth. Be very
careful when you overate yourself. Usually, you have to underrate
those around you.

Only faith has the power to walk in the land of hope.

Do you see a person wise in their own eyes? There is more hope for
a fool than for them. (Proverbs 26:12 NIV)

MAY 27

*H*ope is more than just a warm feeling for future events. Hope has its own life force. The positive energy of the life force of hope is found in Me. I walk hand in hand with hope, anticipating what we can do in your life. If you have breath, you also have hope. If you have a beating heart, you can also feel the pulse of hope throbbing in your soul.

I give all My children the gift of hope because I know the endless flow of negative energy that can infiltrate your life. Hope cleanses the soul of this day's negative and sometimes evil energy and opens you up for tomorrow's positive spiritual energy flow. To live, you must have a beating heart. To thrive, you must have a positive spiritual energy flow of hope.

Too many of my children fall into the trap of letting the world soil their souls. Unfortunately, there is a snowball or dirtball effect when you let the world overcome your hope. It doesn't take long before the mud of a relentless world covers you with its desperate dirt. Hope keeps your head above the demands this world may place upon you. The world may rob you of today, but I have all your tomorrows.

Hope cleanses the soul.

Anyone who is among the living has hope—even a live dog is better off than a dead lion! (Euclasites 9:4 NIV)

MAY 28

*I*t is vital to worship Me whenever you can. Rise this morning with worship on your mind and Me in your heart. Singing praises to Me unites us in a spiritual link. We are united as one as you sing your morning songs of praise. Our life together on this earth must be marked by these simple yet holy encounters of worship. Your morning song of praise will do much to illuminate a dark day. As you worship Me find the offering of hope I leave behind. This offering of hope is to be your guide for the day, focus on the future, and compass for life. As you are faithful to Me so I am faithful to you. My hope will help you see the hidden treasures of life that I will leave along the road of your life's journey. Listen for My song of hope as you travel this road.

Hope is the offering God gives to you.

For the grave cannot praise you, death cannot sing your praise; those who go down to the pit cannot hope for your faithfulness. (Isaiah 38:13 NIV)

MAY 29

The body wears down each day and must find its time for rest. The mind is overburdened with too many life events to manage or daily problems to solve. The soul has its own burdens as well. The sinful sick soul sinks under the weight of a hard life. Hope is lost when one hard day resembles the other hard days before. I intended life to be a joy ride, not a hamster wheel.

Place your hope on Me, and I will give you rest for your soul. Life is not meant to be an endless line of burdens passing by like a picket fence of despair. Place your hope in Me, and you will learn to fly over the burdens of life like a majestic eagle. You can observe your problems without carrying them around like a burden-laden pack mule. Renew your body, recharge your mind, replenish your soul, and soar like an eagle.

You were created with physical, emotional, and spiritual limits. On your own accord, you will never be anything other than what you or a life coach can make you. If you want to live a life beyond the limits, you must consider what I can do for you. One flash of hope is worth countless inspirational and motivational encouragements from your life coach. If you want to be inspired to go far beyond what you imagined, you must be in "Spirit" first. I don't motivate you, I move you.

Hope allows us to soar over our burdens and walk and not be faint.

But those who hope in the Lord will renew their strength. They will soar on wings like eagles; they will run and not grow weary; they will walk and not be faint. (Isaiah 40:13 NIV)

MAY 30

*I*njustice breaks out far too often on this planet. My children are treated harshly and forced to live in impossible situations. Poverty is an injustice that can be fixed so all can meet their basic needs. Racism is a deadly injustice that can be stopped so all My children will be treated with dignity. Discrimination is an injustice that can be disallowed on this earth.

Injustice is a choice, but so is hope. Choose hope and stop choosing injustice. It really is that simple of a life choice for all My children to act with love toward each other. Never force others to live in injustice if you are unwilling to join them. Live together in My hope. If you live together, in my hope, you will not be able to treat each other unfairly, with injustice, malice, or harm.

Injustice is a roadblock to hope. You must see that everyone deserves justice, fair treatment, and, most of all, love. I desire to establish justice on all the earth, but it cannot be done without my children's help. Remember that the blessed Savior died to tip the scales of justice in your favor. All have sinned and fallen short, but I love everyone just the same. You are My greatest hope to establish a just earth. Please help Me, My child.

Both hope and injustice are a choice. Always choose hope.

MAY 31

*W*orry can weary your strength faster than any physical activity or hard work. Worry is a spirit killer and a slayer of hope. Before anything even happens, or the entire event unfolds, a sudden injection of worry can contaminate any possibility for hope. Never say, 'It is hopeless.' What may seem hopeless to you is just a new beginning to Me.

Hope brings spiritual energy to the soul and restores it for optimal performance. Now those huge gates of despair appear as the tiny specs they really are. Your life is centered around your perception of how you think things appear to you. Sometimes the ant may appear as a giant because your faith has failed to draw upon My hope. Start each day in My hope, and you will end each day renewed and strong in spirit.

I know it can be very difficult for you to stop worrying, My sacred heart, but there is a way out of the worry wart trap. Whenever you feel your mind slipping into worry mode, start to pray. Prayer engages the soul with greater power and control over you than your mind. But if the mind stands in line first, it will jump right in and worry. Clear your mind, calm your day, and caress your soul. Your soul has no worries when caressed in the hands of faith.

Faith is the path to hope.

You wearied yourself by such going about, but you would not say, 'It is hopeless.' You found renewal of your strength, and so you did not faint. (Isaiah 57:10 NIV)

JUNE 1

*M*y hope brings its own rewards and its own treasures. Continue to stand faithfully in My hope and stand firm in your conviction for My peace. Healing will come to My children when peace covers the land. Stay encouraged if the peace movement appears too slow for your liking. Deep wounds take longer to heal.

Rise this morning, thinking you will be the first to bring healing to the people. Give pardon instead of holding a grudge. Speak in soft tones of My love instead of clanging sounds of hate. Become an elixir of healing and an instrument of My hope, and your world will soon find the peace you so desperately seek.

Rather than thinking of healing peace originating in some distant corner of this earth, can't it begin with you, My child? I know you are not the cause of the world's problems, but you certainly could be the beginning of the cure. Hatred, bigotry, injustice, or social diseases are bread too quickly in My children. It only takes a few people to stop the viral explosion of hatred. One kind heart and loving soul can halt the onslaught of hatred. Allow healing peace to live in your heart, My child.

Hope brings healing peace to the soul.

We hoped for peace but no good has come, for a time of healing but there is only terror. (Jeremiah 8:15 NIV)

JUNE 2

The land of the lost is filled with dark gloom and misty miseries. Do not choose this land, My child, for neither hope nor peace can be found there. Too many of My children have chosen this dark path of despair rather than following My path of light and hope. Light and hope will come when you glorify Me each morning when you rise from your sleep. Begin each day by simply saying, "Glory be to God."

Glorifying Me is as much for your benefit as it is for honoring Me. When you give glory to Me, you shine My light on your world. You will find the light of hope within your words of praise. Your foot will not stumble, or your soul loses hope in the dark land of despair. Your night will turn to the morning with one quick utterance of My name. Yes, this praise can be done before your morning coffee.

The purpose and focus of spirituality is to enliven your awareness of Me in your life. You must remember that I am the energy life force that gives power to your soul and life to your being. When you place your focus on your inner being, you begin to walk very close with Me. All spiritual acts such as prayer, meditation, and Bible reading are simple attempts to draw closer to Me. I am where your spiritual light will shine the brightest.

Glorifying God brings hope to your life.

Give glory to the Lord your God before he brings the darkness before your feet stumble on the darkening hills. You hope for light, but he will turn it into utter darkness and change it to deep gloom. (Jeremiah 13:10 NIV)

JUNE 3

*D*o you notice the gentle miracles that occur in your life each day? The rain does not have to fall to earth, but it finds its way to water all life on this planet. The sun can choose to hide its shining face, but every morning life is blessed with its golden kiss. These are not just haphazard happenings. The glory of nature is My daily gift to you.

Do not take life for granted; receive everything life offers as a gift from Me. By observing the blessings in life, you will know that every-thing comes from My generous hand. Hope lies in realizing that all you have comes from Me, and I hold all that you will have as a bless-ing. The rain will fall, the sun will shine, and you will be blessed.

I know you think all these blessings are just ordinary common occurrences. Your local weather person can forecast approaching rainstorms with some accuracy. Yes, they have the ability to fore-cast, but they do not have the power to make it rain. You live under the blessings of my hand. I remind you that everything comes from Me, not so you will feel thankful, but that you will know you are loved.

Hope is the realization that God holds tomorrow's blessings in His hands today.

Do any of the worthless idols of the nation bring rain? Do the skies themselves send down showers? No, it is you, Lord, our God. Therefore, our hope is in you, for you are the one who does all this. (Jeremiah 14:22 NIV)

JUNE 4

*T*he future is the greatest gift I can give to any of My children. A promise of another tomorrow is priceless. My promise for another tomorrow is buried deep within My treasure of hope. Without hope, there can be no promise of tomorrow or hope for a prosperous future.

I have plans for you, My precious child. I have plans to help you prosper and grow.

My plans include a future full of earthly comfort and spiritual blessings. Please know that I always want the best for you, and the best is yet to come. Never give up hope for the future because I hold your future in My hands. Receive My gift of hope and know that your future is bright.

Have you come this far just to go this far, My sacred heart? You are the one praying for a miracle breakthrough. Your heart and soul call out to Me to attend to your needs and requests. Unfortunately, you do not have much of a say in the unfolding timeline. You have desires and dreams for your life. I have fulfilling plans for your future. You hope for things to happen, and I am making them happen. Stay with my ultimate plan to make you prosper. It will be worth the wait, My child.

God's plans to prosper are written on the tablet of hope.

For I know the plans I have for you," declares the Lord, "plans to prosper you and not to harm you, plans to give you hope and a future. (Jeremiah 29:11 NIV)

JUNE 5

*D*o you notice the gentle miracles that occur in your life each day? The rain does not have to fall to earth, but it finds its way to water all life on this planet. The sun can choose to hide its shining face, but every morning life is blessed with its golden kiss. These are not just haphazard happenings. The glory of nature is My daily gift to you.

Do not take life for granted, receive everything life has to offer as a gift from Me. By observing the blessings in life, you will know that everything comes from My generous hand. Hope lies in realizing that all that you have comes from Me and I hold all that you will have as a blessing. The rain will fall, the sun will shine and you will be blessed.

Hope is the realization that God holds our blessings of tomorrow in His hands today.

Do any of the worthless idols of the nation bring rain? Do the skies themselves send down showers? No, it is you, Lord, our God. Therefore, our hope is in you, for you are the one who does all this. (Jeremiah 14:22 NIV)

JUNE 6

*M*any will bring you bags filled with false hopes and empty dreams. Do not be eager to follow these shallow promises, for they only will lead you down a dead end. These pail prophets' visions are nothing more than an illusion or sleight of hand. Their lips move, but no truth can be found in what they speak. They are nothing more than puppets speaking the lies of and untruths of the father of lies.

Faith speaks the language of hope. Believe with all your heart, mind, and soul that I am working to prepare the way for you into a glorious future, and it will be as you believe. Hope can never be false if it is grounded in your faith in Me. Rise this morning knowing I will keep and fulfill your promise.

You are living in an age of false prophets, scammers, and liars. Your internet has brought you closer together in many wonderful ways. Unfortunately, some of My children choose to use this information highway for their own gain. Be wise and proceed with due caution on whom you let into your life. They may seek something beyond mere friendship if they want to get to know you better. No one can sell you the future; it is Mine alone to give to you.

God can bring your future hope.

This is what the Lord Almighty says: "Do not listen to what the prophets are prophesying to you; they fill you with false hopes. They speak visions from their own minds, not from the mouth of the Lord. (Jeremiah 23:16 NIV)

JUNE 7

The future is the greatest gift I can give to any of My children. A promise of another tomorrow is priceless. My promise for another tomorrow is buried deep within My treasure of hope. Without hope, there can be no promise of tomorrow or hope for a prosperous future.

I have plans for you, My precious child. I have plans to help you prosper and grow.

My plans include a future full of earthly comfort and spiritual blessings. Please know that I always want the best for you, and the best is yet to come. Never give up hope for the future because I hold your future in My hands. Receive My gift of hope and know that your future is bright.

Have you come this far to go this far, My sacred heart? You are the one praying for a miracle breakthrough. Your heart and soul call out to Me to attend to your needs and requests. Unfortunately, you do not have much of a say in the unfolding timeline. You have desires and dreams for your life. I have fulfilling plans for your future. You hope for things to happen, and I am making them happen. Stay with my ultimate plan to make you prosper. It will be worth the wait, My child.

God's plans for your future are written on the tablet of hope.

For I know the plans I have for you," declares the Lord, "plans to prosper you and not to harm you, plans to give you hope and a future. (Jeremiah 29:11 NIV)

JUNE 8

*I*t is hard to believe that good can come from bad or that life can come from death. Both of these statements are true, however. The blood of the blessed Savior spilled from his death upon the cross is what saved you. You are forgiven of all sins through this sacrificial act of divine love for you and all My children. The very act that took the life of Jesus redeemed your life from sin.

Ponder these words deeply in your heart this evening. Let the terror of the sacrifice also reflect the depth of divine love and grace. Understand that this is the depth of My love for you, that neither life nor death shall ever separate us. The loving things I do, I do for you. The heart of My grace knows no bounds.

No matter what your financial status is in life, My sacred heart and my grace are beyond any imaginable wealth. My grace comes to you as a free gift of My love. My grace was paid for in advance by the death of the beloved Savior. Divine blood bought your forgiveness and paid the way for salvation. The greatest act of love is the giving of oneself to another. I gave Myself to you, My child.

Redemption through the blood

In Him, we have redemption through his blood, the **forgiveness** of sins, in accordance with the riches of God's grace. (Ephesians 1:7 NIV)

JUNE 9

*R*ise this morning with and search your mind and soul for reasons to have hope. Call to mind all those occasions that I came to you to bring you comfort for your physical suffering and relief from stress for your soul. These were not just casual half-hazard happenings; My intentions were very deliberate. Give prayers of thanksgiving as you remember these events that marked My encounter with you.

Past events give a reason for future hope. I was working in your past; I am with you in this present moment, and I will be by your side in the future. This chain of events directly leads to hope for the future. Follow this progressive chain with your mind, and it will lead you to assurance of all future hope. Do not lament or fret over past events and difficulties. Remember the minor victories; they are what got you to this moment: Place your hope on those victories.

  My servant Jeremiah is lamenting because he remembers My blessed children's past sins. In remembering their transgressions, he finds hope for the future because of what I have done. Find ways to call to mind the blessings I have already given you. Each blessing is a pedal of the flower of my love. If you can recount my blessings from the past, it will transform your future into a vision of hope. I am always before you; you must find ways to remember forward so you can expect My holy presence even in the darkest times.

Remember the good God has done in your life, and expect even more.

Yet this I call to mind, and therefore I have hope: (Lamentations 3:21 NIV)

JUNE 10

Too many of My children have been placed in a hopeless position. They see the tragedies and dilemmas of life and give up all hope. When hope is gone, your life is over. When hope is gone, all that remains are the torments of the past and the fleeting moments of this day. Your future has been blotted out and lies hopelessly disabled in a pile of forgotten and unfulfilled dreams.

Never give up, and never give in. Diminished hopes and dashed dreams can become a strong lion roaring at the gates of the future. Begin this day with My hope at your side. Let go of the hope killers of despair and receive a new vision and hope for your life. I have the ability to replace your dead dreams with the hope for a new vision of what your life can be in Me.

If only I could show you the most hopeless situations and how I restored hope to struggling people. The Scriptures were gathered and distributed so you would have evidence of the depth of my love and the commitment to how far I will go to help My precious children. Nothing in heaven or the earth, between glory and the valley of the dead, can stop my commitment to reclaiming the hopeless, helpless, and lost. The blessed Savior is a visible sign of the great depth of My love for you. My sacred heart.

What is the true depth of God's love?

When they say, "He went up," what does it mean but that He had first gone down to the deep parts of the earth? (Ephesians 4: 9 NIV)

JUNE 11

*D*o you see them dry bones? Do you hear their dry bones rattling and clanking to the dance of death and destruction? Do not look and do not listen; the dry bones are only an illusion in your life that sing and dance to the shallow songs of hopelessness. Cast the light of hope on the dry bones of life, and they scatter and hide from My glorious light.

Life becomes hopeless only if you think it does. Your mind is tricked into singing and dancing to the rhythm of the dry bones tune. I sing a different song. I sing a song filled with hope and a future where dreams are fulfilled. I sing the endless song of spiritual harmony where dejection is never part of My repertoire. Sing this song with Me this morning, and it will enliven those dry bones to dance a ballet of hope.

Dance of hope among the dry bones

Then he said to me: "Son of man, these bones are the people of Israel. They say, 'Our bones are dried up, and our hope is gone; we are cut off.' (Ezekiel 34:11 NIV)

JUNE 12

*H*ope that is not yet will soon be. Learn to wait with excited anticipation for the arrival of My Hope. I have heard your morning call, and I am preparing My response in its own divine time. I remember your prayers and petitions; all requests must be wrapped in the promises of hope if they are to be received by you. Wait for the very thing that you hoped for.

Do not try to force things to happen; that moves the hope you have in Me to the unsettled, nervous energy of your own soul. You can either have hope in Me or trust in your own unbridled energy; you can't have both at the same time. The choice to have hope in Me and I will make the wait worthwhile. All good things take time to build and age; the same can be said of hope. Pray, watch, and hope for all good things to come in their own time.

Be patient for what you hope for; God has heard your prayers.

But as for me, I watch in hope for the Lord, I wait for God my Savior; my God will hear me. (Micah 7:7 NIV)

JUNE 13

*M*y hope is that My people will learn to live and work together. That they would learn to love each other as I love them. My people would see that their differences are more forms of distinction that serve to distinguish them rather than signs of separation. Hope rises when common goals are held and shared. Let all the nations place their hope in Me.

Rise each morning, hoping that the world will one day be of one Spirit. I speak many languages and thrive in a variety of cultures. I can open the eyes of the hearts of every nation and show the people the great possibilities that My hope can bring them. My hope will bless the entire planet with peace, love, prosperity, and the power of nations living and working together. I am the hope of the nations and the future of your life together.

I gave a name carried by the blessed Savior so you can all have a common point of reference. Jesus is the name that unites the nations and places you all in My love and care. Do not hesitate to use his name every morning in prayer. Utter his name as you go about your day to reassure you of his holy presence. Greet one another in his name so you will remember you are kindred spirits. Jesus is your name forever, My sacred heart.

Hope comes in Jesus for all the people of this earth.

In his name, the nations will put their hope." (Matthew 12:21 NIV)

JUNE 14

*D*o not hope so much for signs and wonders to be performed in your life. Rather, walk down the path that each day will follow to the future. Hope is less about seeing major miracles and more about experiencing My presence every day of your life. Signs and wonders are breadcrumbs dropped along the path of life to let you know you are headed in the right direction. True hope rests in the assurance that I am with you every step of the way.

Learn to hope for the blessings in your life that will remind you of My presence. Know that I am with you as you love your soul mate. I am present as you experience the holy blessing at the birth of a child or grandchild. Hope rises from living in My divine presence each day, not in witnessing a sign here or there.

Look for Me in the folded hands of prayer. Prayer is an outward and visible sign and wonder of My holy work in My blessed children. Do not calculate the power of one pair of folded hands emptying the heart in prayer. Signs and wonders may only be visible to an open heart and a steadfast soul. I can stand right before you, but if your soul is not attentive, you will walk right by me. History is dotted with hopeful souls looking for a peep show of God. Unfortunately, they missed the command performance in the spotlight directly before them.

Looking for signs and wonders?

When Herod saw Jesus, he was greatly pleased, because, for a long time, he had been wanting to see him. From what he had heard about him, he hoped to see him perform a sign of some sort. (Luke 23:8 NIV)

JUNE 15

*W*hen all hope seems lost in your life, look deeper into the cave of death and despair. The disciples thought that the body of the Savior was destined to remain in the tomb of death. A thousand lifetimes trained them to rely on what they knew. One death would alter their understanding of reality and the scope of My hope. Never short-change your faith by restraining your hope.

Hope rose from the dead on that first Easter morning. It was not a hope based on ancestral faith, it was a hope based on My promise to love My children from birth to life and into life everlasting. I remind you to broaden your concept of hope. My hope has no limitations or walls. The only thing that can restrain My hope is your lack of faith in Me. Dare to roll away the stone from your faith and set My hope free in your life.

Sometimes the greatest signs and wonders will appear in plain sight. Some need to have stones of death rolled away from their lives. Others need a gentle touch on the cheek to remind them that I am still here. Signs and wonders are only necessary if there is a lack of faith or a desire to be entertained. Remain faithful, and you will sustain hope.

Never let your lack of faith fail to soar to endless heights.

But we had hoped that he was the one who was going to redeem Israel. And what is more, it is the third day since all this took place. (Luke 24:21 NIV)

JUNE 16

*M*y hope gives you the power to let go of the things you cannot control. If you haven't figured it out yet, most of life is beyond your control. Your body wears itself out trying to make a living in a fast-paced world that is speeding up every moment of the day. It is easy to lose hope when the thundering herd of society is trampling you. You lose ground as fast as you try to stay on pace.

Find rest for your troubled heart and give your life over to me this morning. The rat race of life can only be won by another rat. Learn to live this life as My beloved child. Use your tongue for something other than cursing the new day when you rise from your sleep. As you learn to praise Me for the gift of another morning, you will find hope in the day ahead.

My early followers had a difficult time finding rest for their souls. The world was against them. The ancient world had no concept of a sacrifice to God. I fulfilled the promise of the Blessed One to dwell in all who proclaim Him as Savior. You, too, will find gladness of heart, a rejoicing tongue, and a body resting in hope. This is what Jesus promised, and this is what I will give you, My sacred heart.

Rest in the hope of God, and your future will unfold before you.

Therefore, my heart is glad and my tongue rejoices; my body also will rest in hope, (Acts 2:26 NIV)

JUNE 17

*Y*our heart cannot hold wicked thoughts and evil desires at the same time it seeks My hope. The mind was not designed to think of evil and hope for good. The mind soon takes over the heart and soul with thoughts that are far from Me and contrary to My ways. Evil thoughts can be like a COVID-19 virus that overtakes the body cell by cell.

My hope will come into your life when you cleanse yourself of troubled thoughts through My forgiveness. Hope has the entire heart to inhabit when the heart is freed from wickedness. If you feel you are losing hope in life, check your heart and mind to see if they have let your soul lose hope because sin has invaded your inner thoughts. Sin happens, but so does My forgiveness.

Sin happens, My child. I understand the folly of sin and the mortal person. I have all the generations ever lived to draw back on and recount their individual sins. Except I don't waste My time unearthing the past. I clear all thoughts and memories from My being to have a clear pathway to you. This is a practice you should discover as well. Keep your heart free from evil and your mind far away from sin, and you will have a clear path to Me.

Sin can destroy hope, so keep good thoughts in your heart.

Repent of this wickedness and pray to the Lord in the hope that he may forgive you for having such a thought in your heart. (Acts 8:22 NIV)

JUNE 18

*I*f making money is your only goal in life, you will soon lose hope in Me. I did not place you on this earth to be a money-making machine. A machine prods through the day without any hope and only focuses on what it was designed to do. You were designed by My hand and articulated by My breath. You were made to walk humbly in life with Me and love your neighbor with the same compassion you love yourself.

I hope that My blessings will be more than enough for you to live an abundant life. Let money, wealth, and riches fall to you like the morning rain. Place your hope in what I can bring to you and not just in what you can make. One day your power to make money may be gone, and your hope will disappear with it. Place your hope in Me.

I know the ultimate value My children place upon their money. I know what wealth, abundance, and massive incomes can do for you. Unfortunately, you may not clearly realize what money can do to you, My child. You believe money will provide everything, but you can only gain something if you earn it and spend it. I freely give Myself to you and place your future in My hands. Earn your money, spend your money, and enjoy life, but learn to trust in me.

When your money is gone, reach for hope.

When her owners realized that their hope of making money was gone, they seized Paul and Silas and dragged them into the market-place to face the authorities. (Acts 16:19 NIV)

June 19

*N*ot all of My children have a hope for a life with Me after death. Please place your faith and hope in my power over life and death, My sacred heart. The resurrection of life is the ultimate hope I bring to every soul that has walked, is walking, and will walk upon this earth. You are an eternal spiritual being walking upon this earth in a physical body at this time. The soul has forgotten, and the body does not know the depth of eternal existence.

I have sealed My promise of eternal life with My glorious resurrection of the beloved Savior. Jesus has paved the way out of the sealed tomb of death. The resurrection can only raise the dead into eternal glory because the Christ event was sealed with My kiss of divine love. My love for My children is the hope for life everlasting. Believe in this great hope.

Here is the blessed part of our eternal relationship, My child. Your faith will not fail you. Our everlasting relationship is only based on one tiny mustard seed of faith. I give entrance into life eternal based on one spiritual spec of faith in Me. You don't have to move mountains; believe that your journey in life will begin at birth and will continue after your death. The blessed Savior showed you the way; follow his steps into the eternal life that awaits you.

The hope of the resurrection of the dead is in Jesus.

Then Paul, knowing that some of them were Sadducees and the others Pharisees, called out in the Sanhedrin, "My brothers, I am a Pharisee, descended from Pharisees. I stand on trial because of the hope of the resurrection of the dead." (Acts 23:6 NIV)

JUNE 20

I do not know what the loss of hope feels like, my sacred heart, but I know what it looks like. I have seen hope slip from the hearts and faces of men deprived of any glimpse of a future. I have witnessed the tragedy of women crushed when hope is stolen from their souls, leaving a deep hole of dark despair. Never give up on hope; when you do, you also give up on Me.

A black storm cloud cannot carry the golden rays of sunlight. A hopeless soul cannot feel the blessings of My glorious hope. When the dark storm clouds of despair surround you, do not look for hope in the midst of the cloud. Hope always lies beyond despair. Hope is never found in the middle of a life struggle, and hope can only be found in Me. Do not look to the storm and yell. "Stop." It cannot stop and will not halt. Look beyond the storm for My hope.

Despair is a raging storm that can easily drown your hope. Don't let the storm of despair wash over your life. Behind every dark menacing black cloud is a shining star or the glimmering sun. Do not be afraid to call out to me; saving souls is something that I do very well. If you take My hand, I will teach you how to walk on the waters of despair.

Hope for things to get better.

When neither sun nor stars appeared for many days, and the storm continued raging, we finally gave up all hope of being saved. (Acts 27:40 NIV)

JUNE 21

*H*ope and faith can work together to stretch even the limits of your imagination, My sacred heart. Did you rise this morning with the expectation that I would lead you beyond all hope into a world beyond your dreams? Only a few of My precious children rise in the morning knowing that even the sun cannot outshine what is about to happen in their lives. Abraham did not know how it would be done, but his faith told him something very great was about to happen. Abraham's faith informed him, and he was led by his hope to become the spiritual father of many nations, people, and religions. I do not think you fully understand the power you hold in your soul. If you did, you would have been up hours ago, ready to seize the day and the hope it brings.

Let me share a spiritual formula with you, My sacred heart. Your dreams are divinely sent. If your dream comes to you as a gift from Me, it has no choice but to come true. Abraham had a divine dream, he doubted; his wife Sarah laughed at the dream, but it came true in spite of their lack of faith or vision. Hold on to all dreams that come from Me; don't let go until I bless you. If your dream was divinely inspired, it is already in the making.

Faith will take you beyond your hopes and dreams.

Against all hope, Abraham in hope believed, and so became the father of many nations, just as it had been said to him, "So shall your offspring be." (Romans 4:18 NIV)

JUNE 22

*R*ise each morning with the knowledge and expectation that I am with you, My sacred heart. Plant this image of My holy presence deep in your heart where your soul can find it. There will be times in your life when that perfect train of life you boarded will make an unplanned stop or become detoured to another destination. Whatever happens, cling tightly to My side.

Your first mistake was to rely too heavily on what you think life should be. You will never get out of life alive by your own means; learn to boast in Me by the faith you have. You have total access to Me at all times; use every moment of your day to seek My wisdom and guidance. Most of all, begin each morning in this sacred hope that I am with you always and that My glory is sufficient for this day.

May I ask you to do a very small thing for me, My child? If you can find it within your heart, can you boast about Me? Many of My precious children can stand in front of huge gatherings and boast of their greatness, but they forget the help I gave them. Come to me with a humble heart and celebrate what I gave you, teach you, guide you, and most of all, the love I bestow upon you. A handful of hearts will always notice what I have done. A heart filled with self-pride will never even know I am here. Always boast of My hope in you for the future.

Never attempt to plan to live beyond the grace of God; it is always ahead of you.

Through whom we have gained access by faith into this grace in which we now stand. And we boast in the hope of the glory of God. (Romans 5:2 NIV)

JUNE 23

*R*emember that at the bottom of a deep dark well lies the water that your thirsty soul seeks. Everyone will encounter suffering in life. Not all sufferings are spiritual testing, but every obstacle in life carries an opportunity for growth. Some will follow a path that leads to despair and self-destruction when faced with suffering. Self-destruction is never the way out of any dilemma. Let your faith lead you down your glory path toward perseverance.

The glory path will turn your suffering into a road map for success. Let your sufferings teach you to overcome the challenges of life. Take My hand and let Me pull you out of the muck and mire of difficult times. Once on the other side of suffering, stand tall and celebrate what you have become as a child of perseverance.

Keep your spiritual compass before you, MY precious child. I have placed many things in your life to help guide, direct, and support you. The blessed savior is your moral and spiritual compass. The Bible holds the GPS you seek to give you practical advice. I am that inner feeling that dwells deep in your heart and soul. I feel your groanings and upheaval of spirit. Prayer will always point true north; learn to use prayer as your spiritual echo locater.

Use your hope in God as your spiritual compass through the challenges of life.

Not only so, but we also glory in our sufferings because we know that suffering produces perseverance; perseverance, character; and character, hope. (Romans 5:4 NIV)

JUNE 24

I come into your life as a divine gift of holy love for you, My sacred heart. Never let a day go by without reflecting and giving thanks for My presence in your life. I am not here by any accident; I come out of love but with a holy intention and a clear purpose. My intention is to love your soul even to death. I will not stray from your side at night's call but remain steadfast with you during the darkest of life's tempests. My love will always abide.

I aim to show you the hope that will lead you through life and step beyond death's door. Never be ashamed of My gift of eternal love or shun My holy presence. I am the eternal hope that lies beyond the mystery of life and death. When the beating of your frail human heart ceases, My love and Spirit force will beat on. This is no shallow hope, My child; this is the eternal promise planted in your heart.

I would like to change how you look at things, My precious child, or in this case, how you listen to things. Listen to the sound of your heart. The beating you hear is not just a physical sound but a spiritual sound frequency. You hear and feel Me with each heartbeat. I poured My love directly into your heart to keep it strong and provide physical and spiritual strength. Your heart not only provides blood to the body, but it also pulses Me through your soul.

Listen for the sound of the Spirit in between your heartbeats.

And hope does not put us to shame because God's love has been poured out into our hearts through the Holy Spirit, who has been given to us. (Romans 5:5 NIV)

JUNE 25

*L*et the morning sun awaken you to the beauty and power of creation. With all of its beauty, creation waits in anxious anticipation for the hope I bring to the world. Hope is realized in the transforming power I bring to all who believe in Me, My sacred heart. You must realize one very important thing, my child, sin and evil have a cataclysmal effect on all the cosmos. Sin does not just sit in a cesspool of life; it festers, spreads, and consumes the very fiber of creation.

The tender transformation of one soul begins the process of healing and salvation for the person and all of creation. Your life has an impact on the physical world and on the spiritual world. Never underestimate your own effect on the divine order of the universe. Plant your seeds of faith in the holy holes of hope and see how all of life will change. If you want to change the planet, change how you live on it first.

The first step is vital if you want to transform who you are as a spiritual being. Put negative thoughts and behavior behind you. This world's negative substances and spiritual forces have loud sexy voices and wear bling and slender that will draw you in. Once you are close enough, they will rob you of your physical, emotional, and spiritual vitality. You cannot change, and the world around will not transform while you keep company with these demons of destruction. Put your childish ways behind you.

If you want to transform the universe, you must begin with your life.

For the creation was subjected to frustration, not by its own choice, but by the will of the one who subjected it, in hope. (Romans 8:20 NIV)

JUNE 26

*L*earn to give thanks for what you already have, for it is the culmination of the hope you once had revealed to you. You now have what you once hoped for; give thanks and celebrate the inbreaking of another miraculous blessing in your life. Learn to receive these fulfillments of holy hope as markers of what is yet to come to you. What you once hoped for now is and what you hope for today will be.

Give thanks for your salvation and have hope for the coming resurrection of all who have hope in Me. Live your life assured that all hope for salvation has been fulfilled. Live your life in the future hope that life does not end in death, for there is hope beyond the door. Celebrate your life today and hope for the life that is yet to come.

Faith is what you do not see; assurance is the reality of a hope fulfilled. Salvation is yours, my friend, do not fear or lack faith; it is yours. Be assured that many of your blessings are placed before you to assure you that I am present and active in your life. Faith and hope are only necessary for believing that what I do today will also be done for you tomorrow. If you look back, you will see your future. Look behind you to find your hope.

Your future hope is based on what God has already done for you.

For in this hope, we were saved. But hope that is seen is no hope at all. Who hopes for what they already have? (Romans 8:24 NIV)

JUNE 27

I have already talked to you about patience and perseverance, sometimes impatient children. Your want and need will not make the universe spin any faster nor bring the rains of tomorrow today. Place the intention of your hope before Me in fervent reverent prayer, and it will be answered in My due good time. You are sometimes short-sighted in that you only look at the cause of your needs; I also look at the effect.

All of life is interwoven, like a precious spiritual prayer shawl. The wool must be considered; the color must be selected the form and fit must be perfected. What you hope for today may unexpectedly influence another life tomorrow. Your prayer is a cosmic spiritual energy of immeasurable power. Only I can measure and fit your prayer to perfect form and function. So, wait for your prayer to catch up to your hope.

I will remember your prayers and petitions; the real question is, do you desire and need what you want enough to remember what you ask for? Place the passion of your spiritual self behind each prayer, and you will drive it all the way to heaven. Hang on to your prayer with endless passion and hope until I bless you. I remember your prayers; make certain that you remember what you asked for, My child. Don't give up, never give in, and what you seek will be found.

Only God has a timeline for hope.

But if we hope for what we do not yet have, we wait for it patiently. (Romans 8:25 NIV)

JUNE 28

*T*ake time for our holy encounter each morning, My child. Our time together can be smooth and manageable. A friendly smile and a sincere prayer from the heart as you move out to encounter your day, is all I ask of you. Be faithfully diligent in your prayers, no matter how short they are. Your prayer life sustains our spiritual connection, seeks help for a loved one, and opens the door to the future.

Prayer is the intimate language of the soul. Your prayers go deeper than words can speak into the inner groanings of your soul. Learn to celebrate answered prayers of past hopes. Take courage in your afflictions; they, too, will pass. Come to Me in the morning light and meet Me in the divine Spirit encounter called prayer. Prayer is the spiritual channel where thoughts pass between us and where you can witness your hopes fulfilled.

Your healing and health are grounded in your prayer life, My sacred heart. Do not hesitate to gather people around you that will assist in emotional, physical, or spiritual healing. Be patient in your affliction as kindred souls surround you with holy, healthy healing prayers. You will know if your time for wellness is at hand if there is witness to My holy healing. I will give health to your body, mind, and spirit so you will feel the blessings of health in your life. Be patient; your time has come.

Three signs your healing is in God's hands.

Be joyful in hope, patient in affliction, faithful in prayer. (Romans 12:12 NIV)

JUNE 29

*R*eceive this blessing as a treasured gift from the ancient texts of ageless Scripture. I send My divine hope to fill your heart with joy and peace. Trust in Me today to bring you joyous hope for tomorrow. Hope is a divine light that shines on everything to bring light to a dingy and dark world. My hope can explode the darkest recess of your soul into light beams of radiant anticipation on what I can bring to your life.

I am the very spiritual power that dwells within you. The more you open yourself to Me, the more room I have to empower you. Trust Me without limits, and I will overflow in your life with abundance and blessings and lead you to what you hoped for. These are not shallow promises; I hope incarnate in all of life.

All of My glorious children were created with physical limitations. There is only so far, your body and mind can take you. There is another world beyond limits: My world of spirit and faith. You can imagine, improvise, dream, and hope in the spiritual realm. Every human reality started out as a thought or dream before it came to be. You recreate the process I employed initially by speaking all things into existence. Embrace the fact that your reality is spawned in your spirit, and you will become limitless, My child.

Joy and peace are blessings from your hope in God.

May the God of hope fill you with all joy and peace as you trust in him so that you may overflow with hope by the power of the Holy Spirit. (Romans 15:13 NIV)

JUNE 30

*I*f you rose this morning wondering how life really works, I will give you the answer to the mystery of life. Life runs on love, pure and simple love. I don't know why this is such a mystery to My children, I have been very transparent in showing the power of love. All life is created from My divine expression of love. Life is the object of My love. Redemptive salvation is a compassionate expression of My love for you and all humankind. Easter morning brought love and hope to the sinful and separated from My love.

Love is the one thing in life that cannot fail if I am the source of love. Through your faith place all of your hope in My love. My love will always protect you and will always give reason for celebration. Heaven and earth may cease to be but My love for you will never end.

Hope is always perfected in God's love.

Love does not delight in evil but rejoices with the truth. [7] It always protects, always trusts, always hopes, always perseveres. (1 Corinthians 13:6-7 NIV)

July 1

*F*aith and hope work hand in hand to create your future. I shared the reality of this dynamic of the power of faith and hope before, My child. Your faith in Me will always bring new hope for your future. I am the divine author of hope for all people. Stay strong in your faith, and the hope of the eyes of your heart will see many splendid blessings on the horizon. Hope will always wait patiently for faith to catch up.

The greatest gift I can give you, My blessed sacred heart, is My never-ending love. My love filled your soul with faith and taught your heart to hope beyond all reasonable expectations. My love is the ground for mercy and forgiveness, creating the open heart of compassionate divine judgment. It is My love that will bind us tightly together forever.

You should know that I loved you before you took your first breath. I delighted over you as I formed you in your mother's womb. I watched with joy as your cells multiplied and you came to life. My love remains strong as I lavish you with daily blessings to enhance your life and strengthen our bond. I loved you with My holy divine love so you could have a purpose in life, my child. Your purpose is to love as I love; you can do no better than that.

God is the divine author of hope and love.

And now, these three remain faith, hope, and love. But the greatest of these is love. (1 Corinthians 13:13 NIV)

July 2

*F*ear is that overwhelming human emotion that enlivens the mind, body, and spirit in the twinkling of an eye and causes the entire being to react to danger in a slit second. Fear is not what I seek; rather, let My love be your motivating factor in your life. Let My love be your guiding light each morning as you rise from bed. Put on My Love like a comfortable old sweater that is as plain as it is worn. My love should be a comfort in your life and not be worn like some ill-fitting sale suit. How you wear My love will inspire others to follow Me because they want our relationship. No need to put on airs or strut around like an illuminated peacock; just be yourself. Hopefully, others will plainly see Me through you.

Love is what I seek, not fear. Love is what I give, not punishment. I placed a record before you, My child. I wanted you to know the life and actions of Jesus through the sacred texts. Jesus is the visible sign of My love. The blessed savior showed you the depth of My love as he hung helplessly on the cross of pain. The resurrected redeemer showed you the glory of My life as I defeated death to unite us forever. You are never far from my love; I am the Spirit of Holiness that dwells within you.

Should you fear God?

Since, then, we know what it is to fear the Lord, and we try to persuade others. What we are is plain to God, and I hope it is also plain to your conscience. (2 Corinthians 5:11 NIV)

JULY 3

The faith you have in Me has direction and purpose in your life, My sacred heart. Your direction in life is to follow the path that leads to My grace. Let this be your first step every morning as you strive to live in My grace. Living in My grace means you will have faith enough to trust My leading in your life. Your righteous living will not bring the salvation you desire. Grace alone has the power to unite you with Me.

Your purpose is to lead a life that expresses your faith in Me by your love for Me, your neighbor, and yourself. Living in this direction and with spirit spirit-focused purpose will bring the hope you desire. Human signs and symbols do not have the power to give you the everlasting life you seek. Only I have that power. You have the power to express your faith in Me through your love.

If you truly want to unleash your spiritual power, My child, you must first surrender your entire life to Me. The focus is Spiritual power, not human strength. If you want to become a spiritual being, you must walk in the Spirit or live in Me. I am the God conduit you so desire. It is easy enough to see if your life is Spirit-led and Spirit-fed. If you live out of My love, you live a spiritual life. Your ego will have difficulty giving up to the spiritual life, but in time the ego will learn to live out of My love as well.

Unleash your spiritual power.

For through the Spirit, we eagerly await by faith the righteousness for which we hope. (Galatians 5:5 NIV)

July 4

There is more awaiting you than you could ever imagine. Spend some time this morning looking backward at your life and count your blessings. The good things that appeared daily throughout your life did not appear to you by mere happenstance. Your blessings came to you from Me as very specific and deliberate gifts. My gift of life blessings was meant to assist you, encourage you, and enhance your life. There are more blessings on the way.

Beyond the blessings of this life lie the untold riches of your inheritance as one of My beloved children. You also received the blessing of becoming one of the holy people. You were made holy by My transforming love. You will remain in My transforming love forever more. The riches of your holy life in Me will never be taken away.

I invite you to open the eyes of your heart, My child. When you see things through your inner spirit eyes, you will have a completely different perspective on life. You will see that you are more than just a spec in this spectacular universe; you are a valued part of a greater whole. You are more than mere space dust; as some would say, you are part human and significantly spirit. When your life ends, you do not pass into nothingness; you receive the glory of this entire universe that I created in honor of my children. Open the eyes of your heart and see what lies ahead of you, My sacred heart.

Open the eyes of your heart and see what God has for you.

I pray that the eyes of your heart may be enlightened in order that you may know the hope to which he has called you, the riches of his glorious inheritance in his holy people, (Ephesians 1:18 NIV)

JULY 5

*T*oo many of My beloved children remain strangers in a foreign land. The struggling strangers have chosen the hard way on the back streets of life. They wander aimlessly through life with no direction, even less support, no helping hand to guide them, or a loving heart to care for them. Never take this life path, My sacred heart for you will find little hope here.

Travel the roads of life that are clearly marked by My covenant of love, and they will always lead you to My hope. You are safely in My world, where the lion and child play together. A universe where peace is as bright as the noonday sun. A place where hope blossoms every morning and is enjoyed with the evening meal. This is not a world of mystery and magic; this is My world - welcome home.

I would hope that My blessed churches would be a welcoming oasis for the spiritual traveler, but many are not. Too many worship centers have become cloistered closets to familiar faces. Become a welcoming heart to a strange soul in your place of worship, my child. Introduce yourself to the stranger, then introduce them to Me. Now you are companions in Christ and not lonely wayfarers on the road alone. They are citizens of your congregation and no longer strangers in a foreign land.

God's helping hand to guide you.

Remember that at that time you were separate from Christ, excluded from citizenship in Israel, and foreigners to the covenants of the promise, without hope and without God in the world. (Ephesians 2:12 NIV)

JULY 6

*T*his is it; you have but one body in this life; learn to care for it and enjoy it. I am it; I am the very Spirit who has called you into a life of holy living; rejoice in this life. Understand that your earthly body is not separate from My holy presence. We live as one because we are one.

Learn to focus your faith in Me and let it lead you to the one hope that all My children share in Me.

Just as you were baptized into the one faith you now have; you are all called to live in the one hope you share in your faith. Live as holy citizens of this earth, for I have called you to all live in Me. No division, separation, or excuses for living a life apart from what I have called you by faith. There can never be one hope in Me if there are several limiting beliefs. There is only one of Me, but there is plenty of Me to unite all of you.

It is very easy for you to become one in the Spirit or one in Me. I gave all of My children the gift of prayer. Do not downplay the power of a single prayer. Never underestimate the unstoppable spiritual force that a unison prayer can become. All prayers are tuned to My spiritual frequency. I hear them; feel them, and react according to the flow of energy they bring to Me. Once you gather tighter in the name of the blessed Savor and pray in his name, you have unleashed power that will move mountains. Did not the Savior explain this spiritual power to you?

There is one body and one Spirit.

There is one body and one Spirit, just as you were called to one hope when you were called; (Ephesians 4:4 NIV)

JULY 7

*H*ope will come to you and all of My children as the good news of My glorious salvation is opened to all the people of this earth. Pound your faith firmly into the ground, and do not let it sway or swagger in the changing winds of challenging times. Times will come and go, and new people will tell you wild stories about who I am and what is right or wrong to believe. Believe in Me and My message of salvation; you will always be right.

Tether your hope to the foundation of faith that was laid in your soul and hang on to the glory of the Gospel message. Seek the wisdom the ancient pages of truth the scriptures bring today. Begin each morning with your heart attentive to what your soul will receive from this holy book. Read, believe, and hope.

I give you hope as a glimmer into what the future can be. Hope wrapped in faith has the awesome ability to see a different outcome than pessimistic human hope. The Bible has countless stories about how faith and hope transformed people and a nation. I am waiting patiently to write the inspiring story of how you put your faith into action and saw your future through the eyes of hope. The future may be in My hands, but it begins in your heart of faith, My child.

The Bible has our hope for tomorrow.

If you continue in your faith, established and firm, and do not move from the hope held out in the gospel. This is the gospel that you heard, and that has been proclaimed to every creature under heaven, and of which I, Paul, have become a servant. (Colossians 1:23 NIV)

If you continue in your faith, established and firm, and do not move from the hope held out in the gospel. This is the gospel that you heard and that has been proclaimed to every creature under heaven, and of which I, Paul, have become a servant. (Colossians 1:23 NIV)

JULY 8

*D*o not neglect your divine seed of faith, My sacred heart. The seed was planted in you by the power of the gospel message. You may not remember when this seed was planted or even who planted the seed of faith within you: yet it is in you. Care for this growing, blossoming, blooming faith seed, which will serve you well. Your belief in Me will grow into a strong tree of hope bearing the fruit of My glory.

Stand back and stay strong in your faith, for it is the beanstalk of a plant without limits to its growth. The message of the mystery of hope for future glory resides in all My beloved children. Bear faithful fruit that will bless your life and glorify Me in the lives of others.

Seeds are meant to be planted so they will grow. All unbelievers deserve to hear the message of hope just as you have. Will the message come from your lips to be planted in their hearts? Each new generation is responsible for ensuring they are not the last generation to spread the Gospel message, revealing the glory of Christ's mystery. If you plant the seed, My child, I will make it grow. I will place you before an attentive ear if you are ready to share your faith.

Look for God's amazing message of hope.

To them, God has chosen to make known among the Gentiles the glorious riches of this mystery, which is Christ in you, the hope of glory. (Colossians 1:27 NIV)

JULY 9

*H*ope through faith is what keeps you connected to Me. Faith without future hope is like a rudderless ship set to sea with no compass for guidance or anchor for a safe harbor. I offer you spiritual guidance for your soul and compassionate love for your heart. Faith and hope are the only cargo you need on your spiritual life journey.

There should never be anything between us, My sacred heart. The veil to the curtain of the inner sanctuary was removed on the day of the blessed Savior's death. The domain of the high priest has been turned into a common gathering place where all can commune in My holy presence. Travel far in life, but remember that you are anchored to Me in this holy sanctuary of My constant love.

You must remember that you will have seasons in your life, My child. Take time to celebrate the great seasons, and try not to worry too much about the seasons of struggle. Remind yourself that I am with you in and out of season. I am only a prayer away from you. I have your hand, I will cover your back, and I will not let go. Just be mindful that your anchor will only hold you as fast as your faith in me. Secure your faith, and you will strengthen your anchor to me.

Hope in God is an anchor for your soul.

We have this hope as an anchor for the soul, firm and secure. It enters the inner sanctuary behind the curtain (Hebrews 6:19 NIV)

JULY 10

*W*hat is it your soul hopes for, My sacred heart? What above everything in this world does your heart long for and ache for? The object of your hope will be your passion in your life. You will strive for what you hope for. Learn to place all hope in Me, and let Me become your passion for life.

Place all the confidence of your faith in Me, and you will have a fulfilled life. Wealth and material possessions are fine; they allow you to see your material success. Your material success is only a small part of a life fulfilled and enjoyed. Have great expectations in the hope for the unseen blessings that await you. Even though you cannot see or count them, be assured that my blessings are coming.

You must realize that faith is far more than believing in me, My sacred heart. Faith is your eyes and the spiritual organ that allows you to turn your perceptions into reality. You can hope for all you want, but without faith, it will never materialize; if it does, you will probably miss the blessing. A blind person can feel the heat from a bright flame. A deaf person can feel the thud of a loud noise. Faith allows you to see the not yet seen through hope.

Faith is your lens to see the hope that awaits you.

Now faith is confidence in what we hope for and assurance about what we do not see. (Hebrews 11:1 NIV)

JULY 11

*P*lace all hope in Me, for you are all My beloved children. The rest of the world may not understand what it means to be a child of God, for they do not know Me. You must understand and live a life that shows the rest of the world what it means to be a child of God. The blessed Savior has shown you what it means to live as a child of God through his earthly life.

Learn the ways of the Savior and purify yourselves through his life. Read the scriptures and gleam every sentence and word that describes the Savior's way of life. Then live your life as perfectly and purely as possible. Even though he was tempted and tested, the Savior stayed true to his calling.

   The savior loved people without restraint. His love and compassion grew as the needs and sins increased with the people he met. The blessed savior knew scripture and put it to work by serving those in need. Love thy neighbor was a lifestyle.   His own greatness humbled Jesus. The miracle worker was only the servant of God. You will purify your life when you focus on service rather than sin. This is the way your Master lived, My child.

Three ways to live like Jesus

All who have this hope in him purify themselves, just as he is pure. (1 John 3:3 NIV)

JULY 12

*T*his was a blessing to Noah and his family. All the plants on the ground, all the animals of the earth, all the fish of the seas, and all the birds of the air were given as a food source for their survival. The earth is given to all of My children as a resource for well-being, comfort, and daily care. I have blessed the earth to carry everything you need for your life on this small blue planet. You must learn to care for the earth as if you were caring for your own future. Remember that I am the divine creator of heaven and earth; you must become the caretaker for your little patch of the Garden of Eden. Coexist rather than rule—Co-create with Me rather than destroy what I have made. Learn to use the planet's resources wisely; your future for your life tomorrow does depend on your actions today.

My servant was given dominion over all the earth to restore and repopulate the earth. You are given reign over the earth to renew it. Your industrial progress has come at a cost to the environment that supports you. My children traded automobiles for fresh air. Clean water for harsh chemicals. Fertile soil for concrete jungles. There is a spiritual solution to your environmental problems. Become the caretaker of My holy creation, and do not worry so much about being the ruler.

How to be a blessing rather than a curse to the earth.

The fear and dread of you will fall on all the beasts of the earth, and on all the birds in the sky, on every creature that moves along the ground, and on all the fish in the sea; they are given into your hands. (Genesis 9:2 NIV)

JULY 13

I will not put you into an overwhelming position that causes you to choose between life and death. How one person approaches life's trials and tribulations may not reflect the same way you approach life's problems. Keep that awe and wonder of Me close inside, and let our dynamic relationship guide your life. Ask yourself, "Would Spirit have me do this?" This question opens a channel between the two of us. On your part, you seek guidance; I will respond with gentle guidance to your life question.

While all things are between the two of us, your direction in life could impact the life of another soul. Proceed with caution and follow My lead. I am always aware of the twists, turns, and intersections when souls travel a similar spiritual path. When the time is right, I will provide alternative options to your dilemma.

I left a book behind to give you written documentation of your life path. Read the Holy Book to give you practical direction. Use your own life experiences to help guide you. Both good and bad life encounters can be valuable for helping you choose which path to select. Pay attention to the passing stranger and the close friend. I enjoy employing people as temporary life guides. A friendly smile, comforting words, and helpful gestures may come as gifts from Me. You are never placed on the life path alone, My child; always seek spiritual travelers to join you.

God will show you the way.

"Do not lay a hand on the boy," he said. "Do not do anything to him. Now I know that you fear God, because you have not withheld from me your son, your only son." (Genesis 22:12 NIV)

JULY 14

*Y*ou may miss My watchful eye while you labor and strain under life's toil. I have not forgotten you. Did I forget to tell the sun to shine this morning? Are the planets still aligned and spinning in orbit in a determined direction? Do the seas still remain retrained and safe in the sanctity of the shoreline? If I remembered all of these things, how could I forget you?

I counted your heartbeats as you awoke from your slumber this morning, My hard-working child. I know the effort you give and the dedication you have for everything you do. Look up from your morning's slumber and behold the inspiration that you seek. I will walk by your side throughout this day.

Just as certain as death and taxes, My love will always be with you. Indeed, My love will outlive the sting of death and outlast the toll of taxes. I never intended you to walk through life empty-handed. Where human love and economic systems may fail you, My love will never let go. I am the better part of you and reside in the innermost part of your being. I placed myself where you could easily find me and where you could feel the depth of My love. I am the only certainty life can offer you, My sacred heart.

Nothing is certain except death, taxes, and the love of God.

If the God of my father, the God of Abraham, and the Fear of Isaac had not been with me, you would surely have sent me away empty-handed. But God has seen my hardship and the toil of my hands, and last night he rebuked you." (Genesis 31:42 NIV)

JULY 15

*S*ometimes drastic and direct actions are required if a dynamic change is going to take place. The little Hebrew child that the quick-thinking midwife saved became a man named Moses. Moses was sent into this world to fulfill His mission to free the Hebrew people and gather them into a great nation. This band of Egyptian slaves would multiply greatly and become My chosen people. The Hebrew people were chosen to carry the awe and wonder of My holy name on their lips and My love in their hearts. Pharaoh tried to stop the progress of My people, but nothing can ever hinder that which is sealed with the divine kiss. Bring this same passion to bear witness to My name and to share My love with the holy people of this world. Nothing can stop you now.

Amidst the clammer and clanging of confusion, listen for the still, small voice to lead you to safety. I speak beneath the sound of a noisy street; I am best heard in the beating of your heart. Loud voices and show barkers will tell you much; only I can lead you where you need to go. If you fail to take time to hear me during your busy day, you will miss My still, small voice trying to whisper comforting words and helpful directions. I am afraid that most of My children listen to the sound of the world passing by and miss Me speaking to their hearts. So, listen to Me, My child.

Listen to the still, small voice guide you.

The midwives, however, feared God and did not do what the king of Egypt had told them to do; they let the boys live. Exodus 1:17 NIV)

JULY 16

*Y*ou should know that My promises cannot be stopped once set in motion. As My promises become reality, all cosmic forces align to bring heaven and earth together so that what I speak will become true. My spoken word is the first utterance that sparks this chain of spiritual forces into motion. The Egyptians knew that what I said would soon become what I did. The Egyptians reacted to My words out of their fear.

Rather than fearing this divine law, learn to embrace the power of its purpose. Come to Me with the wide-eyed expectation that what you speak in your morning prayers will be fulfilled in My hearing. Prayer is your daily channel to ask Me to create what your soul asks for. There is no great mystery here; praying things into existence is a power that all My children have.

  When you pray, you tap into the spiritual power I gave you through My promises proclaimed generations ago. Pharoah's officials feared this spiritual power; Israel would learn to tap into its living stream of energy. My promise has no expiration date. What I promised Moses and Israel, I freely give to you. What the blessed Savior lived and died for he rose from the grave to bless you today. My promises are more than holy words; they carry divine spiritual energy.

You can't stop God's promise.

Those officials of Pharaoh who feared the word of the Lord hurried to bring their slaves and their livestock inside. (Exodus 9:20 NIV)

JULY 17

*D*o not do things out of the fear and trembling of Me. Rather, become awe-inspired in how you react to Me. The fear of the Egyptians had become a dread and trembling of Me, whereas the fear of the Hebrew people had become an awe-inspiring trust in Me. Do not fear Me because you fear what you think I might do; learn to trust Me because you believe what you think I will do. Always perceive Me in the heavenly light of the divine power within you. Do not let your fear of Me engage your psychological fight or flight response. Rather, let your awe of Me engage your stay and pray spiritual response. Stay safe and strong in your faith, and believe that I only want the best for you, and I am working to send you, My best. I cannot receive your best if you hide behind a cloud of fear. When you begin to trust in me and place your faith first, fear will become a secondary response to most of life. When you see Me as loving, generous, and committed to helping you through life, you will begin to see the world in a less fearful way. When your faith becomes your lens to the world, it will seem far less frightening and much more glorious, just as I created it.

Choose faith, not fear.

And when the Israelites saw the mighty hand of the Lord displayed against the Egyptians, the people feared the Lord and put their trust in him and in Moses, his servant. (Exodus 14:31 NIV)

JULY 18

I have chosen you this morning, My sacred heart, to be My disciple on this earth. I have seen the inner depths of your heart and know your greatest desire. I have scanned your soul from top to bottom and heard the slightest groanings of your spirit. I have measured and weighed you inside and out, and I proclaim you sufficient for your earthly calling to serve Me and the people I love. Your official calling is to encourage the downtrodden and uninspired people who live in spiritual darkness. You are to raise the broken-hearted people who gave up on life because they believe life has already given up on them. Learn to widen your circle of influence as you give meaning to shallow and seemingly empty lives. Speak My words, heal with My hands, and love with all of My heart. The world needs us now more than ever.

You are called to lead through your service to My beloved children. I placed you as a leader to love them first, care for them always, and never forget that I hold each child in My sacred love. Leadership means you know the well-worn path to My love. My leaders know how to access forgiveness. True spiritual leaders know the sweet taste of My grace. I know you have gifts and graces to be a leader, but I rely on you to be a person who knows the direct route to My love. When My children find My love, the rest of my life seems to fall into place.

God selected you to change the world.

But select capable men from all the people—men who fear God, trustworthy men who hate dishonest gain—and appoint them as officials over thousands, hundreds, fifties, and tens. (Exodus 18:29 NIV)

July 19

*D*o not let the smoke and mirrors of nature scare you away from My presence. Many things around Me can be scary, but they are only the window dressings to who I am. Thunder and lightning make for a great light show in the evening sky, but they are only a small part of My creation. Smoke and fire bellowing up from a mountaintop will scare the birds away, but you should never fear My holy presence.

Do not look toward the sights and sounds of nature and expect My glorious revelation. The universe operates under My tutelage, but it is not Me. Respect natural forces, but look beyond them to experience My presence in your life. Learn to listen to that still, small voice in your soul's center. No smoke or volcanic clouds will appear, just the whisper of My lips saying, "I love you. My sacred heart."

Remember, my precious child, that much of life's burdens are your own making. Taking on more than you can finish, owing too much money, and extending in far too many places are mostly your life choices. I am not blaming you, but look at your lifestyle and then reverse engineer your way out of the stressful situation. The fear of the thunder and lightning of an overwhelmed life can soon be quelched by unloading some of the extra baggage you carry. The closer you remain to Me, the softer the sound of thunder and the duller the lightning flashes will appear.

Never feel overwhelmed by staying closer to God.

When the people saw the thunder and lightning and heard the trumpet, and saw the mountain in smoke, they trembled with fear. They stayed at a distance. (Exodus 20:18 NIV)

JULY 20

I have placed limits upon all of life. Natural forces of age, biological functions, disease, environment, and spiritual health all have an impact on your longevity. These natural limits can be altered and stretched by your own human behavior. Place yourself in a healthy physical, psychological, and spiritual setting. Pour good things into your body, mind, and spirit, and great things will stretch the limits of your existence.

If you want your day to go well, begin each morning with the physical, emotional, and spiritual food to fuel a positive day. If you look for them, you will only see dark rain clouds on the horizon. Practice the life disciplines that will enhance your today and prolong your tomorrow. Do not fear the limits of life, I have come to show you how to increase the number of your days and enhance each day of your life.

Some of My lovely children think I am a taskmaster because I restrict them from certain things. The things I restrict all of My children from can lead to a life of sin. Sin can damage human cells, destroy thought processes, and steal you away from Me. Sinful, unholy habits will never lead you to a long and happy life. My restrictions are warming signs telling you that his life path will not lead you to where either of us wants to go. You need never fear your life when you keep me close and stay far away from destructive devices. I am here to help you live long upon this blessed earth I created just for you.

Things that increase your lifespan.

Moses said to the people, "Do not be afraid. God has come to test you so that the fear of God will be with you to keep you from sinning." (Exodus 20:20 NIV)

JULY 21

*Y*ou live in a world of checks and balances, My child. Nature has its own way of trying to keep this planet in balance. Hot and cold, dry and rainy, summer and winter, and night and day all sit opposite ends of nature's natural seesaw of life to keep life balanced. There is little you can do to disrupt this balance but be aware that unbridled human consumption of natural resources can destroy My perfect plan for natural harmony in this world.

Also, be aware that all human relationships are connected to Me. Whatever you do to even the smallest of My children, you have done to Me. Human sin does not see the Spirit of the Divine that dwells within each of My children. My spirit force empowers each human heart and fills every human breath. The pain you inflict on another soul shoots directly into My heart. Love one another even as I love you.

You must follow the lead of the Messiah when you do wrong to another person. The blessed Savior showed you that seeking for- giveness for transgressions, sins, mistakes, and unkind acts will help wright the world. Indeed, the Savior came to show you the way to salvation by offering you My grace for your sins. Jesus' suffering on the cross was his way of offering a sorrowful act of pardon on your behalf. When I forgive you of sin, we reunite as one in Spirit, My child.

Accept another person for who they are and the Spirit of God within them.

Do not take advantage of each other, but fear your God. I am the Lord your God. (Exodus 25:17 NIV)

JULY 22

*G*ood morning sacred heart. I hope your night went well. I come to you this morning to talk about your future. Don't worry; it is nothing bad or something of concern. I just wanted to point you in the right direction for a few moments. Start each day by making room for My holy presence in your heart and soul. Awaken that part of your heart that is still slumbering at early morning sunrise, and pay attention to Me.

Walk each day in holy righteousness and pay attention to the life patterns you have set in place. You will soon lose Me in unholy habits, and it will be difficult for you to stay on a spiritual path. Your spiritual path is your primary direction, not your work, family, or play life. All other situations must stem from your spiritual life; If I am not your primary focus, your life will soon lose focus. Your future will always go well when you trust in Me.

I created all of My children with a life purpose and mission. These are not deep dark secrets of your soul; I made them easily discoverable. Come to Me daily to unlock your access to understanding your life purpose and mission. I will gladly tell you what you need to know and how to achieve what you are looking for. Use the tools of your Christian heritage to unlock the future. Millions use prayer, Bible reading, worship, Christian service, and other spiritual aides to act as a spiritual life GPS. What you do today will greatly influence your tomorrow.

Live your future today.

Oh, that their hearts would be inclined to fear me and keep all my commands always so that it might go well with them and their children forever! (Deuteronomy 5:29 NIV)

JULY 23

I have no grandchildren; each child must come to Me of his or
her own volition. Understand Me; you are vital in raising your
children to follow Me on their faith path. There comes a time,
however, when each person must make the decision that is right for
him or herself. The best you can do and the most you can do is to
live a life that models what a righteous life with Me will look like.
By showing your children or any child what faith looks like, you have
opened the storehouse of blessings to the next generation. Tell
them, teach them, show them, and give them the ability to come to
Me in their own faith. I will gladly welcome them into My glorious
family, where they will prosper and live a fruitful life of faith. Is this
not the same way you became a member of the family of God?
  Many of My beloved children grow up in loving Christian families
but do not find the path to Me on their own. Once the children leave
the surroundings of the family, they no longer choose to follow me.
Faith is not genetic. Faith can be passed along from one family
member to the next, but each person must come to Jesus on their
own. You can plant the seed in them, but they must accept the
planting and care for the seed of the faith on their own. You were
born a child of God, but you must choose to be a follower of Jesus.

God has no grandchildren.

So that you, your children, and their children after them
may fear the Lord your God as long as you live by keeping all his
decrees and commands that I give you, and so that you may enjoy a
long life. (Deuteronomy 6:2 NIV)

JULY 24

*S*hare your story of faith often, My child. The stories of your life with Me may be the very thing someone is waiting to hear so that he or she will accept Me and know My love. Never be afraid of boldly proclaiming your faith in Me. I am always looking for ways to brag about you to the world. My bragging voice can best be heard in the blessings I give you and the love I show you.

Help others come to Me out of love so their hearts will be moved to joy and not filled with fear. People fear Me because they have erroneous thoughts about who I am. They have heard that I am a God of judgment, but those words may come from someone who has not felt My grace. You know what My grace feels like and what it does to alter life. Tell your story of faith and share My grace. Your faith story carries My grace from heaven to earth.

Boast of Me as well, My child. Be grateful for what I do in your life. Daily blessings are no accident; they come to you with great intentionality and all of My love. When you give thanks, you show Me that you recognized what you received as a blessing from Me. When you are grateful, you will feel the warmth of gratitude within your heart and soul. Talking about the blessings you receive is not boasting. You merely report that you are a recipient of my grace and love.

God will show you blessings and love.

When we heard of it, our hearts melted in fear, and everyone's courage failed because of you, for the Lord your God is God in heaven above and on the earth below. (Joshua 2:11 NIV)

JULY 25

*O*ther people may run for cover and cower with fear that the first sign of trouble. You, however, stay strong and be courageous of heart at the impending storms of life. Faith, trust, and hope always work together to create the possible in the face of the impossible. Other people will give up and give in when their short-sighted view of life does not allow room for Me. Their Jack-in-the-box thinking will only jump up and scare them to death when their own fears open the lid on their lives.

If you follow Me, you will always remember what your future holds. As dark as the morning day may be, you will always remain in the sanctity of My divine light. Your heart can hold onto many human emotions, My sacred heart. It can hold courage just as easily as it carries fear deep inside. Remain close to Me; your heart will run over with spiritual courage.

  You will only be as spiritually strong as you are spiritually fit. The work you put in now will be your defense in the future. Your prayer time, meditation, Scripture reading, and devotionals all compound to strengthen you for what will come. If you do not spend time seeking me now, it will be difficult to find My strength when difficult times surround you.

Stay spiritually strong in the face of fear.

But my fellow Israelites who went up with me made the hearts of the people melt in fear. I, however, followed the Lord my God. (Joshua 14:8 NIV)

JULY 26

*L*eave a good lineage of spiritual stories behind as an inheritance to your children and grandchildren. Let their inheritance come from your connection to Me and the life you led as one of My beloved servants. Show them how to live, teach them how to grow, and talk to them about Me. Let them know how important a spiritual life can be for them, just as it was for you.

Your children and grandchildren can either follow the spiritual life you model for them or the life the world shows them.

I recommend teaching your descendants to follow Me. A finite worldview of life has crippling limitations. A limitless spiritual connection to Me will lead your descendants to a life of daily blessings and My limitless love. When your children ask, "What do you have to do with the Spirit of Life?" you can show them.

You may not realize it, My precious child, but The greatest gift you can leave behind to your heirs is the faith stories of how you walked with Me. When you share your personal stories of faith, you also point directly to Me to the reader or listener. You bring the gospel to life by aligning it with your connection to Me. Too many of My beloved children believe that the Bible is just a dusty record of the past. When they see your stories of faith, they will realize that the ancient stories can be relived in this generation.

The importance of faith in God is a gift we can leave others.

"No! We did it for fear that someday your descendants might say to ours, 'What do you have to do with the Lord, the God of Israel? (Joshua 22:24 NIV)

JULY 27

*D*o not hang onto the helpless and heartless former gods of your ancestors. Do not let the sins of previous generations destroy the blessings of today and the fulfillment of My promises for tomorrow. I have seen it far too often where countless generations become trapped in the deadly patterns of their foreparents.
Cling to Me and follow Me out of the land where the gods of poverty, hunger, disease, suffering, and pain rule this world's lost and lonely souls. I want the best for you, do not settle for less because it is easy or the only thing you know. Grow beyond your past limitations and take on a new spiritual life. Welcome to My land, which flows with milk and honey.
  Life is more of a choice than you may realize, My sacred heart. Some of My precious children choose their gods as quickly as they select their clothes or mouthwash. Gods are anything you give power to and end up ruling you. Money, prestige, fame, and power are names of gods you may recognize. If you let them, these gods will control you and often lead you to ruin. I do not want to rule you, My desire is to bless your life richly. Where the lesser gods fail you, I am always faithful.

Remain faithful to God because God will always be faithful to you.

"Now fear the Lord and serve him with all faithfulness. Throw away the gods your ancestors worshiped beyond the Euphrates River and in Egypt, and serve the Lord. (Joshua 24:14 TLB)

JULY 28

*D*o not let the world steal pieces of Me from you, My child. You are not here to battle against the world; learn to befriend My glorious creation and live in peace and harmony with it. The physical world, however, is not all there is to your life. If you emphasize this physical plane, you will miss the other side of life in the spiritual world.

When the Ark of the Covenant was taken from the people of Israel, they felt that My very presence was stolen from them. I do not live in boxes; I dwell in the hearts and souls of people. The Ark contained the Ten Commandments; your heart contains Me. Remain strong in your spiritual life as you walk this earth.

Be mindful that I am that still small inner voice that nudges and speaks to you in only words we share. Even if all of your religious symbols are gone, you still have Me, My child. I created nature as a Rembrandt reminder of My holy presence, but I am not nature. The blessed Savior gave you the church as a spiritual portal, but the church is not Him. Enjoy the physical reminders and signs of my holy presence, but I am always closer to you than my hands and feet and more a part of you than life itself. I am always never more than a prayer away.

Spiritual and physical forces live in harmony in you.

When he arrived, there was Eli sitting on his chair by the side of the road, watching, because his heart feared for the ark of God. When the man entered the town and told what had happened, the whole town sent up a cry. (1 Samuel 4:13 NIV)

JULY 29

*A*ll of life must be held together with the divine essence of creation. Life must flow under My physical laws and spiritual commandments. My holy order has been put in place for a reason. The reason is that everyone must work together to make life equitable for all people. No one is to be considered greater than another person. Leaders are in place to lead and unite you, not enslave you.

I give Myself freely to all people so that all My people will live freely in Me. Freedom of humanity will only be achieved if all humans give themselves to Me. Good things happen, blessings abound, and love rules the world when you follow Me. I am not a hard taskmaster but a loving Spirit who wants the best for you.

I placed the government of this world in the hands of leaders. Pray for them, My child. Leaders are in place to help unite you, guide you, and support you. Keep all the leaders in your prayers so that they will seek Me for their wisdom and spiritual strength. Kings, queens, judges, and rulers have all gone before the current leaders. They began to lose the ultimate purpose when they lost sight of Me. All leaders are in place to safely guide you to My beloved children. Pray for your leaders as if they are guiding you to Me.

Living as one in the Holy Spirit.

If you fear the Lord and serve and obey him and do not rebel against his commands, and if both you and the king who reigns over you follow the Lord your God—good! (1 Samuel 12:14 NIV)

JULY 30

$\mathcal{S}$erving Me is a 24/7 calling, My sacred heart. Rise each
morning with Me on your mind, compassion in your heart,
and faithful service in your soul. The spiritual path has a twofold
direction to the divine flow of energy. Give yourself freely to others
in My service, and all good things will return to you in even greater
proportion.

Look back on your life this morning and celebrate all the blessings
that I have given you. My blessings are not rewards or payments
for service rendered. My blessings are the divine energy flowing
back to you, its original source. What you give to others through Me
comes back to bless you. Practice this spiritual law daily, and abundant blessings will return to you.

Never confuse My blessings with the material world. When you
focus on the material and physical rather than the spiritual and love,
you will lose track of Me. When you lose sight of me, you will soon
fall in love with the blessings or things I gave you. You are only the
first stop for My blessings of love. Keep them as you need them, but
share them with others who may be in need.

Serve God by caring for others.

But be sure to fear the Lord and serve him faithfully with all your
heart; consider what great things he has done for you. (1 Samuel
12:24 NIV)

JULY 31

*F*ear is a powerless nuisance with no ability to hurt or harm you. Laugh at fear; it will turn tail and run like a vagabond dog with no dignity or destiny. Fear circles you like a buzzard looking for any entry point into your life so it can sow unpleasant thoughts and whisper lies to you. Nothing fear does or nothing fear says has any reality or truth. Once given any entry point into your life, fear can cripple you emotionally and rob you of your faith in Me.

Do not give into fear. You have a better choice. Stay strong in your faith in Me, and fear will have no choice but to pass you by like a swarm of pesky barnyard flies. I have seen even My strongest servants fall victim to the claws of fear. Once strong, vital people gave way to fear and became nothing more than an empty shell and curled-up corpse of a being. If I am present in your life, fear will always remain powerless.

How do you overcome fear and remain spiritually energized even during difficult moments? You must strengthen your faith before you face a fearful situation. When you look at an overwhelming obstacle, it will seem impossible to defeat if your soul is spiritually dry. When you fill yourself with Me through prayer, worship, gratitude, and daily celebration, there is no room for fear. You are never enough of have enough to face life alone. Only I can fill you with the spiritual life energy to move mountains and defeat giants.

Faith in God has no fear.

Immediately Saul fell full length on the ground, filled with fear because of Samuel's words. His strength was gone, for he had eaten nothing all that day and all that night. (1 Samuel 28:20

AUGUST 1

*et your faith be the foundation for this day, My child. Rise from your slumber this morning and firmly place your feet of faith upon Me. I am the Terra Firma for your faith and for your life. I am the Rock of Israel and the foundation of your sometimes failing faith. Even the simplest days can bring unexpected and unseen moments for your foot to slip, causing you to fall to the ground in a heap. Falling face down on the path of life can happen to anybody, but not everyone will take My hand so I can help them back up.

When you live a righteous life centered in My love and blessed by the gift of My salvation, your life will become startling different. Where others try to walk a tightrope in life with no safety net, you will have My strength to lift you up. Some will retreat to a cold empty cave for protection from life's storms, but you have the comfort and warmth of My love to surround you. I freely offer My comfort and love to all of My children; I delight in any who accept My invitation to stand firm in me.

I know you live in a fast-paced whirlwind of a world, My child. It may seem that the only constant in your life is change. I have seen the winds of change blow by for billions of years, yet, My love for My beloved children remains the same. The blessed savior told you that heaven and earth may pass away, but divine love will always live. Even if the cosmos collides, and the solar systems cease to be, I will always be here for you. Place your faith upon Me.

Place your faith firmly upon the Rock of Israel.

The God of Israel spoke, the Rock of Israel said to me: 'When one rules over people in righteousness, when he rules in the fear of God, (2 Samuel 23:3 NIV)

AUGUST 2

*S*eek asylum and safety in Me, My sacred heart. Run into the inner sanctum of My sanctuary of love and peace for safety and protection from whatever frightens your soul. Unfortunately, there will always be occasions when the soul is troubled, the heart disturbed, and the mind depressed. You usually will not find your way out of overwhelming situations by remaining in the middle of the darkness of the storm. I can keep you safe from the storm and guide you into the freeness of a new dawn.

I have given you all the faith you will need to encounter the troubles and tragedies of life fully. Prayer engages your faith, so call to Me for guidance and protection. Use your prayers to Me to be like the horns of the altar of the Tabernacle where asylum and safety were offered to the fearful soul. I talk to you often about fear because fear can take many forms to fool you and rob you of your faith. Listen to My voice and refrain from hearing the sounds that foolish fear whispers in your ear.   Let faith and not fear rule your life, and you will always remain safe in My love.

You must remember, My sacred heart, that there is nothing closer to you than Me. You never face the world alone; I am always with you.   I created a safe place for you and all of My precious children. Faith is the safest place you will find. The more you believe in Me, the less the world will overwhelm you. The stronger your faith, the weaker the lies of the evil one will become. Faith is not magic; it is simply seeing Me in your life.

Our safe place is faith.

But Adonijah, in fear of Solomon, went and took hold of the horns of the altar. (1 Kings 1:50 NIV)

AUGUST 3

*B*uild your house on the foundation of faith, not fear, My faithful child. Open your doors wide so the world may enter your home and see that I live there. Let them feel My holy presence in your home and see how easily we live side by side. Let them see the spot where we gather every morning for devotions and prayer. Help the stranger visualize how you read from the Holy Book and let the words of the ancient past speak clearly to you each morning. Help the stranger become a friend of faith so that there will be no strangers or foreigners among us. An outsider can just as easily understand my spoken word as you. An unbeliever can just as easily receive my eternal love as you feel it. Let your home and church bear the name of the one who loves you, and you worship. Let your lips express the love your soul feels.

  You must sometimes consider altering your life path and faith course, offering spiritual hospitality to the stranger, and refreshing old faith patterns. You are not the showcase in your home, I must be. If all the stranger sees are your fingerprints and misses, My footprints, how will they know this is My home?   Leave lively hints that I dwell with you and encourage the visitor to create a similar place for My dwelling in their life.

There are no strangers or foreigners in God's house.

Then hear from heaven, your dwelling place. Do whatever the foreigner asks of you, so that all the peoples of the earth may know your name and fear you, as do your own people Israel, and may know that this house I have built bears your Name. (1 Kings 8:43 NIV)

AUGUST 4

*G*iving praise to Me and seeing the wonderful things I do in your life is the act of a thankful heart. As you recognize My movement of love in your life, you will suddenly see all I do for you. Seeing My movement is a spiritual quality that you should practice daily. As you arise each morning, keep your eyes open to what the day will bring. Look for my blessings and receive each one as a heavenly gift.

Practicing thanksgiving is the quickest way to understand Me and see My work in your life. Giving thanks to Me connects your physical world with your spiritual life. You soon realize that I am available in both worlds, and I bridge the gap between the two realms. You should also realize that I have all power over heaven and earth. No force on this earth can match My divine power or equal My endless love for you. This is the created order of all things in heaven and earth.

  You don't have to give up the physical world to engage in the spiritual. On the contrary, you live in both worlds. Becoming more spiritual means that you take more time for Me. You practice the things that draw you closer to me, like singing, praying, dancing, or talking with others about me. You are not a spiritual being trapped in a physical body; you are a complete being living in a world of body and spirit. Learn to experience me and My creation with all you are, My child.

Connect mind, body, and spirit.

For great is the Lord and most worthy of praise; he is to be feared above all gods. (1 Chronicles 16:25 NIV)

AUGUST 5

*N*ever let the fear of external forces rule over your faith. There will always be distracting voices who tell you that faith is for the weak and lowly person who is not strong enough to make their own way in life. Many will laugh, and some will even scoff at you as you leave your home and drive to your place of worship. I am so very saddened at the actions of some of My children. Do not let their heartless actions sway you from worshipping Me.

Show any and all detractors the better path to life by gathering with others for worship. Through your worship and love for Me, the onlooker may come to see what you see as you engage in worship. The center of worship is not song or sermon but finding My love in your heart. The outsider has trouble finding the love that I have to offer them. Show them a more excellent way, My beloved child. You were all born to worship Me.

If you do not feel My holy movement during worship, you pay too much attention to the trappings. If you can't feel the sacred kiss from the savior as you receive body and blood, your ears are closed to his words. "Do this, in remembrance of Me." I rushed into the apostles' lives on Pentecost Sunday; their lives were ever changed because they felt My presence. You have heard the stories of My presence during worship, now believe it can happen to you, My sacred heart.

Finding God through worship is not a mystery but a spiritual blessing.

Despite their fear of the people around them, they built the altar on its foundation and sacrificed burnt offerings on it to the Lord, both the morning and evening sacrifices. (Ezra 3:3 NIV)

AUGUST 6

*M*y sacred heart, rise every morning with your life plan and path in mind. Your life plan should include following Me with your whole heart, your spirit's dedication, and your mind's submission. But, plan to follow Me each day down the path I will lead you. I do not promise this will make life an easy cakewalk for you; life will always be a faith walk. Plan as you will, follow Me as best you can but trust Me with unshakable faith.

Don't think that one bad day in your life will derail your entire life plan. You can either grow and learn from life's disappointments or curl up in a ball and let life run you over like a speed bump in the road. Your faith will always direct you to what awaits you on the other side of any daily dilemma. But know this one very important thing, I am with you in your struggles and support you in your failures. That is My life plan for you.

You share one very important spiritual plan with all of My children. You all need to reflect on Me in your daily lives. Share the stories of the blessed savior with as many people as possible. You are the greatest influence I have on this earth. I often try to talk to My children, but they don't always listen. Perhaps they will hear your words where mine fall short.

God does have a plan for you.

In the land of Uz, there lived a man whose name was Job. This man was blameless and upright; he feared God and shunned evil. (Job 1:1 NIV)

AUGUST 7

*N*ever intermingle faith and fear; they create an unhealthy situation that destroys the very fiber of our relationship. Do not be afraid of Me, My child. I have the power of life and death and My disposal, but I have chosen to give life in every instance. Let awe of Me replace any fear of Me. Be in awe of what I can bring to you in life, but never be surprised by what I have done. I give and bless you out of the fulfillment of the promises of My love.

Do not listen to the whisper of the distracting lies of evil spiritual forces that attack your faith. The air is filled with the passive pollution of slandering spirits that chant and chatter meaningless words. There is only one voice that you should be in tune with, and that's My voice. You will know it is always Me speaking to you because I speak at the same frequency as the sound of divine love. No one can speak this sound wave of love but Me. Listen to Me and drown the deadly drone out.

I place all kinds of reminders, people, and envoys around you so you will feel My love and never forget how much you are loved. There are worldly and spiritual forces that would have you think differently, but I assure you, My love is real. The sacred scriptures recount My love in countless ways. Your life is filled with loving experiences that affirm that My love is in action. I even died for you, My sacred heart. I speak the language of love, so we will never miscommunicate.

Can you hear the voice of God speak the language of love?

"Does Job fear God for nothing?" Satan replied.   (Job 1:9 NIV)

AUGUST 8

*Y*ou are never powerless in this world, My sacred heart. You are not a pawn slapped on the board of life with no control of say so in your movement through life. I do not push and pull you against the forces of evil like two dogs fighting over the same old bone. You are a child of free will and a person of personal purpose. Do not let the perception of how you think others were treated cloud your judgment of Me. You must first learn the inner truth before you make an outer judgment.

Do not blame Me for disease, poverty, hatred, bigotry, or suffering. These are all aliments of an earthlier design. Rather, look for My hand guiding the medical team to find disease cures. Watch as I call relief teams to feed the poor. I will never use you like a pawn in life, but I will call you to care for the struggling people of this world. I rely on all My righteous children to change the world. Always remember that I am only a prayer away.

Do not think that I have placed you in a difficult situation. Rather, believe that I am guiding you out of your struggle. Listen to that still, small voice; I shout to your soul to help guide you. I speak directly to your heart. I can't answer if you don't ask. Search scripture daily. You are not the first person to travel through difficult passages. You stand in the footsteps of several Bible giants.

Three Powerful ways God guides you.

Then the Lord said to Satan, "Have you considered my servant Job? There is no one on earth like him; he is blameless and upright, a man who fears God and shuns evil. And he still maintains his integrity, though you incited me against him to ruin him without any reason." (Job 2:3 NIV)

AUGUST 9

*F*ear can shake and rattle you down to the very bone. Awe of Me has a way of touching your heart and soul so that you are moved and inspired by Me. I not only give life, but I also inspire it. I animated you with the very breath of My being when you were born. I can tingle your soul with inspiring breath so you will do more and accomplish greater things than you ever imagined.

Never think that you have to undertake the challenges of life alone. Your largest challenges may also be your greatest achievements. Take a deep breath of Me before you move that mountain or before you undertake the unthinkable. You set your own limits; I will help you find a way beyond your fearful restraints. Trust in Me and have faith in yourself; you can shake the world.

Let your faith become your vest life tool, My child. Faith will help you see the possible hidden behind the impossible. Have faith in yourself and believe you can do far more than you thought. If you have as much faith in yourself as I have in you, you will be amazed at what you can accomplish. Somehow you tend to think you are the only one with problems. Everyone has problems; you can either face life challenges with or without Me. I encourage you to connect to Me and the people of faith I placed around you. Together we can do far more than you can alone.

You have the faith to reach mountain tops.

Fear and trembling seized me and made all my bones shake. (Job 4:14 NIV)

AUGUST 10

*O*nly My word has intrinsic power. While the spoken word of a misguided human heart can belittle, disgrace, damage, and even cripple the heart and soul of the listener, it has no power if you do not listen. Deadly words fall on deaf ears if you turn your back and walk away from the useless utterings of a sour soul. My words have their own power, whether they are heard or not.

The universe did not hear "Let there be light" when I spoke the phrase. Yet light appeared in response to My word. Do not listen to the flapping of lapping tongues who like to hear their words. If you do not listen to them, they fall like melting ice dripping to the ground in the noonday sun. "I love you, My sacred heart." These are the words you should listen to; these are My words that I want you to hear. Rise each morning with My words in your heart.

  As you go about your day, let your words create holy moments when you can share My divine image and love with those you en-counter. Try to create divine love in the hearts and souls of those you encounter. You have that ability, my child. Speak helpful and not hurtful words to everyone. Act, speak, touch, listen, and live like Me. I give you My permission to be a loving representative and living reality of who I am.

You are the living reality of God's spoken word.

You will be protected from the lash of the tongue and need not fear when destruction comes. (Job 5:21 NIV)

AUGUST 11

*J*ust as My spoken word has its own power, kindness has a kinetic
energy that replicates itself the more it is employed.   Kindness
is of My creation. It is a quality of the divine heart that seeks to
find the center of the human heart. Kindness is My divine love in
action. Kindness is not self-seeking but is always looking for another
heart to touch and another life to encourage. Never hold back your
random acts of kindness because you restrain Me if you do.
Kindness changes lives. When you start to act like a kind person,
your behavior will soon alter the structure of your heart and soul.
Loving and caring kind acts will flow from your heart and hands like
an overflowing stream of My spiritual blessings. Nothing can stop
such a great force once set into motion. Don't dam it up by greedily
withholding an act of kindness that has its own power to accomplish a goal. After all, kindness is not you at work; it is Me working
through you.

Do not think kindness to be too slight a thing, My child.   Kindness
does not make the nightly news like crime, but it has a more positive,
powerful effect. You can change a life, foster a strained relationship,
and make someone's day. You bear My holy name, serve with the
hands of Jesus, and may represent the God someone never knew.
One solitary act of kindness can send a tsunami of goodness across
the land. Always be kind.

Kindness is not your work but God working through you.

"Anyone who withholds kindness from a friend forsakes the fear of
the Almighty. (Job 6:14 NIV)

AUGUST 12

*D*oesn't it feel good to rise each morning with the feeling of a life freed from fault and sin? You have that feeling because you have placed your life into My care. You still have your faults and continue trespassing against your neighbor. Your freedom comes from living and loving in Me. I forgive all sins; therefore, you are freed from the shame and shackles of past sins. As you slumbered, your soul was cleansed, and your spirit rose with a life renewed in Me. So, stand up firmly by the side of your bed, and I will support you throughout the day. Begin each day with this spiritual freedom and strength in mind. Lift your face toward the sun and enjoy whatever this day has in store for you. I will keep your feet firmly planted on the ground; you need not worry about slipping or tripping. Enjoy the blessings of this day; they are made just for you.

  No matter how hard you try, you will slip up and sin. I do not desire that you find ways to sin against your neighbor, Me, or yourself, but I am prepared to help you, my child. I give all my children the freedom to do what they want, but their wants and desires often lead them from me. The blessed Savior offers you the way back to My grace. You are never far from My love, but grace will draw you into My heart. Sleep and rest in the comfort of My loving grace. You have found rest for your soul in My forgiveness.

Always look up because that is where your life is headed.

Then, free of fault, you will lift up your face; you will stand firm and without fear. (Job 11:15 NIV)

AUGUST 13

*S*ome of My children continue to live in needless fear of Me. I don't understand where I may have gone wrong. I have chosen to dwell in you, My child. I am closer to you than hands and feet and more a part of you than life itself. I am not a distant deity dwelling in the outer regions of space. My space is in you. I take up the area between your cells and the time between each heartbeat.

If you still yourself and listen to your inner space, you will truly hear and feel Me. I am not heavy-handed but light-spirited, so feeling something lighter than atoms or air takes practice. Fear of Me will dissipate when faith in Me increases. Let your faith inform you that I am here to fill you with My love. Never be afraid of the one who loves you and gives you life.

Pay attention to the inner feeling bubbling up inside you; it is probably My still, small voice trying to speak to you. Be keenly aware of your surroundings; you are often in the right place at the right time for Me to guide you. Your friends, family, and coworkers often carry a message of love from Me to you. There is no limit to how I can touch your heart and soul; remain open to Me talking to you in soft tones of love, My child.

God's hand is as light as love.

No fear of me should alarm you, nor should my hand be heavy on you. (Job 33:7 NIV)

AUGUST 14

*R*ise every morning without the fear of countless foes forming around you. Fear exists in the lives of the fool-hearted who think they can control life and all spiritual and life forces. Your control over life is as limited as your ability to snuff out the shining of the stars. You are limited but not helpless. Your human limits become divine opportunities in Me. I can take over where you left off. Fear will make you as short-sighted as a stone statue. Faith in Me will give you the eagle's view of life.

So do not fear the assembled assailants that surround you. They are just bystanders gathered to witness the daily parade of your life. They watch and wonder because you have chosen the faith path for your life where you will always travel safe and secure in My love. Just wave as you pass them by and toss out testimonies of where your strength comes from.

  Never forget the supportive value of a faith community. Churches and spiritual groups allow you to lean on others in times of distress. People of faith can surround you with spiritual strength and support that the rest of the world cannot give you. Most of all, you will find hope peeking up from behind the crowd of anxious onlookers. A faith community can elevate you above the dark and bleak vision you can acquire in times of stress. Once elevated, you will be able to see Me holding your hope.

Never let life surround you.

I will not fear though tens of thousands assail me on every side.
(Psalm 3:6 NIV)

AUGUST 15

*I*f you eat only the food of the good earth, you will never be completely filled. No matter how good, regardless of the nutritional content, food is not a lasting substance. What you have for breakfast this morning will barely keep you until lunch. You need to eat; food fuels the body and builds a strong body. There is more than just food for the body; you must also learn to feed the soul. I am the source of life for your soul. As you rise each morning, learn to eat and drink from My blessings for spiritual health. Seek Me in morning prayer, I can easily be found as the sun kisses the earth with its golden rays. Listen for My ancient voice whispers to you from early morning Scripture reading; what I shared in the past can be heard again this morning. There are as many ways to feed the soul as there are to feed the body, be diligent in finding healthy sources in both accounts.

  You must take physical means to connect to Me through spiritual prayers. Folding your hands may make you feel more comfortable. Some bow their heads; others look up toward heaven. Do what you must to feel comfortable physically, but know I am in you and a part of every cell in your body. Prayer feeds both body and soul and con-nects deeply with Me. You will know if your prayer time is well spent when you feel like your heart is strangely warmed. Don't worry. It is just me talking back to you, My sacred heart.

Prayer will feed your soul.

"Son of man, tremble as you eat your food, and shudder in fear as you drink your water. (Ezekiel 12:8 NIV)

August 16

*P*eople are often afraid of what they don't know and what they can't understand.   Fear overtook the immediate followers of the blessed Savior, but fear was replaced with total awe as they came to love him. Ghostly shadows cloaked in the darkness of fear soon become inviting figures when bathed in the light of love. Never stand in the shadows to view Me, My sacred heart. Come into whole light and see My radiant beauty.

My form and figure will shape as you learn to identify My love for you. My love is found in the morning blessings of sunlight and fresh air made daily for you. My love is identified in the whole light of the noonday sun as it shines upon the world around you. My love never rests even when the sun sets at the close another day. These are daily patterns of My love. Look for them often.

   Try to think of me as an ordinary God who does extraordinary things for those who receive My love. I am as ordinary as dirt and as common as air, yet My love can help you move mountains or find rest for your soul. I am as common as the sunrise and as reliable as the winter breeze. You will unlock the secret to My extraordinary love when you learn My common patterns. The secret is really very simple; I am in everything you encounter and behind every blessing you receive.   Look for My daily patterns of blessings: My love notes to you, My child.

God's Daily Patterns of Love.

When the disciples saw him walking on the lake, they were terrified. "It's a ghost," they said and cried out in fear. (Matthew 14:25 NIV)

AUGUST 17

I know how scary it can be to be completely transparent and open to Me, My frightened child. Confession is a total unveiling of your heart and soul for the purpose of cleansing the spirit. Being completely truthful with yourself is a practice that sometimes illudes My children. I don't know why My children shy from sharing a truthful heart; I am fully aware of all human actions. A truthful heart makes way for the penitent soul. You cannot repent unless you confess from your heart.

The purpose of confession is to be forgiven. Confession is not punishment or fault-finding; it opens the door for My grace. You need to hear your confession so you will feel My words of forgiveness. The process is not for My benefit but for the benefit of the release of sins from your soul. As difficult as it may seem, telling the whole truth about your earthly life opens the door for My heavenly blessings. Go ahead; I am listening.

Confession brings the things bubbling up inside you to the outside, where you can deal with them. The only force stronger than sin is the guilt that attaches itself to sin like a soul-sucking leach. Guilt is the client killer of the soul. Guilt is like a heart attack waiting to rob your life of its pleasure and purpose. You committed the sin, don't let the aftereffects linger in your soul. Confession releases you of your sin and purges you of any self-imposed guilt. Remember, my grace is free; guilt is optional.

Never be afraid to confess to God that which God already knows.

Then the woman, knowing what had happened to her, came and fell at his feet and, trembling with fear, told him the whole truth. (Mark 5:33 NIV)

AUGUST 18

*N*ever fear the unknown, My child. If you tightly lock yourself into a predetermined set of limiting beliefs, you will miss My movement in your life. The unknown is a blank canvas of knowledge just waiting for you to see its beauty. As your eyes are opened, you will see an entire world of beauty blooming and blossoming out of the darkness of the unknown. Some see to believe, you must learn to believe, and then you will see what was once hidden.

The blessed Savior brought the world the New Good News of divine salvation. It was not a totally unknown or unexpected message. My prophetic messengers carried my words of hope centuries before the earthly virgin gave birth. Many were frightened because they were uncertain of this unknown message of My grace. Their eyes could not see the beauty of My message being born before them. Stand in the middle of the unknown with awe and wonder and let your eyes see what I am doing in your life today.

It is not enough to believe in Me. You must also realize that what I do is commonplace in your life. Salvation is the gift of life for your soul. You could not listen to My words without the precious gift of salvation. Without the death of the Messiah, you would not know the love of Jesus. If your savior did not spread his arms wide on the cross, there would be no room for me in your heart.

Do you know where to find God's greatest gift?

The chief priests and the teachers of the law heard this and began looking for a way to kill him, for they feared him because the whole crowd was amazed at his teaching. (Mark 11:18 NIV)

AUGUST 19

*I*t may be hard to determine where I start and the human stops. Clearly, there is an indistinguishable intertwining of human and divine in the eyes of many of My children. The reality is that all earthly things are of a heavenly origin. You cannot separate what I made into categories or divisions. You are of the body and of spirit. Both come as a blessing to Me. You are born of earthly parents, but I dwell in your body of flesh, blood, bone, and spirit.

Never try to guess what is of body or Spirit; I dwell in all My children. My children are called to reflect on Me in their ministries to one another. Learn to look for My face in the eyes of a hurting soul. Learn to listen for My hunger pains in the stomach of a starving child. Learn to hold the hand of a dying person and hear My song whispered in their last gasps of air. Listen for My voice in all of life.

Remember, My sacred heart, if I am closer to you than hands and feet and more a part of you than life itself, I am likewise in all of My precious children. Listen for My voice in the inspired songs of choirs singing My praise. Watch My Hands guide the skilled surgeon in removing a toxic cancer. Pay close attention to My overpowering smile as I burst through with laughter from a toddler chasing a puppy. Look for the divine origin in ordinary human life. You will often find Me there.

God is closer than you think.

But if we say, 'Of human origin' …" (They feared the people, for everyone held that John really was a prophet.). (Mark 11:32 NIV)

AUGUST 20

Whish, roar, and blow are the northern winds' sounds. "Silence" is the sound of My voice. The mighty northern winds slip into quiet rest at the command of My voice to silence their howling noise. What sound does your faith make? Is it the sound of a little child frightened by the darkness of the night? Does your faith sound like the thunder booming of the canyons of life?

Learn to allow the sound of your faith to resemble My voice.

Talk in quiet, caring tones to the hurting people of this world. Bellow and bark at injustice, prejudice, and hatred. Speak in inviting tones and welcoming words to the lost souls of this life. Learn to speak words of love to everyone you encounter. Freely talk lovingly every day to everyone, for that is exactly how I would talk to them.

You can change the world if you can learn to speak in my love tones. The world speaks far too harshly and has not learned the language of speaking to each other with truth and love. The truth will disarm you and remove any fences or blocks between you. When love is spoken, bridges of peace and harmony soon appear. These are not difficult tools to master but require daily attention and practice. Love is the greatest display of faith you will ever show another person, My child.

Love is the tone of God's voice.

"Where is your faith?" he asked his disciples. In fear and amazement, they asked one another, "Who is this? He commands even the winds and the water, and they obey him." (Luke 8:25 NIV)

August 21

*I*t is such a sad day when people exile the presence of the divine from their lives. It happens every day, however. You remembered where your car keys were this morning, but did you remember to encounter Me in holy prayer? You had your quick morning gulp of breakfast, but did you sit just for a moment to encounter Me in the glory of the morning sun? I do not say these things to make you feel guilty; I mention these things to help you remember that I am here for you.

Some people hesitate to draw near to Me because they fear. Most people fail to find Me daily because they are too busy. Don't lose yourself in the busy tangled web of life; rather, free yourself in Me. Learn to fear My absence, and you will soon appreciate My presence.

Do not let your perceived lack of time alienate us, My child. Time with Me may be the most important thing you will do all day. Remember that while I am always with and thinking about you, our time together is purely for your benefit. I have counted and numbered each hair on your head. I named each cell in your body, but you barely know Me. I will gladly set aside any spare moment and make it our time, My sacred heart.

God is never too busy for you.

Then all the people of the region of the Gerasenes asked Jesus to leave them because they were overcome with fear. So, he got into the boat and left. (Luke 8:37 NIV)

AUGUST 22

*Y*ou cannot hide from Me, My blessed sacred heart. Darkness affords no cover for the fearful soul. Nighttime is not a cloak that can hide your deeds from My observing and loving heart. I am the light that burns so brightly in your soul. I am the ray of hope that bursts open the hidden recess of a troubled heart. You have no place to hide because I am with you always. What you think you are getting away with has already been revealed to Me through your inner thoughts.

I remind you of these things so you will know I am your guiding hand in life. I am speaking to you now if you feel the tug and pull of your inner conscience telling you to avoid what you are about to do. Listen to Me, and you will avoid many self-inflicted problems in life. Follow Me, and you will remain free of the hidden snares that My children sometimes find in life. Do good, shun evil, and follow Me always.

  Most importantly, My precious child, trust in me explicitly. Trust is the next step beyond faith; faith believes I can and will do something. Trust believes and hopes it will be. Manifest as you think and pray. This is a very important spiritual law for you to place in your master plan for life. When you place something in My hands with full trust on your part, you move your hopeful prayer from a thought to a reality. The only thing that separates your thought from manifested blessings is your trust in Me that it will be so.

Trust God, and good things will happen.

And when the Israelites saw the mighty hand of the Lord displayed against the Egyptians, the people feared the Lord and put their trust in him and in Moses his servant. (Exodus 14:31 NIV)

AUGUST 23

*D*o not let fear lock the door to My holy presence. The fear the first followers felt was against human agents. They feared because the disciples knew their beliefs were ahead of their time. The Good News, the blessed Savior, was too far ahead of the thinking of that day. So, the fearful band of faithful followers fortified themselves in an upper room. Surprise, there was no place to hide from that which is holy.

Fear has the ability to shut you off from Me because it turns all of your senses toward the object of your trembling soul. Let Me remind you that there are three responses to all fears. Fight, flight, and faith are all My children's human responses. Learn to face fear with faith first. Believe that I am with you, and you will soon have peace in place of fear. Know that I am with you always, and you will find a spirit of determination and resolve to overcome your need to fight or flee any situation. The first followers of Jesus found their faith by receiving peace from the blessed savior. I am that peace that passes all understanding, My child.

Choose faith in the face of fear.

On the evening of that first day of the week, when the disciples were together, with the doors locked for fear of the Jewish leaders, Jesus came and stood among them and said, "Peace be with you!" (John 20:19 NIV)

August 24

*F*ear overwhelms many of My churches today. There is a definite shift in how the people of this world connect to Me and worship Me. Congregations are in flurry mode, trying to reach out and make new disciples. Countless dollars are spent annually advertising that their church has the best spiritual options. Too many of My beloved churches hide in the corner, shrivel up, and die. It saddens Me when once lively churches give up, give in, and opt out of serving My children.

All churches have a life cycle of birth, life, and death. The life cycle of a church depends greatly upon the spiritual vitality of the worshippers than anything else. Are you bringing spiritual vitality to your church home? Gather together outside of worship for prayer, invite nonmembers to attend your church, and get inspired by connecting with Me daily. Let your church act as if I am at the center of their worship because I am. Do not be afraid; believe, pray, act, and invite.

Remember that the Church is the Body of Christ physically on this earth. The Church stands for everything Jesus did to ensure your salvation. I move and dwell within each church to empower the worshippers to encounter Me in ways unlike anywhere else. The church is where heaven and earth meet, enter this holy portal often, My child.

Are churches struggling to stay afloat?

Great fear seized the whole church and all who heard about these events. (Acts 5:11 NIV)

AUGUST 25

*Y*our biblical ancestors are named and defined in the Bible. They were people blessed, inspired by Me, and sent into the world to serve in My name. Read the spiritual accounts of their lives and marvel at how ordinary people were moved to do extraordinary things. I am the compelling and inspiring force behind their lives. Through Me, your spiritual ancestors made a difference in the time period in which they lived.

Now, it is your turn to create a lasting mark in someone's life through your ordinary living. You. may not be called on to part the waters of the sea, turn water into wine, or raise the dead. But I call you to care for the sick, feed the hungry, and clothe the poor. These are ordinary acts of kindness that will take on extraordinary form when done in My name. They will remember your kind love for the next generation.

Rather than repeating that I am the God of Abraham, Isaac, and Jacob, they will use your name. It doesn't take much to have a generational impact on someone's life. All you have to do is talk about Me, live like you believe in Me, and love everyone like I love you. Too many of My lovely children are worried about passing down the riches of gold and silver. I encourage you to pass along the blessing of knowing Me. It may be the greatest gift you leave behind.

Find your spiritual ancestors in the Bible.

'I am the God of your fathers, the God of Abraham, Isaac and Jacob.' Moses trembled with fear and did not dare to look. (Acts 7:32 NIV)

AUGUST 26

*I*f Noah had not acted in faith, no ark would have been built. If Noah had remained still in his beliefs, he would not have taken faith's course and gathered animals two by two into the ark. If Noah had not acted on his faith, you would not be here to listen to My voice this morning. Faith is the easy part of your spiritual journey with Me, My sacred heart. Acting on what you believe is an invitation to a pious life that I send to all of My children. Have you heard My call to live a righteous pious life?

Walking the pious spiritual path does not mean you are better than anyone else or that you know more than other people. Piety simply means you have devoted your entire life to following Me with your whole heart, your vast mind, and the very depth of your spirit. A pious life means you have chosen to walk with Me, talk with Me, and serve Me by serving My children. Piety is not a call to perfection it is My call to action. Noah was far from perfect, but his faith led him to lead a pious and righteous life by serving Me.

It is difficult to find a pious person because they are always doing God's work.

By faith Noah, when warned about things not yet seen, in holy fear built an ark to save his family. By his faith, he condemned the world and became heir of the righteousness that is in keeping with faith. (Hebrew 11:7 NIV)

AUGUST 27

*M*any have suffered the ridicule that sometimes comes from following Me. Do not fear the people who slander you with the slings and arrows of desperate detractors. They jeer and jest you out of their own fear and ignorance of Me. The fear has little to do with you and falls fully on Me. I am the object of their fear and focus on their lack of knowledge. I weep for all My children who fester in the fear of faith because they will never know Me as you have come to know Me.

Try not to fight back out of your fear, learn to defend yourself in faith. Fighting fear with fear only fosters more fear. Fight fear with faith and pray for My blessings on your detractors. If your assailants receive Me and My blessings then fear is conquered and faith rules their hearts. Stand firm in your faith and everyone will see that I am the source of your strength. Faith is your best defense over both their fears and yours.

Faith is the best defense against fear.

But even if you should suffer for what is right, you are blessed. "Do not fear their threats; do not be frightened." (1 Peter 3:14 NIV)

AUGUST 28

*G*ive no quarter to fear in your life. Fear is a useless foe that tries to disarm your faith and rid you of your spiritual defenses. Fear does not have the power to enter into My circle of divine love, my sacred heart. Rise every morning and step boldly into My circle of love. My circle of love is the holy place I have prepared for you and all of my blessed children. My love is perfected by My grace which I extend to all who seek My forgiveness.

Perfect divine love sees no spoil or spot of a sin-stained soul. Your sins are forgiven so you have nothing to fear or any bad memories to haunt you. You are forgiven, blessed, and loved in My perfect circle of love. You have no need to fear your past. Receiving My love is far more than just a faint feeling of your grateful heart. My love brings total transformation through the complete forgiveness of your sins. I do not hold onto your past so you have no need to fear the shadows of the former days that lie behind you in the dust of life. I do not punish; I bless everyone with My love.

Were are perfected in God's love when we let go of our fears from the past that haunt us.

There is no fear in love. But perfect love drives out fear because fear has to do with punishment. The one who fears is not made perfect in love. 1 John 4:18 NIV)

AUGUST 29

The trumpeter will always make a triumphant sound to summon My children to gather in My holy name. You need not fear Me if you have remained in the inner circle of My divine love. As you abide deep in My love, gather as like-spirited souls to worship Me in perfect harmony and love. I do not come to destroy, but to restore. Perfect love can never destroy the beauty of its' own creation. I will move across the waters of the deep once again and restore the pilled pollution to human discard and decay. I will raise the glory of the mountains above the flattened plains of human need. My holy hand will touch the heavens to brethren the brilliance of the stars and bless each ray of sunshine. Mostly, I come to cradle you in My love and surround you in My hope. Listen for the sound of the heavenly trumpet calling you to gather under My wings where you will be renewed and restored in My love.

You do not have to fear the judgment of God when you are held in the beauty of divine grace.

He said in a loud voice, "Fear God and give him glory, because the hour of his judgment has come. Worship him who made the heavens, the earth, the sea and the springs of water." (Revelation 14:7 NIV)

AUGUST 30

*S*tay close to Me and have no fear of Me or the world around you. Rise this morning knowing I am with you always and My love does not rise and fall like the morning ocean tide. Stay close to Me and worship Me each morning to set the direction and focus of your day. Once you leave My sanctuary of worship the day will have its own demands for you. Listen to Me first before anything else can clutter your mind or cling to your soul.

Rising to worship Me each morning is the best thing you can do for your head, heart, and soul. Keeping this pious pattern of spiritual discipline restores and enlivens your entire being. It is easier for you to remain spiritually strong than to try and restore your fatigued soul. Spiritual vitality comes from practice and usage. A spiritual couch potato will never have the strength to face even the smallest of life's challenges. I will reveal the path of a healthy spirit as you worship Me this morning. You are on the right path at this very moment.

An active spirit does not seek a place to sit. It's time to move your soul.

Who will not fear you, Lord, and bring glory to your name? For you alone are holy. All nations will come and worship before you, for your righteous acts have been revealed." (Revelation 15:4 NIV)

AUGUST 31

*F*ear is never welcome when you enter My sanctuary of divine love. Fear becomes awe and wonder as you gaze upon My beauty and glory. I look upon you with the proud eyes of your heavenly creator and My heart overflows with love. You are the vessel of My glorious creation. What I imagined and what I spoke became fulfilled in you. I so wish that you could see yourself through My eyes and feel the great depth of love I have for you.

The praise I hear from the sound of your sweet voice fills Me with joy, it is what I live for. Your voice takes on a different timbre and the stature of your soul takes on different heights, sounds, and shapes are altered when you praise Me in worship. When you worship Me there is a total transformation of your earthly being. You are temporarily transformed into a heavenly being. Listen for the sound of the voice ceiling you to worship and gather with like-spirited souls to praise Me. In that moment you will see where heaven and earth meet and all is made one in Me.

Then a voice came from the throne, saying: "Praise our God, all you his servants, you who fear him, both great and small!" (Revelation 19:5 NIV)

SEPTEMBER 1

*C*ome to Me in the early morning dawn and drop the cloak of darkness that hid you throughout the night. See yourself in My light as I brighten your soul through the forgiveness of sin. Forgiveness is the Spirit Force of My love. My Spirit Force of forgiveness flows out from Me as easily as the human heart pumps blood to the entire body. Forgiveness is a divine function of My holy loving being.

Forgiveness also ordains you as one of My holy servants. My forgiveness is less for My own sake as it is for your sake and the benefit of all My children. You are forgiven so that you can drop the heavy load of guilt you carry so your hands will be free to serve My children. Sin burdens the soul and restricts human service. Forgiveness places you into My holy sacred service where you will serve Me and my children with joy.

Forgiveness places us in God's sacred service.

But with you there is forgiveness, so that we can, with reverence, serve you. (Psalm 130:4 NIV)

SEPTEMBER 2

*T*he promise of forgiveness for your sins was purchased with the price of the Savior's blood. This is the price for divine love—the total giving of the holy self to the sinful human. There are no regrets about giving the total divine self, and it is My nature to give completely without regard to personal cost or loss. The divine nature made flesh out of holy love and existed to show My perfect love.

The covenant promise is relived whenever you take the treasured chalice to your lips. You drink from more than just the fruit of the vine; love fills your veins just as it fills the life of the Savior. Communion is often in this sacred meal, and drink fully from the cup of salvation. Let the vine's fruit pass to your heart and soul as it enters your body. It is not a drink to quench the thirst of a parched body; it is divine food for the starving soul.

Be mindful that when you surround yourself with spirit-minded believers, you become the living body of Christ or the church of Jesus on earth. A mystical, spiritual transformation occurs when you gather in love to take the cup and share the loaf. Jesus is made real in your presence, just as he shared the same meal with his disciples. This meal is to fortify, inspire, and transform you into modern-day disciples who are being sent into the world to become the body of Christ to the world.

The Cup Of Christ's Blood: Our Salvation

This is my blood of the covenant, which is poured out for many for the forgiveness of sins. (Matthew 26:28 NIV)

SEPTEMBER 3

*I*t took countless generations and fully devoted servants to prepare the way for you, My child. The appearance of the Baptist on the horizon was the loudest noise I could make and had the greatest impact on the world then. Generation after generation came before you to create this time for your forgiveness of sin. Do not take it lightly, or that asking for forgiveness is just a formality of our holy relationship. I moved heaven and earth into perfect alignment and harmony so that forgiveness of sin would be as available as the fruit on a tree at harvest time.

Forgiveness is ready for you this morning. It will cleanse your soul like the morning shower washes your body. Forgiveness will nurture your spirit with the vitality of a new life freed from past hardships and pain. My forgiveness will clothe you with the righteousness of holy livening that will be with you throughout this day. Listen, and you will hear the voice of the Baptist calling to you this very morning.

Watch as I descend upon you from the heavens and light upon your soul like a marvelous dove. Listen, and you will hear My voice saying, "You are My beloved Christian child in whom I am well-pleased. You are never far from the acts of the Baptist; he still speaks to your soul and calls you to repentance from sin. I am still here to grant you My grace through the loving arms of the blessed Savior.

How To Get Forgiveness from God According To John The Baptist

And so John the Baptist appeared in the wilderness, preaching a baptism of repentance for the forgiveness of sins. (Mark 1:4 NIV)

September 4

*L*earn to share the great knowledge of wealth you have in your treasured store house of information about Me, My sacred heart. Don't hold back any of your life experiences. Talk about Me to the generation that follows your spiritual path. Show them what a saved and redeemed life looks like. Bless them with the knowledge you have accumulated over the years. Tell them how you have felt My hand of grace and My loving kiss upon your forehead.

I am counting on you to be My beacon of hope to the lost and lonely souls of this world. Their darkness will only part when they are illuminated with My salvation. My saving love is not to be held as a treasure; it is to be shared as a sacred meal. Do not hold back on who you invite to this holy gathering, My salvation is meant for all to enjoy. Pass it on.

The knowledge of salvation is not to be held onto; it must be passed to the next generation.

to give his people the knowledge of salvation through the forgiveness of their sins, (Luke 1:77 NIV)

September 5

*G*ranting forgiveness from sin is an easy endeavor on My part, My child. The difficulty comes when you receive My forgiveness. I forgive all of you for all that you do. I forgive without limitation or hesitation. My love is easy to forgive and My heart will always forget any trespasses or wrongdoings. Divine forgiveness must maneuver over many roadblocks before it can reach the depth of the human soul.

Forgiveness must move past the traps of the mind that will always question and forever wonder if I really forgave you. The human heart blocks the blessing of My forgiveness because it holds its own hatred for those who have wronged you and hurt you. If I am able to make it past the mind and heart the soul has its own recoiling resistance to My blessing of forgiveness. The soul must receive the Good News of salvation as truth. Relearn the pattern of My forgiveness and you will create a direct pipeline from Me to your soul. All roadblocks to forgiveness come from you, let go of them and receive what awaits you.

There is nothing that stands between us and God's forgiveness, except us.

And repentance for the forgiveness of sins will be preached in his name to all nations, beginning at Jerusalem. (Luke 24:47 NIV)

SEPTEMBER 6

*M*any voices have imitated the voice of My beloved servant over the years. Peter called out for repentance so that everyone would receive the divine gift that marks and seals the glorious covenant of grace. Just as I rested over the head of the Savior at his baptism, so I will find My way to you through the cleansing brook of blessed baptism. The water of baptism holds no mystery of magic. Transformation of the human soul occurs when you accept the message behind the method of baptism.

The message is simple. Repent and turn your life over to Me. Be baptized in the waters of divine salvation. Receive Me as your eternal gift and spiritual companion. There is something that hides beneath the surface of the waters of baptism that you may not see at first. My love is carried in the depths of the waters of baptism. My love is released to transform you into what you were meant to be. You were called to be My beloved child, servant, and companion.

The waters of baptism carry the gift of the Holy Spirit and the fullness of God's love.

Peter replied, "Repent and be baptized, every one of you, in the name of Jesus Christ for the forgiveness of your sins. And you will receive the gift of the Holy Spirit. Acts 2:38 NIV)

SEPTEMBER 7

*M*y divine grace and everlasting love are far-reaching. Rise each morning knowing that what was proclaimed through the prophet centuries ago is now released to you. I relied on the prophets of old to carry My message to many people of countless generations. I now call you into the role of holy messenger for the contemporaries of this day. The very name of "Jesus" is the portal between the past and present and heaven and earth. I invite you to carry the holy name as you carry any form of identification. Jesus holds the mark of salvation and the sign of divine love. As you carry the blessed name of the Savior you also carry Me as your life force and constant companion. Do not be amazed or mystified at My teachings, they are as old as the hills. Just testify to what I am doing in your life today. I bring you My grace for the forgiveness of sin and I bless you every day with My holy presence. You are my modern-day prophet who will carry My message of love to all the nations.

You are the modern-day prophet who gives witness to the blessed name of Jesus.

All the prophets testify about him that everyone who believes in him receives forgiveness of sins through his name." (Acts 10:43 NIV)

SEPTEMBER 8

*A*ll I needed was one strong voice to tell the world of My plans to forgive sins by the love of My grace. I knew My plan would work if that strong voice was connected to a compassionate heart that had a passion for loving people no matter what the cost. My divine plan would unfold to the world if the voice was connected to a Spirit of love dedicated to reaching the brokenhearted and those who have a crushed spirit.

The voice of forgiveness, compassion, and love has made its way to you this morning. You are set free to follow your day knowing that the Savior has made forgiveness possible. The blessed Savior has also blessed you with the presence of My indwelling. I am not a distant voice calling from the past but a very real voice speaking directly to you this morning. I rise with you this morning to remind you that your sins are forgiven, your heart is cleansed and your spirit is set free. Listen to My voice each mooring as I remind you of My love for you.

The Spirit of God reminds us of the forgiveness from sin that Jesus brought us.

"Therefore, my friends, I want you to know that through Jesus the forgiveness of sins is proclaimed to you. (Acts 13:38 NIV)

SEPTEMBER 9

*I*t is difficult to open your eyes to the brilliance of the rising sun after you have spent the night in the stillness of darkness. Your eyes are accustomed to the dark and recoil at the immersion of daylight into their darkened world. At night, darkness is the norm. During the day darkness must retreat to give way to the magnificent light of the day. This is the pattern for the natural order of things on this blessed earth.

The pattern of the soul need not remain in the flow of darkness and light. I place My forgiveness before you as a beaming porch light so that you will always see My light even in the deepest darkest night of the soul. Your faith in Me will continue to keep this light burning throughout your life so you need never fear the darkness. My light of salvation will lead you directly to My forgiving and loving heart. Remain in the center of My love and you will be bathed each day in the glory of the light of pure salvation.

The light of God's love will always lead you to God's grace.

to open their eyes and turn them from darkness to light, and from the power of Satan to God, so that they may receive forgiveness of sins and a place among those who are sanctified by faith in me.' (Acts 26:18 NIV)

SEPTEMBER 10

*D*o not take anything I have done as happenstance or some sort of cosmic accident. I totally realigned heaven and earth to and posted My intentions in the night sky over Bethlehem. Each star, every orbiting planet, and the drifting debris of space moved over so that My divine intentions could unfold before My beloved children. This was no accident that all that was and all that is and all that will ever be came to rest in one acute moment in time.

I know that this is a lot for you to take in on this early morning, but I want you to know the truth. Redemption comes to all of My children as a deliberate divine gift of My love. My redemption for all of My children is poured out as heavenly blessings onto earthly souls. I bless you with the richness of My love which is beyond compare and is above any measurable value. This was no accident; this is what My grace looks like as it comes to you from My love. I did all of this just for you as one of My beloved children.

Redemption through salvation is God's plan for forgiveness from sin by grace.

In Him we have redemption through his blood, the forgiveness of sins, in accordance with the riches of God's grace. (Ephesians 1:7 NIV)

SEPTEMBER 11

*H*ave you forgiven yourself, My sacred heart? I have shared the path to forgiveness with you often. I have spoken of how I reached out in love through the price of the blessed Savior to draw all My children close to Me. I hope forgiveness is a living reality to you and you know that the door to My love is always open to you. But have you forgiven yourself? You cannot feel the fullness of My blessings unless you let your soul feel the touch of My love on your heart.

You remain the greatest block to this divine feeling in your life. You must forgive yourself for all that you are. Don't let doubt hold you back from receiving what I want you to have. Too many of My children struggle to forgive themselves. Let go of past sins just as I let them float by like a leaf floating on a gentle stream of cleansing water. I forgive you, now you must practice this spiritual art of self-forgiveness. Let go of your past and live in the glory of this moment.

God forgives your sins; you must do the same. Practice self-forgiveness.

In whom we have redemption, the forgiveness of sins. (Colossians 1:14 NIV)

SEPTEMBER 12

*T*he past and the present come together to create a new celebration. The sacrifice of animals was once required by the law. Innocent blood was shed on behalf of the unholy actions of the trespasser. The blessed Savior shed his divine blood for your sins. This was the one-time universal sacrifice for all sins, of all people for all time. Come to the table of forgiveness with this in mind, the love offering held in the cup and the bread is the sacrifice of divine love that holds the reemergence of this sacrificial act.

Gather as often as possible to share in this communion meal. You will witness minor miracles as you look in the eyes of the sinner gathered next to you. You will witness the transformation of the sinner into a saint as the holy meal is shared. There is no shedding of blood required, only the union of the communion of saints in My forgiving love. Let this holy meal restore your soul and renew your life.

Gather often to receive the sacrifice for the fogginess of sins that holy communion offers us.

In fact, the law requires that nearly everything be cleansed with blood, and without the shedding of blood, there is no forgiveness. (Hebrews 9:22 NIV)

SEPTEMBER 13

I know how difficult it is for My children to let go of their earthly life. They cry and scream, shiver, and shake like a water-soaked dog trying to shake the water out of his or her coat. Many of My children cling to their lives as if they wanted the refuge of their mothers' wombs. Let Me speak to you clearly this morning, My blessed child. You cannot see heaven's door from where you are standing. What is born of this world remains in this world. The vantage point to seeing Me comes only when you step into My world.

All of creation belongs to Me, but you will only experience half of what I offer if you are not born into the life of the Spirit. Once you are born into this spiritual life you must attend to your spiritual needs just as you care for your home or car. Being born again does not place you into some secret society, it awakens that sleeping side of your spiritual life that too many have forgotten. So, rise and shine like a newborn babe and receive the spiritual milk that I offer to all of My growing children. Grow in My likeness.

Human eyes only see earthly things, spiritual eyes experience Godly wonders.

Jesus replied, "Very truly I tell you, no one can see the kingdom of God unless they are born again." (John 3:3 NIV)

SEPTEMBER 14

*I*t may be too early in the morning for you to understand the theology of spiritual rebirth, but a theologian's approach to rebirth is not necessary. You are not studying Me; you are giving your life over to Me. There has been a great deal of study on this subject of being "Born Again." The study has created a vast variety of camps that proudly raise their victory flags claiming they have vanquished the subject. Being Born Again is not just a topic for debate, it is the spiritual pathway to Me.

Just as I created the heavens and the earth, I recreated your earthly form into My divine likeness. You will continue to look like the culmination of your parental genes, but you will act more like Me. Yes, you will fall back on your old path of human behavior. I fully expect temporary lapses of spiritual direction to happen. That is why I give you My forgiveness. Place your face pointed down the path toward Me and walk with Me. Awareness of Me is the first step in spiritual rebirth.

The Spirit of God gives us spiritual rebirth, we must act like we now live in the family of God.

You should not be surprised at my saying, 'You must be born again.' (John 3:7 NIV)

SEPTEMBER 15

*T*here are many paths to rebirth, My sacred heart. Take the path of least resistance and it will bring you directly to Me. Some have chosen the hard path that is covered with rough stones and paved with potholes. They trip and fall and cartwheel their way toward Me, but they find M nonetheless. Being born again need not be as painful as being born of a physical birth. Great pain is placed on the earthly mother and the physical child through into a temporal birth. Spiritual rebirth brings joy to Me and to you as you are reformed spiritually.

Every person is born of the perishable seed of human origin. Unfortunately, your earthly parents will perish with the dwindling days of decaying dust as time goes on. Just as I spoke and all this was created, My spoken word will give rebirth to you and your earthly parents. The Good News of My Gospel brings everyone the message of being born again. Hearing My Good News is the spiritual path to new life in Me, follow this path with ease and you will be born again in spirit.

The Gospel is the imperishable seed that sows spiritual rebirth.

For you have been born again, not of perishable seed, but of imperishable, through the living and enduring word of God. (1 Peter 1:23 NIV)

SEPTEMBER 16

*H*ave you forgotten to look for My massagers in your life, My sacred heart? My angels are spiritual beings sent to bring you My heavenly message. Many believe that angels are interesting beings restricted to Bible times and no longer viable in this modern world of technology and instant data.   I do not come to you this morning to prove or disprove angelic existence. I come to tell you to be aware and on the lookout for My messengers. My message has not stopped regardless of what some may think of the existence of those who carry My divine message today.

Celebrate the message and think less about the form of transportation My words of inspiration utilize. My living word brings you the same power whether they arrive through angelic form or by sled dogs. The message I want you to hear today is this "I love you and I want to spend eternity with you." Few can refute that this is a message sent by Me through My angels to you. After all, they received the same message.

Angels bring God's spiritual message to be heard by an earthly ear.
Listen to their message.

The two angels arrived at Sodom in the evening, and Lot was sitting in the gateway of the city. When he saw them, he got up to meet them and bowed down with his face to the ground. (Genesis 19:1 NIV)

September 17

*Y*ou will not always recognize that the angelic messengers who stand before you are blessings sent from Me to you. The important part is not the messenger, but My message. Sometimes My words of warning come at just the nick of time. At times it is not a verbal warning that seeks your attention, it could be a stop light that runs a heartbeat longer and saves you from an accident. It could be the coworker who offers you a doughnut when you are dealing with a difficult issue at work that brings you a message of momentary joy.

Angelic forces abound all around you. I am always sending you messages; I am always trying to get your attention I constantly want to communion with you. Angels take over when you fail to remain alert to My holy presence. If you fail to pay attention to your inner spirit, I will continue to send messengers to get the attention of your outer perceptions. Hurry, and rise from your bed this morning and know that I await your presence, My holy connection cannot be completed without you.

Angels exist to help bring us back to the holy presence of God.

With the coming of dawn, the angels urged Lot, saying, "Hurry! Take your wife and your two daughters who are here, or you will be swept away when the city is punished." (Genesis 19:15 NIV)

SEPTEMBER 18

*T*he stairway to heaven is a well-traveled path. My angelic messengers are constantly coming and going with My heavenly messages to My beloved children. Invasion angels caring your prayer request up this latter to heaven. The words spoken by your heart and soul are lovingly brought before Me cradled in the arms of My angelic messengers. Invasion as well, messages from heaven being brought to you and laid at the seat of your heart and soul. Jacob's ladder is a dramatic dream of a spiritual reality.

Massages do indeed flow from you to Me and from Me to you. This spiritual ladder is our connection. It is as busy as you desire, it is as empty as you make it. Make good use of this spiritual tool of constant communication with Me. Pray without ceasing and you will fill every rung and rai on this heavenly path. Keep the river of spiritual energy flowing between you and Me by utilizing your spiritual gifts and employing your daily blessings. All dreams can become reality to those who know how to interpret them and put them into practice.

The spiritual ladder to heaven carries your hopes and dreams for tomorrow.

He had a dream in which he saw a stairway resting on the earth, with its top reaching to heaven, and the angels of God were ascending and descending on it. Genesis 28:12 NIV)

SEPTEMBER 19

I do not speak to you about angles and heavenly messengers to try to prove or disprove their existence. Angelic spiritual forces will exist with or without your approval. You must be aware that many of My ways are above and beyond your ways. There is more to heaven and earth than you ever imagined even in your wildest dreams. These Biblical texts come before you as a way of opening the height and breadth of your faith. Your spiritual ancestors were as spiritually stuck as you can be, My blessed child. It took spiritual encounters of a holy kind to change their thinking and enlighten their spirits.

Countless words have been written and spoken for and against every imaginable spiritual topic. You are your own best authority on what you will or will not believe. If you do not believe something exists, it most certainly will not be present in your life. Do not be surprised if one of your unattainable unbeliefs meets you on the road someday. Many of My children have been greeted with a smile from something they were certain did not and could not exist. The things you once were certain did not exist are just as surprised to meet you as you are to see them.

Your faith can either heighten or hinder your perception of the world.

Jacob also went on his way, and the angels of God met him.
(Genesis 32:1 NIV)

SEPTEMBER 20

*A*ll power under heaven and upon the earth and throughout the vast universe must stand before Me sooner or later. Angelic beings and demonic forces have their own path in this world. Just as all of My children have the freedom to choose whom they will serve. The short-sighted do not have the vista vision to see beyond their own noses at times. Short-sighted spiritual vision restricts your service to the darker recess of this universe. Do not restrict yourself and thus restrict Me.

Be mindful of your self-serving habits that may lead to destructive practices. Money is meant to serve you. Money and financial resources are only some of the ways I can bless you. The love of money can enlist you into a service that does not honor Me and has little regard for you. In all things keep Me before you and serve only Me. In this manner, the universal forces will become your partners in life and not your masters.

Do not let anything stand between you and God, all things must stand before God.

One day the angels came to present themselves before the Lord, and Satan also came with them. (Job 1:6 NIV)

SEPTEMBER 21

*R*ise this morning and sit by My side. You may not realize it but your morning practice is a time-honored tradition throughout the universe. I come to you every day, however, so you do not have to come and present yourself to Me. I want our spiritual connection to be strong and to grow as your life on this earth increases as well. I do not wish to do battle with you or to make you submit to My divine power and authority. I want you to love Me and have ultimate faith in Me, just as I love you and have faith in you.

Our time together is not a royal audience where you have to curtsey and bend before Me. I seek the reverence of your heart and the sacrifice of your soul. When you present yourself to Me in this manner, we are one in this moment of time and united in each other's presence. Make each morning special by seeking My holy face even as you look to awaken your sleeping face in the shower. The spirit must be enlivened even as the body is awakened.

> Your time with God is not so much a royal audience as a sacred moment.

On another day the **angels** came to present themselves before the Lord, and Satan also came with them to present himself before him. (Job 2:1 NIV)

SEPTEMBER 22

*Y*ou do not walk this earth alone, My sacred heart. Never leave your home thinking that you are sent out as a single soul in this big cold world. You have more help than you think. Spiritual and physical sources are charged to watch over you. Most people think little about this spiritual and physical reality. If you leave your home each morning with your mind centered on the world around you you will perceive very little of the world around it. It is not that you live in two different worlds, you dwell in the center of two worlds united as one.

The sacred spiritual life you live has an impact on your physical body life. You cannot escape the physical and just dwell in the spiritual, you must live in the holy union of both realities because you are of body and one spirit. I send you out each day trusting that you will look for Me in the most common of places, I will send My servant messengers before you to help point the way.

God trusts that you will travel the spiritual path, you are given helpers to assist you in your journey.

If God places no trust in his servants if he charges his **angels** with error, (Job 4:18 NIV)

SEPTEMBER 23

*E*very day is fresh and new, every day is a new beginning for a fresh start. Do not let days gone by rise each morning with you. Let yesterday remain on your pillow with your evening's sleep. Look at each day as a totally new creation. The morning sun brings new possibilities unhampered by yesterday's problems. Listen less to the constant replay of past problems looping round and round in an unending sequence of hurt and pain. Listen to the angles' song. The angelic song has been sung ever since the first sunrise and is the same angelic song sung at the birth of the blessed Savior. With every new sunrise, a heavenly shout can be heard across the entire expanse of the vast universe. Listen with newborn ears and the breath-taking sounds of angel songs will greet you each morning. The glory song is repeated daily with the unified voices of angels and bright morning stars. Are you ready to rise now?

The angels sing a new song with each sunrise. Learn the tune.

While the morning stars sang together and all the **angels** shouted for joy? (Job 38:7 NIV)

September 24

Never think too little of yourself, My lovely child. You may be of earthly birth but you are also created from a heavenly origin. Your body is created from the red clay of the earth and the stardust of the cosmos. You represent the culmination of heaven and earth's" holy union. You are a person of the world but you are also a living being of My spiritual essence. My angelic messengers are beings of light and love who have been called into My holy service.

You were created to reflect My holy image on the face of the earth. I have crowned you with My own glory as I am a living part of who you are. You honor Me when you act in ways that reflect My holy image in your earthly world. You may have been created just a little lower than the angels, but your divine calling is just as valued as theirs.

You were created just a little lower than the angles to fulfill your divine earthly calling.

You have made them a little lower than the **angels** and crowned them with glory and honor. psalm (8:5 NIV)

September 25

*E*ach day brings its own types of troubles and new problems that stretch you to your limits and pull you to your wit's end. These are the days that will test your faith and tempt your soul. Do not let temporary struggles create lasting difficulties in your life. Problems, difficulties, and life stresses come and go like ocean waves. If you give into them it is very hard to get rid of them. Problems soon take you over and they find room in your soul to set up a perinate residence.

If you take the wrong step at the wrong time to try and avoid your life issues you will find yourself free falling onto even harder places. Trust Me always. I am here to provide the help, strength, and courage to help you get through the difficult times all of My children's faces. You will have My angelic spiritual help mates to assist your every move and to support your every step. Life can seem to be impossible when you face it alone. Stand by Me and we will face it together.

We have the promise of a spiritual solution to our worldly problems.

"If you are the Son of God," he said, "throw yourself down. For it is written: "'He will command his **angels** concerning you, and they will lift you up in their hands, so that you will not strike your foot against a stone.'" (Matthew 4:6 NIV)

SEPTEMBER 26

*T*rials, temptations, impulses, and inclinations are just temporary moments in your life. They are like buzzing bees, frantic flees, and annoying gnats that demand all of your attention. They fill the air with their perfume of fear just to distract you from Me. Try to pay little attention to their deadly drone because they have nothing of value to offer you. Muster all of your spiritual forces to bear at any given moment when you are faced with temptation. Learn to focus on the sound of My voice and the din of the day will fade and fall into nothingness.

You have help. Rely on the spiritual support you have before you. Read My Word to block temptations. Pray without ceasing and listen to My voice and impulses will fade. Heaven and earth are at your disposal cling to the spiritual sources available to you. Claim your victory when your temptation is vanquished and My angles will attend to your needs.

We never face temptation alone; God will always give us the support we need.

Then the devil left him, and **angels** came and attended him. (Matthew 4:11 NIV)

September 27

*T*he saving grace proclaimed and promised by the blessed Savior moves through every generation. The Good News is the angelic form of My living word. Evil shrinks and shrivels at the hearing of the message of salvation for all people every time. The hearts of the wicked are purified in the living waters of baptism. The souls of the evil are crushed but raised to a new life as they are born again through My grace. Forgiveness roams the land looking for the penitent heart.

I do not vanquish evil by destroying human life. I destroy evil by purifying the tormented souls of a lost generation. Each generation is lost because they have not found direction through My Good News. Each generation is redeemed when the Good News of My saving grace becomes theirs. Angelic messengers take form as they stand before each sinner and offer them the path to sainthood. Nothing in heaven or on this earth has more power to transform the human race than My divine love offered through the forgiveness of sin.

Evil is destroyed when God's grace is received.

The Son of Man will send out his **angels**, and they will weed out of his kingdom everything that causes sin and all who do evil. (Matthew 13:41 NIV)

SEPTEMBER 28

*N*ever fear, My sacred heart your children are in My care. Heavenly spiritual forces guide and guard all of My little children. These angelic energies have charge over each and every small life on this planet. They are accountable to Me but they can always use your assistance. While the angels in heave have charge over the souls of the blessed children, I am giving you and your brothers and sisters on this earth charge over their earthly lives. My little children carry the sacred future and hope for this world make sure that they can fulfill the future.

I want you to pray for the alleviation of poverty the smallest and most fragile of My children are forced to suffer. Became active in feeding the roaring hungry stomachs of My beloved children, the stomach also nourishes the soul. Offer warm clothing to their tiny shivering bodies as they fight for warmth every night. Together you can all create an unimaginable miracle as you rid the world of the deadliest disease known to humankind. The disease of forgetting the plight of the suffering children.

The disease of forgetting and ignoring human suffering is always terminal.

"See that you do not despise one of these little ones. For I tell you that their **angels** in heaven always see the face of my Father in heaven. (Matthew 18:10 NIV)

SEPTEMBER 29

*T*here are inner secretes that are not amiable to you, My child. I revealed the depths of feelings from My heart. I have told you about My forgiving grace, My daily blessings and reassured you with My undying love. I opened up to you the secrets of the Book of Life and shared the path to eternal glory. You were given an understanding of the spiritual power that you hold within your own soul. These are just some of the spiritual secrets revealed through the ages and reaffirmed in your hearing.

There is a place were heaven and earth cannot meet and the secrets of the universe remain hidden. It is not for you to know the appointed times of life and death. Time is what I give to all of My children as they are born into this world. The gift of time is the one gift I share with all individuals and is kept between them and Me. Neither heavenly beings or earthly souls have the power or insight to see within this precious gift of time. I will share one insight with you this morning, My sacred heart. You will never have enough time to so the things you want to do in this life unless you start to do them today.

Time is a gift from God to each one of us. Use it wisely.

But about that day or hour no one knows, not even the **angels** in heaven, nor the Son, but only the Father. (Matthew 24:36 NIV)

SEPTEMBER 30

*O*h, how I wish you could have seen this glorious Christmas sight. Heaven reached down to kiss the earth with a holy blessing straight from My heart. An angelic choir sang the. Glory song that pieced the heavens and filled the vast recess of the entire universe. The night air tingled with the spiritual energy of the precious birth of the beloved Savior. I choose an open field for My birth announcement because the walls of a royal palace would fall down in praise of the blessed birth.

The holy birth which was conceived of heaven and born on earth was found in a lowly and humble place. Creation itself had to be humbled in order to receive the glorious offering from heaven. The mountains were made low and the paths made straight as all of My creation fell in humble awe as the greatest gift ever given was born in the heart of the universe. Oh, that you could have seen this glorious sight. Open the glory of the story as told in the Bible, and you will have a Shepheard's eye view of that wonderous night.

The Bible allows you to relive the glory of the birth of Jesus through the Shepheard's eyes.

When the **angels** had left them and gone into heaven, the shepherds said to one another, "Let's go to Bethlehem and see this thing that has happened, which the Lord has told us about." (Luke 2:15 NIV)

OCTOBER 1

*S*ing as loudly as possible this morning as you give praises to Me. Your voice must echo beyond the mountain tops and piece the center of the universe. Don't hold anything back but belt out the grandest sound you can muster. Reach deep down into the bottom of your soul and blast out My praises from the bottom of your spiritual diaphragm. Don't worry about your neighbors, if you sing loud enough and long enough, they will join in singing the song of your soul.

This is the pattern I take every mooring as you rise from your sleep. The blessed Savior has brought your name before all the heavenly hosts so we sing your salvation song. The salvation song is a unison song heaven sings when My children find the path to My love and grace. As you proclaim Me, so heaven proclaims you a thousand-fold. So, sing your mooring praise as loudly as you can and rejoice in the glory you have fond. Heaven's voice will echo back its heavenly refrain.

Sing boldly of your salvation and listen to heavens refrain.

"I tell you, whoever publicly acknowledges me before others, the Son of Man will also acknowledge before the **angels** of God. (Luke 12:8 NIV)

OCTOBER 2

ou must seek the depth of total conviction that filled the heart of My beloved servant Paul. The blessed Savior took all restraints that block divine love to the grave with him, when he arose, her carried the pure undying divine love with him. Love is the perfected part of Me that connects with the peracted part of you. The holy circle of this love is the sacred place where angles dare not go. Angels are not pure enough to trespass My love without being sent by Me. Daemons are held at bay like barking dogs helplessly restrained by chains unable to enter My holy circle of love. Past, present and future are only limited tenses of time posted on a writer's blog. The one thing that you carry now and will always carry is My love. Love is the undying essence that will bind us together forever. If you must know, My love is what created the universe in the first place. I did not move over the face of the deep because I was curious to see what was there. I moved over the unformed chaos so that I could find you. My love for My children was the compelling force of creation.

God's love is the reason for all of creation.

For I am convinced that neither death nor life, neither **angels** nor demons, neither the present nor the future, nor any powers, will be able to separate us from the love of God that is in Christ Jesus our Lord. (Romans 8:38 NIV)

OCTOBER 3

*Y*ou must have the divine driving spiritual force of love for all that you do and speak, My sacred heart. I just told you that all of creation is based on My divine love. So is all of life to be based on My divine love. Love is a language that needs no interpretation. You do not have to guess at the body language of someone to see if they are acting out of love. Their loving acts will need no interpretation. Regardless of its origin, love can be understood in any language. If you speak in English, Spanish, or German love has its discernable dialect. The high-frequency songs of the angles are easily understood when they speak with words of love. Learn to speak out of love and live out of loving everyone. Doing less than love will make you little more than a noisy baby's rattle. The rattle makes noise but it does not carry the love of the beautiful child that shakes it. Make less noise and live and speak more out of My love.

God's love is the language of all generations. Learn to speak it and live it daily.

If I speak in the tongues of men or of **angels** but do not have love, I am only a resounding gong or a clanging cymbal. (1 Corinthians 13:1 NIV)

OCTOBER 4

*A*re you truly happy this morning, My child? Are you happy when you find a good place to park your car when you are downtown? Your continuance falls when you receive a parking ticket because your good parking place was a "No Parking" Place. If your happiness flutters and fades with the prodding and poking of external forces then you are not truly happy. You are only happy in the moment but your joy does not carry over to the rest of your life. Happiness flows from the inside out not the outside in. People with very little material wealth have learned to live a happy life because they don't let external forces steal their joy. They have found their life blessings in the wealth of loving Me. When you love Me, I promise I will never disappoint you, make you sad, abandon you, or make your life miserable. I will alter the way you perceive things, however. When you experience the world from the inner presence of My love, your outer world will become your friend and not your foe.

Happiness comes from the inner joy of God's love.

Haman went out that day **happy** and in high spirits. But when he saw Mordecai at the king's gate and observed that he neither rose nor showed fear in his presence, he was filled with rage against Mordecai. (Easter 5:9 NIV)

OCTOBER 5

*H*appiness follows good works and good ways. Righteous living paves the way for future happiness, while Living a life contrary to My teaching will soon follow the path that leads to regret. Joy flows over the soul when a pious spirit finds its way into this world. Remorse is the feeling that fills the soul when the heart finally realizes a life lived apart from Me.

Happiness can always be found in Me. When you live a life dedicated to following Me there are no regrets to look back on or foolish behaviors that will cause you shame. You will live in happiness because your past deeds are forgiven and your future path remains certain by My side. You may continue to do sinful things from time to time, but remember, shame is the optional feeling of your choice, I always forgive with My love. Your shame is always your option, My love is always My blessing.

God's grace opens the door to happiness, shame is a door of your choosing.

But may the righteous be glad and rejoice before God; may they be **happy** and joyful.
(Psalm 68:3 NIV)

October 6

*P*eople can see how you feel as you leave your home each morning. Let your face reflect the feeling of your heart, just make certain that your heart is bathed in the fullness of My love. It is difficult for the casual observer to tell that you are one of My blessed children when your face is lifeless and dull. Let the love I have for you fill the fullness of your face. A heart made happy by My Love should reflect what is happening on the inside of the soul. Shine brightly and sing loudly from the very depth of your being.

I know that the weight and worry of life can bring you to your knees at times. You have an unfair advantage when you fight life's battles on your knees. With knees bent you are in the perfect position to come to Me in prayer. I will comfort your aching heart and renew your crushed spirit. I want your heart to be happy so that your face will be cheerful as much as possible. Be happy in the good times and seek Me in the difficult times.

You are the mirror that reflects the happiness you have in God.

A **happy** heart makes the face cheerful, but heartache crushes the spirit. (Proverbs 15:13 NIV)

OCTOBER 7

I do not come to you each morning trying to build you up with false hopes or silly slogans. I want you to know that the inner happiness and joy you feel in your life is a blessing from Me. I want you to feel the joy that I felt when I created the heavens and the earth. Joy is the spiritual energy that flows back to you as you create good things in your life. I was pleased with all of My creation and deemed it to be "Very Good" and the positive energy bounced back to bless Me with happiness and joy.

Don't think that the joy your heart feels is limited to human beings. You do not hold the patent on all the happiness and joy felt in this universe. Joy is a universal feeling felt by celestial and terrestrial life. Heaven rejoices and is filled with joyful happiness just as easily as is the earth. This is the pattern of life, create good and you will feel the joy that bounces back to you.

Celebrate your labors by feeling the joy that comes from your creation.

I know that there is nothing better for people than to be **happy** and to do good while they live. (Ecclesiastes 3:12 NIV)

OCTOBER 8

*L*earn to enjoy what you have as a gift and blessing from Me. I always want to give you the best that you deserve and you do deserve to have the very best. I know how hard you work and the amount of effort you put into everything that you do. There are no shortcuts or easy approaches to your work or your life. The things you do and the things you have will only bring you joy if you learn to appreciate your life path and the possessions that flow to you.

I have already blessed you with the ability of appreciation, you just need to practice the art and craft of enjoyment which will lead to happiness.

Begin each day with a prayer of grateful thanksgiving. Prayers of thanksgiving are the quickest way to see and appreciate My blessing that flows to you. You may have more than you think, but I know you miss many of My blessings that come your way each day. A grateful heart that practices prayers of thanksgiving will always be content with the quality of what they have. An ungrateful heart always looks for more quality to fill the vast emptiness of their life. Happiness is based on enjoying what you have not reaching for what you don't have.

Look to fill your life with happiness and not just material possessions.

Moreover, when God gives someone wealth and possessions, and the ability to enjoy them, accept their lot, and be **happy** in their toil—this is a gift of God. (Ecclesiastes 5:19 NIV)

OCTOBER 9

I make all the days that number your life, My sacred heart. Like this morning each day starts as a gift from Me. The gift of each day comes to you unwrapped and unopened; it is up to you to select its contents. If you select the contents of each day be careful how you perceive everything you select. One person may have a great desire to have what you deem as bad and discard it. Another person may see your daily contents as trash as you proclaim it to be treasured.

Be happy in good times and in what you call bad times. Each day comes as a gift to you and it is up to you to fill it with the blessings that flow to you. Receiving today as a gift for tomorrow is never promised to any of My children. I can only promise you My undying love which exists beyond all tomorrows. This is the day I have made for you, rejoice and be happy in it.

Each day is a gift from God, it is up to you to select its contents.

When times are good, be **happy**; but when times are bad, consider this: God has made the one as well as the other. Therefore, no one can discover anything about their future. (Ecclesiastes 7:14 NIV)

OCTOBER 10

*I*n the most difficult of times in life, the smallest gift from Me may seem like a boundless blessing. Learn to appreciate all of My gifts and your entire life will seem like a boundless blessing. It takes very little comfort from Me to ease your pain while you are under the pounding rays of the noonday sun of despair and grief. It takes a great deal of coaxing to get your attention to notice any meager blessing from Me while you sit on top of the sun in your own glory. My blessings flow to you at just the right time so that you will enjoy just what you need in that moment.

Learn to appreciate My leafy plant blessings and then you will be able to see and enjoy the jungle garden blessings that I send to you. Your happiness need not depend on the size of the blessing. Each of My blessings carries its own joy if you receive it with thanksgiving. I am not trying to trick you by sending you less in times of great need. I am just trying to alert you to the fact that I carry every blessing to you. Enjoy Me and be happy.

God gives us just what we need at the time we need it. Not what we want at the time we want it.

Then the Lord God provided a leafy plant and made it grow up over Jonah to give shade for his head to ease his discomfort, and Jonah was very **happy** about the plant.
(Jonah 4:6 NIV)

OCTOBER 11

*S*ometimes even the most difficult of situations can lead you down the path to a happy life. Repentance is the spiritual conviction of the affairs of the soul. The eternal struggle between good and evil and life and death give way to salvation's glory. You can remain in your sick sorrow of sin or you can do something about the grief you feel for your sins. Grief, sorrow, and shame can give way to happiness and joy when your sins are forgiven and forgotten by Me.

Remember that the loving formula of forgiveness has worked in you throughout the night. You pray for forgiveness at the evening's call, and you rise from your slumber refreshed, renewed, and forgiven. You slumber as a sinner; you rise to glory as a saint. Never let the night overtake you, confess the sacrifice of your heart and all will be forgiven all of your trespasses and transgressions. Sleep well and rise in My forgiveness.

Your sins from the day will bring you no comfort at night. Confess your sins and awaken to the gift of God's salvation.

Yet now I am **happy,** not because you were made sorry, but because your sorrow led you to repentance. For you became sorrowful as God intended and so were not harmed in any way by us. (2 Corinthians 7:9 NIV)

OCTOBER 12

I have provided ways for you to express yourself in good times and in difficult dilemmas. Let the sorrow and struggles of each day drive you to My side. Seek My face and come to Me in prayer. Prayer is an open channel to My heart. I am always attentive and always eager to listen to you. Let the rise of the sun morning sun be your call to prayer. Go into the world knowing that your prayers have been heard and that the help you seek awaits you.

When happiness finds your heart sing boldly and proudly of the joy you have found in Me. Practice connecting the joy you feel in your heart to the blessings I send to your soul. This simple practice will multiply your perception of the blessings that I give to you. Let your voice become a siren song to attract others to share your joy. Joy is never a gift to be relished by one person, joy is to be shared with as many as possible.

Joy is as infectious as any virus and can cure satedness faster than any vaccine.

Is anyone among you in trouble? Let them pray. Is anyone **happy**? Let them sing songs of
praise. (James 5:13 NIV)

OCTOBER 13

*G*rief is My divine feeling replicated in your heart and soul, My sacred heart. The depth of your loss is felt first in Me. I know the depth of the great love you shared with your soul mate. I know because I brought you together to be helpmates and companions throughout your time on this earth. I also realize that understanding your grief will not provide any solace to your soul or heal your broken heart. I do want you to know that I carry the pain your loss has brought you. You do not grieve alone; I am here to help you carry the challenging load and burden that death has delivered to your door.

Grief may cloud your eyes and bring pain to your heart, but I am here to bring comfort to the depth of your soul. Although you walk in the valley of the shadow of death, I will bring comfort to you in due time. For now, grief had rushed in to fill the vacuum left by your dearly departed. For now, we share the pain of grief. Do not despair, for I have saved all of the love of your beloved. As grief takes its course, I will release the loving and lasting memories your loved one left in My care.

Grief is a divine feeling felt by both you and God.

My eyes have grown dim with **grief**; my whole frame is but a shadow. (Job 17:7 NIV)

OCTOBER 14

Do not be afraid to let grief enter your life, My blessed child. Grieving is what all of My children do at the loss of a loved one. Grief rushes into your heart and soul the moment your loved one dies. Greif rushes in to fill the vacant places in the heart and soul where love once lived. Grief is that natural human emotion all of My children feel at love loss. The heart and soul have no recourse but to grieve when the object of their love is gone.

I bring My mercy to comfort the sudden sorrow you feel due to the loss of love in your life. My grace and comfort will slowly lift the curtain of grief so you can once again feel the joy of the love that remains with you. My children all die, but the love they carry does not die. All love lives on eternally in Me. Although the body is gone, love abides in Me.

Grief will take its due course, but love remains forever.

Be merciful to me, Lord, for I am in distress; my eyes grow weak with sorrow, my soul and body with **grief**. (Psalm 31:9 NIV)

OCTOBER 15

*G*rief bubbles up to the surface, doesn't it, My sacred heart? Just when you think you have beaten the sorrow that filled your aching heart, it finds its way back to the surface. Grief may find its way up in the middle of your laughter as the heart remembers a special moment you shared with your loved one. I remind you of one extraordinary reality. The grief you feel will draw you back to the love you once shared. As grief finds its way back to you, try to be open to the reality that there is something you need to remember or reexperience.

Grief is rarely a good feeling, but reexperiencing the love you shared with your loved one is a blessing. Let your grief show you the way to the love that you continue to share through Me. I hold the key to life and death, and I am the vessel of eternal love. I hope you will find new laughter in your life; I also hope you will remember the laughter you shared with the person who loved you so very much.

When grief knocks, let love come in.

Even in laughter, the heart may ache, and rejoicing may end in **grief.** (Proverbs 14:13 NIV)

OCTOBER 16

I bear the grief you feel from the loss of your loved one. The sorrow I bring is not a punishment but a way of dealing with the pain of losing love. I bring grief to you because I care about you and love you so very much. I would never leave such an important task to someone who does not hold the same love I have for you. I bring you grief, so your sorrow will cleanse your heart and soul. While I carry grief in one hand, My infinite loving compassion comes to you in the other hand.

When you give yourself to another person in love, they hold a significant part of you in their heart and soul. When your loved one dies, the love you gave them seeks to remain united in you. This is the natural spiritual pattern of love. Love does not die but must be reclaimed by the recipient of love. Once reunited, the love you receive will once again bring peace to the heart and comfort to the soul. The grief I carry acts as a lamp so love can find its way back to you.

God places grief in your heart so the love you once shared will find its way back to you.

Though he brings **grief**, he will show compassion, so great is his unfailing love. (Lamentations 3:32 NIV)

OCTOBER 17

You will never grieve if you never love. When you give yourself to someone in mind, body, and soul, something must replace the love you share when they pass from this world. Love does not exist in a vacuum, but love creates a vacuum when your beloved dies. Grief is the cost of profoundly loving someone. I do not torment you with grief; grief naturally flows in when love flows out. The depth of power that grief brings is directly proportionate to the love that is lost. But there is a vast difference between grief and love.

Grief is always temporary, waning, and will diminish day by day. Love never dies. Because love never dies, grief must temporarily find its way to fill the hole in the heart. Human emotions are complex; the human spirit is even more challenging to understand. Please know this, My child, the grief you feel is holding the place for the love you once felt. Grief will let go of its grip as love makes its way back into your heart. I promise.

The temporary feelings grief brings will be replaced by the eternal feelings of love.

For he does not willingly bring affliction or **grief** to anyone. (Lamentations 3:33 NIV)

OCTOBER 18

*Y*our grief will turn to joy as your heart finds its path back to your loved one and Me. I know how tough it is for you to see the world going about its daily business as if nothing happened. People continue to go to work. The TV continues to podcast whatever it had programmed for the day. Cars run, clocks tick, and the world spins without missing a beat. But your heart has stopped with the screeching ache of grief.

It is not far that your world is halted by grief, and the rest of the world enjoys the day oblivious to your loss. I know your loss, and I feel your pain. All I can promise you is that your grief will turn to joy as love finds its way back to your heart. As love returns and grief subsides, you will once again spin in unison with the rest of the world, and joy will be found in the rising of the morning sun.

Grief will give way to joy as you remember the love you lost.

Very truly, I tell you, you will weep and mourn while the world rejoices. You will **grieve,** but your grief will turn to joy. (John 18:20 NIV)

OCTOBER 19

*T*he blessed Savior showed you the path to My eternal love. The Savior gave you his life as a straightforward way to Me through the divine gift of salvation. Follow this path of eternal love. When you give your love to someone, the love is eternal. Feelings of grief rush in to fill the void when the object of your love is lost. Do not worry; your love is not lost; it is bound in the glorious resurrection of the blessed Savior. Death may temporality separate you from your loved one, but you remain united in My love forever.

Your time for grief may be at hand, but your joy is on its way. The soul of your loved one is held in the holy center of My heart. My heart is where love and eternity gather together in due time. Do not fear I have the soul of your loved one in My heart; there is no safer place to store it. Your loved one is not lost but held in My safe grace for eternity. Let grief take its path, but know that My joy waits patiently for you. When you are ready, open your heart to receive the love and memories I hold.

The glory of the resurrection holds the power of joy over grief.

So with you: Now is your time of **grief**, but I will see you again, and you will rejoice, and no one will take away your joy. (John 16:22 NIV)

OCTOBER 20

*A*ny loss of things you attach yourself to can bring you grief. The death of a loved one has its level of suffering, but anything you give your heart and soul to can create despair when it is no longer in your life. Be very careful where you lend your heart. Money has no good or evil attached to it. Money is just inert paper and or a passive plastic means of payment for goods and services rendered. If you link your heart and soul to the things money can bring you, the dynamic will change dramatically. Simple transactions become life fixations when you connect your passion to cash.

Grief will overwhelm your life the second your money stream dries up. Never place your faith behind the numbers on a credit card. Always trust in Me and the power I have to bless your life. You may not have everything you want in life, but I will bless you with everything you need. Material wealth will never bring you lasting comfort. At best, wealth will only give you the momentary illusion of joy. It is challenging to enjoy life from a full pocketbook when the heart and soul remain empty.

Grief is the interest rate paid on loving money once it is gone.

For the love of money is the root of all kinds of evil. Some people, eager for money, have wandered from the faith and pierced themselves with many **griefs**. (1 Timothy 6:10 NIV)

OCTOBER 21

*T*he path of grief is well traveled, My sacred heart. It is impossible to live a life that does not encounter grief along the way. That is because there is a price for love, the price is called grief. Again, grief is not a punishment rather, grief is what must rush in when love I lost. You cannot give away the depth of your soul to someone and then remain unchanged when they die. The sudden loss of love pulls at the very fiber of your being. Grief gives purpose and direction to the loss of love.

I will help you live in this limbo of the shadows of love. I know the trials and tribulations you are going through. I have seen these encounters with grief before in those who have walked this way before you. Please be aware of one important hang, My child. Love walks this path as well. I will teach you how to reconnect with the love you have lost. I will fill your soul and heart with long-lasting memories of the one who loved you. You will feel love once again.

Pay attention as you travel the path of grief, you will encounter love there again.

In all this, you greatly rejoice, though now for a little while you may have had to suffer **grief** in all kinds of trials. (1 Peter 1:6 NIV)

October 22

*T*he words of the psalmist are much easier to read than to live. Most of My children have great difficulty being still. Being still means that you let go of the world for a moment and cling closely to Me. You must slip away from the gravitational pull this material planet has upon you. Slip into my divine presence this morning and you will know Me as never before. You will know Me because your stillness creates an emptiness for Me to fill with My presence. You must become empty in order for Me to fill you. This is not too difficult a thing for you to attempt. Emptiness comes when you pour out of your heart and soul to Me in prayer. Your thoughts and desires flow out of you into Me and a holy union is created as you pray. Practice emptying yourself through prayer every morning, and be still and know that I love you.

Prayer empties the heart so that God has room to dwell.

He says, "Be **still**, and know that I am God; I will be exalted among the nations,
I will be exalted in the earth." (psalm 46:10 NIV)

OCTOBER 23

*Y*ou are to see the world of shape, substance, and spirit through My eyes and not just your eyes. You see your material world through the lenses of your perception. When you receive Me and walk with Me, you begin to see both material and spiritual things in a different light. If this were not so, then why are there disagreements, arguments, and even wars? Every image, smell, sound, taste, and feel are subject to your interpretation. I see the world I created and the people whom I love through the eyes of divine love.

You can see as I see, but you will never know as I know. You are to rely on Me for all of your insights, knowledge, understanding, and love. The path of all creation travels through the creator. You were not created to have the height, breadth, or depth of the One who made you. You are limited to what I give to you. But know this, what I give to you is all My love.

You were created in God's image to act like God, not know what God knows.

"For **God knows** that when you eat from it your eyes will be opened, and you will be like **God**, **know**ing good and evil." (Genesis 3:5 NIV)

OCTOBER 24

I will impart to you skills and abilities and gifts and graces that will help you make your way in this world. Rise each morning, knowing that you are fully empowered to face the challenges of the day. You were created in My image to fulfill your divine calling. Your holy calling is to be a continued creator of this earth. You are to continue to develop and tend to the needs of this planet and its people.

You are given the tools of a servant to care for the needs of your community. Your skills are not just self-serving implements but instruments of saintly service. I fill your life so that you will fulfill your mission of serving My people. Use all of your divine gifts to the best of your ability.

You are filled with the Spirit of God to fulfill your divine calling.

And he has filled him with the Spirit of **God**, with wisdom, with understanding, with **know**ledge and with all kinds of skills— (Exodus 35:31 NIV)

OCTOBER 25

*A*s you rise each morning, know that I wake in the center of your heart. Sometimes you will forget to find your center in holy prayer. I am already in your center listening to the inner groaning of your heart and soul. Do not be afraid of sharing the very depths of your soul, because I am already present in your most inner thoughts and feelings. You cannot hide from ME because I am in the very center of your being.

I do not live as a part of you because I demand to know all the things that you think or do. I dwell in the core of the soul so that can comfort your troubled spirit. You need not look hard or travel far to find me. I am present even before you know what is happening to you. We share no secrets when you remain united in My love.

God will always know the secrets of your heart.

Would not **God** have discovered it, since he **knows** the secrets of the heart? (Psalm 444:21 NIV)

OCTOBER 26

I know the very depths of your spirit, My sacred heart. I know you inside and out. I understand the hidden chambers of your heart. I move within every minuscule molecule of you and have peered into the tiny atom to see your DNA. Every hair on your head and every freckle on your face has been counted and numbered by Me. I move within you so that you will make the Spirit Connection with Me.
I want you to know Me as well as I know you. You will never know everything I know, but you can know Me by My love. Love dives deeper into the heart and soul than knowledge can ever go. Love reveals the blueprint to each human soul so that every corner and cranny of your soul can be loved.   It is through divine love that we connect spirit to Spirit. Yes, My child, I know your guilt, but I see you through My holy eyes of love.

Love allows us to see God face to face and Spirit to Spirit.

You, **God**, **know** my folly; my guilt is not hidden from you. (Psalm 69:5 NIV)

OCTOBER 27

I do withhold some inner knowledge from you, My child. Be assured of one essential thing this morning, I love you. I cannot say "I love you" enough. I hope you are enjoying herring My words of love as much as I want to speak them. My language of love spoke the world and the entire universe into existence. You were created by My divine breath and formed by My heavenly voice.

Love is an elementary language to learn. It will only take a little time out of your busy day to practice My three sacred words. Practice saying "I love you" to as many people as possible. You will be amazed at the impact it has on both your life and on their lives. Practice random acts of loving-kindness to the stranger and see how My love of light will shine all around. Gather together like sheep in a green pasture, and I will love you all at once. Love is the holy manna of all My children.

Let God's love be your daily bread.

God's love has the power to unite all people.

Know that the Lord is **God**. It is he who made us, and we are his; we are his people, the sheep of his pasture. (Psalm 100:3 NIV)

OCTOBER 28

*A*nxious thoughts come from an impatient soul. I am not speaking of the anxiety of the mind that afflicts many of My beloved children. I am talking to you about the anxious moments your spirit often feels when your world seems to lag behind your expectations. The longing of your soul wants all things to happen in your good time. But everything happens in My due time. There is nothing you can do to force things to happen before their appointed time.

You have your life planned out from your limited point of view. I must consider all things from My worldview of your life. Spiritual anxiety ceases when inner faith makes room for Me to do My work. I have searched you and know your inner thoughts and deepest desires. Now you must trust in Me to deliver the prayers of your soul in My time—Wait for the next best thing to happen.

Spiritual anxiety is caused by an impatient soul. Learn to wait for your blessings.

Search me, **God**, and **know** my heart; test me and **know** my anxious thoughts. (Psalm 39:23)

OCTOBER 29

*D*o not overthink your connection with Me. Many of My
children will whisper in your ear the way to the proper path
to understanding who I am. Learn to gather together as My holy
children and worship Me with song, word, and deed. Allow My
children to bless you with their insights and share their stories of
faith with you. Learn to sing in blissful harmony and dance together
in joy as I lead in the holy worship.
Pay close attention to the words of the blessed Savior, and he will
lead you to Me. The words of the Savior are the markers that will
lead you to Me. Holy words take no notice of human status; they are
to be heard by all of My children. Read, listen, and follow the path
that lies before you.

Learn to swing and sway in tune with the Spirit of God. It is the only
dance you will ever need.

They sent their disciples to him along with the Herodians. "Teacher," they said, "we **know** that you are a man of integrity and that
you teach the way of **God** in accordance with the truth. You aren't
swayed by others, because you pay no attention to who they are.
(Matthew 22:16 NIV)

OCTOBER 30

*T*here is an incredible power that comes from knowing the
Scriptures. Breakfast breaks the fast from your physical sleep.
When you read from the Bible in the morning, you awaken from
your spiritual fast. Both the body and soul need to be alert to the
possibilities of each new day. Your food fortifies your body, while the
Scriptures revitalize your soul. Eat and read plenty so you will have
all the physical and spiritual energy you need for the day.
Do not be bashful or shy when you sit at My holy table. Read until
you are full of My Word. If you continue to hunger and thirst for
more of My pure spiritual milk, feel free to ask for seconds. Having
a double dose of My Morning Blessing will nurture your spirit and not
affect your waistline. Go ahead and eat until you become full of My
Word, then you will come to know Me.

Reading the Scriptures reveals the power of God. Take a second
helping.

Jesus replied, "Are you not in error because you do not **know** the
Scriptures or the power of **God**? (Mark 12:24 NIV)

OCTOBER 31

*Y*ou can find Me in many places, My sacred heart. I can be found in the whales and dolphins' sounds as they sing songs to My Glory. The eagle and the hawk whistle their tunes of praise and adoration as they fly beneath My Majesty. The elephant and the ant fill the air with their hymns to honor Me. All of My earthly creatures point in My direction with their honor and praise of Me.
Only the blessed Savior can show you who I am. All of creation holds the essence and fingerprint of My power, but none of divine design can show you who I am. Only the blessed Savior can lead you to the beginning of knowing Me. The Bible holds the material key to the spiritual understanding of who I am. Read daily from the Scriptures and grow in your knowledge of Me.

The Bible is the physical key to the spiritual knowledge of God.

No one has ever seen **God**, but the one and only Son, who is himself **God** and is in the closest relationship with the Father, has made him **know**n. (John 1:18 NIV)

NOVEMBER 1

*W*orship and prayer are natural occurrences in fulfilling the
human desire to know Me. Worship gives you a sacred place
to encounter Me. Prayer gives us holy ground where you can speak
to Me and listen to what t I have to say to you. Both worship and
prayer are remedies for the soul's painful maladies, pining to be with
Me.   Just as the body yearns for food and air, so the soul desires
to live in My holy presence. Worship and prayer help fulfill the needs
of the suffering soul.

You can find Me in My house of worship, or I will reveal Myself to you
in your home so you can worship Me in this place. As you worship
Me and pray to Me each morning, you will find that I already bless
your day. You need not bow down to worship Me; I will come and
sit by your side so I can hear every word you breathe. Let Me bless
your soul in this holy moment.

The human heart and soul need to worship and pray just as they
need food and oxygen.

Then the man bowed down and worshiped the Lord, (Genesis 24:26
NIV)

NOVEMBER 2

*R*ise from your slumber and greet the morning sun as it streams in to brighten a new day. The rising of the sun is the first act of creation. The moon and the stars bow to the beaming sunlight flowing throughout space. Sleeping plants stretch and reach to touch the golden rays of the sun, which whipper My name. Sleeping jungle beasts and the napping house pets rise to sing and dance to the tune of a new day.

All of creation was made to worship Me. Worshiping the creator's glory is in every fiber and cell of every life form on this planet. The human heart is the only living thing on this earth that forgets to worship Me each day. Let your heart remember, and your soul rejoice as you worship Me this morning. Let morning worship become your daily practice, and pass it done to the next generation. I will meet you each morning in the new light of the day.

Let the morning sun be your daily call to worship.

And I bowed down and **worshiped** the Lord. I praised the Lord, the God of my master Abraham, who had led me on the right road to get the granddaughter of my master's brother for his son. (Genies 24:48 NIV)

NOVEMBER 3

*Y*ou do not need a holy mountain to worship Me, My sleepy child. A grand cathedral is a spectacular place to meet Me in majestic worship, but such a lofty place is not a prerequisite for our encounter. Modern giant worship centers are impressive with their multiple worship experiences and multimedia expressions, but none of those shiny things are needed this morning.

Come to Me each morning with a humble heart and loving soul, and you will have all you need for the morning's worship. The ground you stand on becomes holy the moment I touch it as I stand next to you. Come to remember My blessings of the past and to celebrate the joys I will bring in the future. Let your morning worship be a sign to you that I will be with you throughout the day.

Your daily worship is a sign that you recognize God's activity in your life.

And God said, "I will be with you. And this will be the sign to you that it is I who have sent you: When you have brought the people out of Egypt, you will **worship** God on this mountain." (Exodus 3:12 NIV)

November 4

*D*o not get lost in the beauty and splendor of My creation. Creation is just a fingerprint of My handiwork; My exquisite design is not Me. I have already shared that creation can act as your call to worship, but by no means is creation to be worshipped. Never let a material image become your focus in worship. Material things will passively demand all that you will offer to them and give you nothing in return.

Place your heart in the center of My love, and you will find the sacred altar of worship. Let the sun, the moon, and the morning stars just be a backdrop for your worship setting. All heavenly bodies must bow down to their creator as they join us in worship. I love the time we spend together each morning. True worship is more about the time you give to Me than the activities that fill the time.

Your time is an essential part of worship.

And when you look up to the sky and see the sun, the moon, and the stars—all the heavenly array—do not be enticed into bowing down to them and **worshiping** things the Lord your God has apportioned to all the nations under heaven. (Deuteronomy 4:19 NIV)

November 5

*F*ollowing Me is not a genetic trait. Following Me is only passed on to the next generation by sharing your love for Me with your children. Faith does not come from any natural selection process of genetic superiority. Faith comes from a holy acoumeter with Me. Do not be distracted or discouraged by the lives your parents or grandparents led.   Your ancestors can show you the way down any path. It is up to you to select the right direction to walk in life. Follow Me. The moment you rise from your bed, follow Me. Follow Me and worship Me with your heart, mind, and soul. Honoring Me is the leap of faith that places you in My holy presence. Worship is always the first significant step of faith.

 Your faith will naturally lead you to worship the God who loves you.

"Now fear the Lord and serve him with all faithfulness. Throw away the gods your ancestors **worshiped** beyond the Euphrates River and in Egypt, and serve the Lord. (Joshua 24:14 NIV)

November 6

When you say your amen, let it be more than a simple statement stated at the end of a sentence. Let your amen become a holy breath word. Breathe in the "A." As in saying, "A: as you take a breath. Breathe out the "men" with a resounding exhale. Breathing in this fashion will involve your mind, body, and soul in your affirmation. If you genuinely believe in what you are saying or singing, let your amen be the breathwork for affirming your statement.

When you worship Me, I require all of you to be present. Place yourself in the living center of worship and open yourself to My movement. I am truly blessed by your presence in prayer or worship. Open yourself to receive the blessings that I will bring to you in worship. Let your breath amen be an affirmation of your holy encounter.

Let the breath of your spirit flow as you breathe your amen.

Ezra praised the Lord, the great God; and all the people lifted their hands and responded, "Amen! Amen!" Then they bowed down and **worshiped** the Lord with their faces to the ground. (Nehemiah 8:6 NIV)

November 7

You do not have to do drastic deeds or follow extraordinary measures to worship Me. Clothing yourself in sackcloth and shaving your head will gain My attention. Tearing your clothes and forcing yourself to the ground will receive more than just a second glance from Me. I notice everything that you do, both the ordinary and the extraordinary. I will always draw My attention to the inner feelings of your heart and soul.

Dress however you desire for worship. I will always look beyond the outer person and find the inner groanings of the heart and soul. Any refinement of building or body in your worship is only for your benefit. I am interested in the outpouring of your soul. As you pour yourself out to Me, I can pour Myself into you. The holy encounter is achieved in worship when we find the path to each other's hearts.

The center of your worship lies at the bottom of your heart.

At this, Job got up tore his robe, and shaved his head. Then he fell to the ground in **worship**. (Job 1:20 NIV)

NOVEMBER 8

*W*hen you worship Me in the morning's light, you honor My holy name. Do not be frightened or afraid of drawing near to Me. You come to Me as My name's sake. All of My children are claimed and named by Me. Every child rises from their baptism with My name washed on their forehead. Every child dedicated to Me bears My holy name in their hearts. The fact is, you were born to worship Me.

Do not think that worship is an act of submission. On the contrary, it is Me that comes down to be with you. When you worship Me, you enter into My divine partnership. In the moments of worship, we are in a holy union. The glory and splendor that you attribute to Me in worship reflects on you. Come and worship Me, My namesake, and stand in the holiness of My presence.

Worship creates a holy spiritual union with you and God.

Ascribe to the Lord the glory due his name; **worship** the Lord in the splendor of his holiness. (Psalm 29" 2 NIV)

NOVEMBER 9

*W*orship not only creates a holy union between you and Me but all are united in our circle of worship. Worship has the power to disarm even the greatest foe momentarily. Enemies become partners in the holy moments during worship. The spirit sees what the eyes have missed. You will see your hated enemy as your trusted friend. Love will replace reproach as strange feelings of love and warmth fill your heart. Look at the person next to you with eyes of love, and you will no longer see any reason for contempt. Remember that I walk among your gathered crowd of worshippers. I stand between you, and I sit among you. When you worship Me, there is no room for anything else but My love. Know Me first, and then you will see Me in the face of the person next to you. Celebrate My holy presence and rejoice in My love when you gather for worship. Look for Me seated among those who worship Me.

Look for God seated next to those who join you in worship.

With whom I once enjoyed sweet fellowship at the house of God, as we walked about among the **worshipers.** (Psalm 55:14 NIV)

November 10

*W*orship creates the holy ground where you can find common ground. Every person is different. Every culture has many differences. Every nation has a vast array of life cultures that vary from another country. Beautiful colors of different skin tones can blend to create a tapestry for holy worship. Learn to see the divine unity that worship can make, and subtle differences will quickly disappear.

Worshipping Me is a spiritual experience, do not struggle with the physical differences.   Enjoy the sound of a foreign tongue singing your favorite hymn. Delight with Me as the man of dark skin receives communion from the lady with the light skin. Smile as the man in the designer's suit stands next to the woman in her nearly worn-out dress. Worship creates an atmosphere where all My children are breathing the same air.

Look for spiritual unity rather than physical differences in worship.

On that day there will be a highway from Egypt to Assyria. The Assyrians will go to Egypt and the Egyptians to Assyria. The Egyptians and Assyrians will **worship** together. (Isaiah 19:23 NIV)

November 11

*Y*ou do not need a reason to come to Me in worship. People have traveled great distances and faced peril to come and bow down in worship. The night sky watchers did not know why they came to worship; they just followed the power that led them to worship. Worship is not something you do; worship is a holy encounter. The first act of worship is stepping from your common ground unto My holy ground.

Once standing on holy ground, My divine power will surround you. Some come to worship the King of the Jews, and others worship the Messiah. They seek My spiritual power through an earthly name. Use whatever name draws your heart closer to Me. People use countless phrases uttered in all languages to call to Me. Your heart will find the right words to speak to Me. I will touch your soul in our holy encounter.

God has many names but only one Spirit. Encounter the Holy Spirit in your worship.

And asked, "Where is the one who has been born king of the Jews? We saw his star when it rose and have come to **worship** him." (Matthew 2:2 NIV)

NOVEMBER 12

I do so appreciate your worldly offerings, My dear child. All your hours of volunteer work and your endless prayers and worship are always appreciated. I count every financial contribution as a blessing from you. I dance with joy as I watch you open up your treasure chest of worldly wealth and pour out a portion to Me. I know the personal sacrifice of your offerings and the joy in which you give them.

I hope you realize that your generous offerings do not flow to Me. I do not need money or gold. Good works are appreciated, but there is nothing you can do to help Me. Your offerings are My blessings flowing out of you to help the churches, communities, and people of this world. The earthly ministries exist because of the blessings that flow from Me through you to them. I am so very thankful that you allow My blessing to flow from you.

God blesses you so you can bless others.

On coming to the house, they saw the child with his mother Mary, and they bowed down and **worshiped** him. Then they opened their treasures and presented him with gifts of gold, frankincense, and myrrh. (Matthew 2:11 NIV)

NOVEMBER 13

*A*ge has a way of robbing the fruits of your youth. What you could do well at thirty seems impossible at sixty. The things you could see last year are but dim shadows today. Unfortunately, the body cannot exist in a youthful state forever. Even the mind will slow down with age to keep up with the body's slower pace. The spirit knows no such limitations or restraints. If anything, the soul finds new life as the mind and body seek a slower pace.

Let worship be your fountain of youth. When you worship Me, you enter a time capsule of holy joy.

If your voice sounds weaker in speech, let it ring out in hymns of praise. If your ears fail to hear the organ's glorious sounds, learn to dance to your tune. When your body no longer has an insatiable craving for food, feed yourself with prayer. When your mind forgets some of the words to your favorite hymn, inject your own words. Your soul will always be present in worship. Do not think of yourself as a physical force in worship, but that worship is a spiritual force in you.

Let your soul lead you where your mind and body no longer can.

And then was a widow until she was eighty-four. She never left the temple but **worshiped** night and day, fasting and praying. (Luke 2:37 NIV)

November 14

*D*o not listen to false profits or satanic singers who offer you the world. The world is not theirs to provide; I am the creator and sustainer of this world. 'These deadly daemons can only give false promises, which will soon die in an empty grave. I do not see an encounter with the dark spiritual forces ending with any good. Runaway from these hideous hellions and come straight to Me. It does not matter what you believe about the darker forces of the spiritual world; you will encounter them in some form or the other. Spiritual forces whisper and hiss to you through your imagination and tell you that they will fulfill your lifelong dreams. Earthly agents acting in their steed will smile and show you treasures you cannot have. If the blessing does not come from Me, do not take it. Keep your attention focused on Me, and the dastardly devils will be as powerless as their lies.

Your attention is one of your most prized possessions, be careful to whom you give it.

If you **worship** me, it will all be yours." (Luke 4:7 NIV)

NOVEMBER 15

*W*orshipping Me is one of the most spiritual acts you can do. Come to Me each morning and worship Me. Do not settle into your day or let your routine overtake you. A mundane and monotonous life will slowly dissolve your spiritual strength. You will lose your soul in the pursuit of the world if you lose your connection to Me. Let your morning worship set the pace for each day. Open your heart in prayer. Release your spirit with sacred songs. Join the heavenly host in giving praise to Me. The body has to follow where the spirit leads it. If the spirit rises tired and worn from the evening's slumber, the body will follow the sluggish steps. Revitalize your soul and awaken your body with worship to Me. I've been waiting all night for you to arise and worship Me.

Let your morning worship be your first encounter with God.

God is spirit, and his worshipers must **worship** in the Spirit and truth." (John 4:24 NIV)

November 16

*T*he impossible begins in Me, My sacred heart. I have moved more mountains than you can count. I opened hardened hearts so that the singly stoic would share their enormous wealth. I have healed the crushed spirit, touched the bruised heart, and brought new life to a battered body. I have healed what the good doctors said could not be cured. I have ransomed the sin-sick soul and released the fettered spirit. None thought this was possible, but I did them anyway.

What is your impossibility? Claiming your impossible dream begins by worshipping Me. Do not fall short in your worship. Worship creates the holy ground from which you can build your impossible dreams. Do not take My words as simple sentences stated to entice your interest. You will never be able to witness the glory of My movement in your life by looking in through a passive window. Come to Me in worship, and your life will change.

You will find the impossible worshipping next to you.

One of those listening was a woman from the city of Thyatira named Lydia, a dealer in purple cloth. She was a **worshiper** of God. The Lord opened her heart to respond to Paul's message.

NOVEMBER 17

*M*y children of ancient days offered sacrifices on their behalf. Animals or plants were sacrificed for the forgiveness of sins or for giving thanks to Me. The need for an intermediary was always necessary so the worshipper could come close to Me. I do not require the sacrifice of plants or animals any longer. I want the dedication of all of you, My child. I created you in My divine image; try to love into that glorious creation. I offer you My mercy, so you do not have to sacrifice animals or plants as a representation of your deeds.

You are a living sacrifice. True worship is the giving of yourself to Me. You honor Me when you place yourself as a living sacrifice before Me. The greatest sacrifice you can give to Me is your time. I know I receive all of you when you offer Me your time.

Time is the greatest gift we can offer to God.

Therefore, I urge you, brothers and sisters, given God's mercy, to offer your bodies as a living sacrifice, holy and pleasing to God—this is your true and proper **worship**. (Romans 12:1 NIV)

NOVEMBER 18

*I*f you do not hide yourself, you will find Me. I am in plain sight. Why are you so surprised when you encounter Me in worship? Did you not know I am present during worship? I don't want to miss a second of your driving sacrifice to Me. I tingle with excitement when you take the time to encounter Me in worship. I am gritty with joy. I am like a young child that cannot sit still.

The only thing that separates us during worship is the veil on our hearts and souls. You cloak yourself from Me, thinking that you will not expose the innermost secrets of your heart. Uncover your heart, and you will see Me. I am really among you. You are the only block that causes separation. Bare your heart and soul to Me, and you will experience the object of your worship.

We experience God in worship when we no longer hide our hearts.

As the secrets of their hearts are laid bare. So, they will fall and **worship** God, exclaiming, "God is really among you!" (1 Corinthians 14:25 NIV)

November 19

*W*hat would you say to Me if you had the opportunity to speak to Me spirit to Spirit? Would you come and sing the song of your heart before My throne? Would you humble your heart and bare your soul to Me in prayer? Would you confess with your lips the sins of your soul? Now is your opportunity to worship Me. Come to Me this morning and sit before Me.

You always have complete access to Me. I will never hinder your approach to worship Me. You bring Me holy joy when you take the time to be with Me. Why would I ever want to stop your loving acts of worship? In between your words of praise, listen to My words of affirmation to you.

God will always allow you to speak, and seize the moment.

The twenty-four elders fall before him who sits on the throne and **worship** him who lives forever and ever. They lay their crowns before the throne and say: (Revelation 4:10 NIV)

NOVEMBER 20

*C*ome to My holy temple and rejoice. Enter the gates with a song of celebration. Do not come by yourself. Bring your neighbor and the person who loves you down the street. Lift your heads high as you enter My sacred sanctuary. I have been waiting for you all morning long. I love to have my children stand shoulder to shoulder in holy worship. I am blessed when the laborer takes time to be the worshiper.

I have measured My holy temple, and I have right-sized it to include you and Me and everyone else who cares to enter. Worship is another act of My creation. The Sabbath rest reflects the perfection I saw on the seventh day and settled in from My labors. Follow this pattern of work and leisure, and you will find rest for your soul. You honor Me and mimic Me when you seek your holy Sabbath rest in worship.

You honor God and participate in creation when you worship together.

I was given a reed like a measuring rod and was told, "Go and measure the temple of God and the altar, with its **worshipers**. (Revelation 11:1 NIV)

November 21

*I*t may be complicated for you to understand how deep and wide the impact of your prayers can have on my sacred heart. You pray for immediate results in your life. I look for long-lasting solutions for the entire world. Your prayers focus on one solution. My answer looks to many possibilities and outcomes. Prayer is far more than just you seeking something from Me. I answer prayer with a thousand responses in mind.

Give yourself over to praying with the answer to your prayers more open to my movement than to your well-defined need. One prayer prayed long ago sought one single possibility. I answered the prayer with the birth of two vast nations. Had I restrained My blessing to the single-minded request, two people groups would not exist today. When you say, your prayer learn to listen for a better answer.

God often answers our prayers with more than we ask.

Isaac prayed to the Lord on behalf of his wife, because she was childless. The Lord answered his **prayer** and his wife Rebekah became pregnant. (Genesis 25:21 NIV)

NOVEMBER 22

*D*o not hide the blessings that come to you in prayer. Be as bold and brash with your acclimations as you wish. You are not bragging about your feats of strength; you are proclaiming My answer to your prayer. People must see the material result of a spiritual blessing. I am not just a Spirit of the celestial world, I am a divine power in the terrestrial globe as well.

Do not limit your affirmations to the size of the blessings you receive from Me. Thunder and lightning create a great show of My creation. The budding dandelion can be just as spectacular to view. So, pray and then rejoice so that everyone will know that I am with you. Do not hold back your praise, and I will never withhold My holy blessings.

The answer to your prayers is a testimony to God's great work in your life.

Moses replied, "When I have gone out of the city, I will spread out my hands in **prayer** to the Lord. The thunder will stop and there will be no more hail, so you may know that the earth is the Lord's. (Exodus 9:29 NIV)

NOVEMBER 23

*L*et your first act of every morning be a call to prayer. I will guide you for the day if you first open your heart and soul to Me in prayer. You cannot know what awaits you in the day ahead. So do not go out into the day uninformed and ill-prepared for lies ahead. Seek Me with the rising of each sun as eagerly as you look for your morning breakfast. The soul hunger and thirst just as much as the body. Feed your body with food and your spirit with prayer. Courage is not a necessary attribute to come to Me in prayer. Prayer opens the door between you and Me. I am always eager to listen to the thoughts of your soul and the desires of your heart. Do not let your hesitancy to pray become your most significant loss of the day. Begin each day with your soul wide open to the blessing that will come your way.

Race the sun to meet God in mooring prayer.

"Lord Almighty, God of Israel, you have revealed this to your servant, saying, 'I will build a house for you.' So your servant has found the courage to pray this **prayer** to you.
(2 Samuel 7:27 NIV)

NOVEMBER 24

*Y*ou are the primary focus of My attention each morning, My child. Do not stand in the shadows like a lost child yearning for My attention. The moment you open your heart in prayer, My full attention turns to you. You are in the center of My sacred circle of divine compassion and love. The world is not your worry or concern in this holy moment. I am all you need to know, and I am your entire focus in this moment.

You have My mercy even before you ask for it. I heard your cry and plea for grace before the first breath of life entered your frail body. You have a clear path to Me, do not hesitate to come before Me. The desire to pray is a human notion that I placed in all of My children. Blessed is the child who feels this desire and comes to Me in prayer.

The need to pray is a blessing from God. Use your gift every morning.

Yet give attention to your **servant's prayer** and his plea for mercy, Lord my God. Hear the cry and the **prayer** that your servant is praying in your presence this day. (1 Kings 8:28 NIV)

November 25

ind your way to My holy temple each morning, My child. I dwell in many temples across this earth. I live in the most incredible cathedrals and the tiniest of churches. I signed My name on the doorways of grand and Gothic structures. My name is rising from the altar flower of the humble rural church. You will find Me wherever My children have built a place to gather for worship and prayer.

I am also by your side and in your heart. Do not hesitate to draw near to Me as the sun pokes through your window. I am with you every night and beside you all day long. The best time and place to connect to Me is in the here and now. Just sit yourself down and share the deepest desires of your heart and soul. I love to hear your prayers; it matters little to Me where you stand when your prayers to Me. Just pray.

Right now, is the best time for prayer.

May your eyes be open toward this temple night and day, this place of which you said, 'My Name shall be there,' so that you will hear the **prayer** your servant prays toward this place. (1 Kings 8:29 NIV)

November 26

*P*rayer is not just a solitary experience. Many families, peoples, and even nations have endeavored into the courts of holy prayer. If one can accomplish much, just think about what many can achieve. I hear the cries of each heart as My children come to Me one by one. I rejoice in every holy gathering of brothers and sisters of kindred spirit. Corporate prayers push aside any division and culminate in a powerful force that even heaven's foundations are shaken.

The union of the human spirit is the most potent force in the universe when grounded in Me. So, come to Me with like minds, kindred spirits, and hearts united. Just the gathering of people in My name causes Me to move and fulfill your prayers and petitions. How can I not answer a request when your prayers are united in love? Gather together in worship and move the mountains that separate you from each other.

The prayer of one has great power, but the prayers of many are unstoppable.

So, we fasted and petitioned our God about this, and he answered our **prayer**. (Ezra 8:28 NIV)

NOVEMBER 27

I have heard your cry for mercy this morning, My sacred heart. Before the sun rose to break the day, I listened to the groaning of your inner spirit. Long before your eyes peeped into the new day, I felt your mercy moan. Never try to hide what you want Me to hear. A muffled prayer or a faint plea for help brings no faith foundation from you. Pray it like you believe it.

Let your words be as strong as your desire to have Me hear your prayer and answer it. You must have as much of yourself behind your prayers as possible. The strength of conviction in your prayers is solely for your benefit. You must believe that I will answer your prayer, or you will miss the answer I send to you. So, pray with all your heart, mind, and soul, and I will answer your prayers with all that I am.

Pray it like you mean it.

The Lord has heard my cry for mercy; the Lord accepts my **prayer**. (Psalm 6:9 NIV)

NOVEMBER 28

*Y*ou do not need to know what the person next to you is praying. Just know that their prayers are a reflection of their heart and soul. The person who sits next to you in worship may have a different ethnic background, but they pray with the same spirit. Their spoken language may be foreign to your ear, but My heart recognizes every word. Folded hands and bowed heads are part of the universal language of prayer that I seek in My children. I also recognize the position of the heart and soul as they align in prayer. I will always accept the holy offerings of prayers and petitions that come to Me from My beloved people. Come into My holy house of worship and join the nations of this world as they pray. Prayer has the power to form a spiritual hose that covers the earth.

God's house of prayer is not so much a place as it is the unity of spirits.

These I will bring to my holy mountain and give them joy in my house of **prayer**. Their burnt offerings and sacrifices will be accepted on my altar; for my house will be called a house of prayer for all nations." (Isiah 56:7 NIV)

November 29

*T*he prayers of a penitent heart will open the path to endless possibilities. Fasting aligns the body with the spirit. Rather than solely relying on the fruit of the earth for nourishment, an acute desire for spiritual food takes over. Dressing the body in sackcloth and covering the head with ashes is an outward sign that you seek to repent for your sins. If these acts of seeking My forgiveness are helpful to you, please follow them. These actions are not necessary if you come to Me with a desire to repent and change your current life path.

Just stand before Me and ask for My forgiveness. Let your prayer come from your heart backed by your emotional and spiritual desire to change. I will always listen to your prayers and petitions. You must learn to listen to My answer. I will constantly affirm your prayer and forgive your sins.

Come to God as you are, and God will forgive what you have done.

So, I turned to the Lord God and pleaded with him in **prayer** and petition, in fasting, and in sackcloth and ashes. (Daniel 9:3 NIV)

November 30

*W*hen you arise each morning, seek the blessings that come from heaven. Call out to My holy name, and I will answer your prayer. Seek to live, love, and work in the garden of My glorious creation. When you step into the garden where heaven and earth connect, you will receive the spiritual bread that I alone can offer. Your daily bread is the manna from heaven that feeds your soul. Blessings will come down each morning to prepare you and equip you for your day.

I know what each of My children needs for the day that awaits them. Take the teachings of the blessed Savior to heart. This prayer is the prayer he used to feed his soul and strengthen his body. Let this prayer be your morning ritual and daily blessings.

The words of the Lord's prayer contain your blessing for the day.

"This, then, is how you should **pray**: "'Our Father in heaven, hallowed be your name, your kingdom come, you will be done, on earth as it is in heaven. Give us today our daily bread. ... (Matthew 6:9 ff NIV)

DECEMBER 1

*I*t is challenging to worship Me when you carry your worldly worries and daily sins into My house. You must learn to let go of the trials and tribulations of your day if you are going to worship Me in spirit and truth. You cannot connect to Me if you are still chained to the worries of the world. You cannot raise your hands in praise if you carry your regrets and concerns in your hands. Unfetter your soul and open your heart so you can worship Me and receive my loving blessings.

The outside world will rob you of your spiritual strength if you allow it to do so. The daily grind can pulverize you into spiritual dust if you are not careful. So, release the forces that drain you and drop you to your knees. Let go of the clods of clay that cling to your soul and seek to worship only Me. Worship is a spiritual encounter, not an earthly reunion. I am here to redeem the spiritual blessings that the world stole from you. Come and worship Me.

The world has a way of taking everything we give. God has a way of replenishing it.

And as he taught them, he said, "Is it not written: 'My house will be called a house of **prayer** for all nations'? But you have made it a den of robbers.'" (Mark 11:17 NIV)

December 2

*Y*our prayer may be generational, My child. Your intention for today may be the answer for tomorrow. Even if the outcome seems unreasonable to you or even highly impossible, let Me do My work. I often begin with the impossible. Take heart in what you ask for this morning. My answer to your prayer may affect children and grandchildren and generations following them. I tell you these things to know that prayer is not an answer to just one plea. My answer may connect many hearts.

Your prayers are a dynamic spiritual force that does not just take shape; prayers create energy. Spiritual energy has no limits. The pneumatic energy flows through the Me unit until it finds its end. What begins with the impossible concludes in Me. Pray from the depth of your heart and soul and know that you have set heaven and earth in motion along My divine course.

Prayer does not create things; it is a dynamic spiritual force.

But the angel said to him: "Do not be afraid, Zechariah; your **prayer** has been heard. Your wife Elizabeth will bear you a son, and you are to call him John. (Luke 1:13 NIV)

December 3

*P*rayer can be a bonding force with your family, My child. Love unites siblings and parents in their hearts, but prayer connects the family in Me. You often tell your family members that you love them and share that you are praying for them. Telling your loved ones that you are praying for them unites you all in Me. Let this be your sacred sentence for this day, "I am praying for you."
This sacred sentence can set the tone for the day for your friends, loved ones, and even your coworkers. Knowing that I follow them with your prayers will certainly help create a better day. Realizing that you have them in your prayers continues the spiritual connection you have with them even when you are apart. Let your prayers be the uniting spiritual force that binds both heart and soul tighter.

Let "I am praying for you" become your sacred sentence.

They all joined together constantly in **prayer**, along with the women and Mary the mother of Jesus, and with his brothers. (Acts 1:14 NIV)

DECEMBER 4

*P*ray for the messengers of My word as they give witness to My love and grace. My messianic messengers plant the seeds of faith that I will grow in the hearts of My beloved children. Pray that their work will be as rewetting as they are tireless in their endeavors. Evangelists have no small task. They must have a voice that is counter-culture in nature. Their words must call people to change their ways and follow a path with blind faith. Do you remember this path of faith you first followed?

Pray for My evangelists and support them daily with prayer and love. They venture out every morning, not knowing what the day will bring, yet one by one, they plant the seeds of faith. When you pray, you are helping Me give birth to a new soul. Their newborn souls are awake to My world of love and grace. The evangelists' plants, but you help the seeds of faith grow.

Pray for the new seeds of faith planted every day.

As for other matters, brothers and sisters, **pray** for us that the message of the Lord may spread rapidly and be honored, just as it was with you. (2 Thessalonians 3:1)

DECEMBER 5

*A*s you grow in your prayer life, you will also increase your understanding and insight of Me. Come to Me with your morning ritual of prayers, petitions, and silent songs of praise. You open the door to increase the depth of your spirit as you settle yourself in your holy habits. I will connect to your heart to heart, and you will feel what perfect love is. Love perfected is more than just a simple human feeling. My perfect love touches the heart and soul so that My grace surrounds every atom and particle of your being. When perfected in divine love, you begin to understand what it means to love the way you love. My love goes beyond any emotional connection and becomes rooted in grace and forgiveness. When you forgive out of the grace of your heart, your soul finds the definition of divine love.   Grace is the highest and most profound love expression because grace does not require you to earn My love.

Prayer is the portal to perfect love.

And this is my **praye**r: that your love may abound more and more in knowledge and depth of insight, (Philippians 1:9 NIV)

DECEMBER 6

*C*ome to Me in the morning light and connect to Me in fervent prayers and petitions. The blessed Savior has set the pattern of prayer for your life. Submit yourself to Me in all things, and then your path to Me will become wide open. Only you have the power to impede your spiritual journey. That the initiative and walk the morning path of prayer daily. Walking the prayer path each morning begins the movement of a closer life with Me.

Complete submission begins with giving Me your valuable time. When you give your time, your life will naturally follow. Time is the most precious commodity you have. I delight and dance with joy whenever you break off a tiny morsel and share it with Me. I know how vital your prayers are because they come from our time together.

Don't waste your valuable time; give it to God in prayer.

During the days of Jesus' life on earth, he offered up **prayers** and petitions with fervent cries and tears to the one who could save him from death, and he was heard because of his reverent submission. (Hebrews 5:7 NIV)

DECEMBER 7

*L*et your feelings and emotions in every moment guide the prayers you share with Me. Whenever the darkness of the day overwhelms you, stop and call to Me in your hour of need. When you have reason to rejoice and celebrate, I will perform the happy dance of life with you.

Do not be ashamed, shy, or scared of your human emotions. I am the one who gave them to you; I fully understand what you are feeling.

Let go of the emotions that connect you to the moment, and feel free to share them with Me. When you share your feelings with Me, I also understand the moment of their creation. So come to Me with your troubles and worries. I will rest My hand on your shoulder as you share each one. Sing your songs of praise, and I will listen in joy to each word. My arms are always open to receive whatever you feel.

Let your feelings guide your prayers.

Is anyone among you in trouble? Let them **pray.** Is anyone happy? Let them sing songs of praise. (James 5:13 NIV)

DECEMBER 8

*Y*our prayers come to Me unfettered and with no restrictions or restraints. Use each morning to your benefit and to care for the needs of others. I do not restrict your prayers to Me, so feel free to pray as your heart leads you. Bring Me the list of blessings from the depth of your soul. Take time to give thanks for the blessings I have given you. Remember to celebrate the life you have because each day is a gift from Me.

Remember to pray for others. The people who surround your life and make each day better are also My blessings given to you. Pray for the infirm, give thanks for the healthy, celebrate every victory, and bless each person by name. Let your morning prayer be a faith offering to Me. Your voice will carry the message of your soul as your prayers resound in My ears like a Temple Psalm. Morning prayer is your time but take time to pray for those who need our help.

Prayer is an expression of faith.

And the **prayer** offered in faith will make the sick person well; the Lord will raise them. If they have sinned, they will be forgiven. (James 15:15 NIV)

DECEMBER 9

I wish that all of My children understood the excellent power of prayer. When souls unite to form a single bond, unbelievable things take shape. To the single soul, many things in life seem unlikely and impossible. To the gathered souls of many, prayer reduces mountain tops to manageable molehills. The greater power transforms the limited perception of one person into a wide-eyed experience of the assembled group.

Unison prayer unites the people of the earth and gathers in the angelic assembly in heaven. Prayer creates a sacred spiritual connection before My holy altar. What you say on earth is heard and multiplied in heaven. So, gather for worship and pray often and know that heavenly forces mirror what is done on earth. Blessed are My people when they gather in My name.

Unison prayer creates a spiritual union before the heavenly altar of God.

Another angel, who had a golden censer, came and stood at the altar. He was given much incense to offer, with the **prayers** of all God's people, on the golden altar in front of the throne. (Revelation 8:3 NIV)

DECEMBER 10

*Y*ou are My modern-day rock, My sacred heart. The stone is your confession of faith your faith in Me. I built My church upon this foundation of faith. Physical places of worship would not exist if it were not for spiritual foundations of faith. Let your faith become the great cornerstone of My church. Neither heaven nor hearth or other forces shall overcome which is built upon your faith.

My church will only be as strong as the saints who gather to worship Me. Commit yourselves to building each other up into a holy people. Confess your sins, lay aside your hates let go of petty differences. Let go of everything that will gnaw at the foundation on which I build My church. Fill My church with diverse colors, foreign sounds, and unfamiliar faces, and I will unite them all under one roof. You build the church, and I will call My people.

God has chosen you as the foundation of the church.

And I tell you that you are Peter, and on this rock, I will build my **church**, and the gates of Hades will not overcome it. (Matthew 6:18 NIV)

DECEMBER 11

*T*ry to care for each other with love and grace. My church on earth reflects My heavenly desire that all should experience My love and grace. Squabbles, feuds, and fights are not a holy representation of My divine will. When My children do not act like the saints they are, they reflect their agenda and not My will. Let My church be the gathering place for sinners and saints to meet to help each other. The church is a house of worship and prayer, but it can also be a spiritual hospital to heal the soul.

Practice pious behavior at all times. Piety has the same life you confess in the church as you live in the world. Let your actions match your confession. Do your best to keep everyone connected to Me. I am the source of strength for life. You are responsible for each other as members of the same spiritual family. Treat each other as you would treat a parent or child.

The church is responsible for their spiritual family.

If they still refuse to listen, tell it to the **church**; and if they refuse to listen even to the **church**, treat them as you would a pagan or a tax collector. (Matthew 18:17 NIV)

DECEMBER 12

*E*ven the most damaging behavior can change. I never gave up on My servant Paul even as he tried to destroy the birth of My lovely church. Hate created an elite mindset that was fearful of what he thought My church would bring. The advent of something new does not always mean it will replace what exists. Paul's eyes were closed so that he could see my movement. Sometimes I have to cover the familiar so that new can spring up.

Keep your eyes wide open to My movement in the church. I have always led saints in dew directions and down unfamiliar paths. Do not believe that something is wrong until you have determined if you are right. If something is of Me, it will happen with or without your support. Prayer is always your first act, and destructive behavior is always the last.

Give new things a chance to blossom into Godly events.

But Saul began to destroy the **church**. Going from house to house, he dragged off both men and women and put them in prison. (Acts 8:3 NIV)

DECEMBER 13

I am your encourager in life. I am the most outstanding cheerleader you will ever have. My encouragement is not for your benefit alone. I encourage you so that you will inspire others. I create a spiritual flow that comes from Me, flows through you, and excites the recipient. Let your church understand this dynamic flow of spiritual energy. The church is like a golden lampstand. You serve to illuminate the world around you. Your flame lights you, and it brightens the world of the person next to you.

You must also carry your light into the dark and dismal world of the lost and lonely. Many of My children desperately seek Me but cannot find their way because they lack the light to illuminate their path. Be My light to the world, oh My bright child. Shine with all the intent and purpose you were given and bring My lonely children to Me.

Blessed are those who illuminate others' paths. They shall be called the lights of the world.

Then the **church** throughout Judea, Galilee, and Samaria enjoyed a time of peace and was strengthened. Living in the fear of the Lord and encouraged by the Holy Spirit, it increased in numbers. (Acts 9:31 NIV)

DECEMBER 14

*Y*ou carry a great name and a holy mark upon you, My child. You are the namesake of the beloved Christ. The word Christ means the "anointed one." The Savior was anointed with the holy oil of divine salvation. All My children carry the spiritual filmily name of Christian. Wear your reputation well, My child. My name will always be visible to the world around you by your loving acts of faith. The holy waters of salvation anointed your head and soul. The name of the three in one unity was proclaimed over your head and upon your soul. You were blessed on the inside while you were baptized on the outside. You are My child from head to toe and heart and soul. Together, you are My church on earth and My blessings from heaven.

Blessed are all who carry the name of Christian. They are the church.

And when he found him, he brought him to Antioch. So for a whole year, Barnabas and Saul met with the **church** and taught great numbers of people. The disciples were called Christians first at Antioch. (Acts 11:26 NIV)

DECEMBER 15

*M*y church is not just a random gathering of people. My church is a holy union of like-spirited people who gather to worship Me and live according to My will. Let your voices proclaim what your heart knows, and your soul feels. You unite out of love for My children and Me. There is no greater force in heaven or on earth than My divine love. My love is the power that moves the church to mission and compels My people to serve. Do not lose sight of your divine purpose.

Your divine purpose is to tend My garden. You no longer live in the Garden of Eden; you have the entire planet and all of its people for which to care. My universal church knows no bounds and has no limitations. You are to be My holy people who cover every corner of this planet to announce the name of the blessed Savior. Be diligent in your work, love with compassion and grace, and serve Me tirelessly.

You are a servant of God's global church.

To the **church** of God in Corinth, to those sanctified in Christ Jesus and called to be his holy people, together with all those everywhere who call on the name of our Lord Jesus Christ—their Lord and ours: (1 Corinthians 1:2 NIV)

December 16

*L*et your soul express the unity of mind and thought. It is challenging to serve as My people when you are not working out of spiritual unity. You will follow any thought or sentence that tickles your fancy. One group will go in one direction, and another group will pull in the opposite direction. At best, you create division among yourself. At the least, you have destroyed your divine purpose for being My church. Everyone loses if you divide yourselves.
Learn the art of spiritual multiplication. Find your holy common ground in Me and start from that sacred place. You all carry the sacred name of Christian; now behave as if you are who your title says you are. Live into your namesake. Your Christian name will flood the earth with My grace, and the world will come to know My love. Become the church I have called you to be.

Christian becomes a verb when you learn to live in unity.

I appeal to you, brothers and sisters, in the name of our Lord Jesus Christ, that all of you agree with one another in what you say and that there be no divisions among you, but that you be perfectly united in mind and thought. (1 Corinthians 1:10 NIV)

DECEMBER 17

I already live and move and fulfill your life, My child. Do you feel My presence this morning? Spiritual maturity means you become more aware, open, and receptive to My holy movement and presence. I dwell in you like your breath and heartbeat. Both give you life, but they are so much a part of you that you rarely provide them with attention. Do not take Me for granted, or you will miss the more significant part of your life.

The more you focus on Me, the more I reveal to you. Learn to take time from your work a day life, and pay attention to your life in the Spirit. Draw close to Me and see what you are missing. I hold a world of blessings for you in My loving hands. All things will be given to you in My due time. All will be granted to you when you make yourself ready to receive. Let the morning light your path to follow Me each day.

Spiritual growth comes with an awareness of God's presence in your life.

Brothers and sisters, I could not address you as people who live by the Spirit but as people who are still worldly—mere infants in Christ. (1 Corinthians 3:1 NIV)

December 18

Leave judgment to Me. It is too easy to judge a person by worldly standards, but I look at them through my love's spiritual eyes. The person begging on the corner may seem like a deerlick to you, but I see deep hidden emotional concurs that need My loving attention. The unruly children on the bus appear to be out of control. The children are wild with fear as they travel to visit a dying grandparent. The drunk on the park bench once lost his family and is now losing his life.

It is too easy to look down your nose at people when you don't understand their life stories. It is far more difficult to minister to the needs of a broken heart and a crushed soul. Take the long path around judgment, and you will find a soul that is waiting for your assistance. Gather your brothers and sisters of your church to try and find spiritual answers to worldly troubles. Judge your ministry readiness to all of My beloved children, and you will soon learn to change the world.

Your judgment alters little in the scheme of things; your service changes lives.

What business is it of mine to judge those outside the **church**? Are you not to judge those inside? (1 Corinthians 5:12 NIV)

DECEMBER 19

I have called you to live your life as a faithful follower. I have called you and commissioned you with My gifts and blessings to serve one another in love and grace. Follow your faith path, and you will always be close to Me. I call My children to be a community of biowaivers who share their spiritual gifts in service to My children and Me. You all have different skills for service, but everyone shares in the same ministry. Your ministry is to serve one other, the world, and Me.

Try not to stumble over the perceived order of importance you believe each of you has. I called you and equipped you for need, not by rank. Try to be the first to serve and the last to complain. Dedicate your spiritual energy to caring for the world's vast needs around you and your brothers and sisters within My church. Do not waste your time trying to change that which you cannot alter.

The church has many servants with different gifts but only one mission. Serve God and the children of God.

Nevertheless, each person should live as a believer in whatever situation the Lord has assigned to them, just as God has called them. This is the rule I lay down in all the **churches**. (1 Corinthians 7:17 NIV)

December 20

*T*he blessed Savior is your model for the Christian life. Follow his heavenly pattern as you walk in faith on this earth.   The church is named, claimed, and proclaimed to glorify the life of the Savior. I am the spiritual force that gives life and love to every being in the church. I am the same spiritual energy that rose with the Savior from the waters of the Jorden River. I led the Savior into the desert of temptation and cared for his needs afterward.

Enter the gates for worship and praise and raise your voice high in songs, hymns, and shouts of celebration. Worship the carrier of your salvation. I will fill your hearts and souls and move in you to make a divine connection. I am the spiritual force that connects heaven and earth at the center of your soul. Come and worship and follow your Savior.

The church is the connecting point for all past, present, and future acts of salvation.

And God placed all things under his feet and appointed him to be head over everything for the **church**, (Ephesians 1:22 NIV)

DECEMBER 21

*T*he church is the My throne on earth. Though My church, all nations shall come to know Me. By My church, all people shall come to worship Me. In My church, every child will know I love them. I placed My church on this earth to be a physical connection to My spiritual presence. The church is the gathering place for all My living saints. Let kindred spirits seeking to find Me gather in My sanctuary for worship and praise.

My church is the earthly portal to My heavenly presence. People from all over the earth can gather in one sacred place and find Me in the holy moments of worship. The unity of My church culminates in the diversity of My children. Rich and poor, young, and every language spoken on this earth is My church. Come and worship Me and seek My wisdom and counsel.

The church is a place of worship and a repository of God's glorious wisdom.

He intended that now, through the **church**, the manifold wisdom of God should be made known to the rulers and authorities in the heavenly realms, (Ephesians 3:10. NIV)

DECEMBER 22

*L*ive according to the faith you have. Unite with other spiritual-minded people to create something greater than what you currently are. When you feel your faith is failing, connect with others for support and encouragement. Every generation has its difficulties and dilemmas with which to deal. No person should be a lonely soul facing life's struggles alone. Gather together, My children, and share the wealth of knowledge and strength of faith you have in each other. Longsuffering and endurance need never be faced alone. I have placed you in a loving community with caring people to make difficult situations more bearable for you, My child. Surround yourself with caring spirits that are accountable to You and supportive of you. My church, you, and I form a spiritual trinity of lasting support and love. Come beneath the shelter of Mt Wings.

The church provides the leverage to ease the stress and strain of daily life.

Therefore, among God's **churches,** we boast about your persever-ance and faith in all the persecutions and trials you are enduring. (1 Thessalonians 1:4 NIV)

DECEMBER 23

*S*hare the blessings and gifts you were given, My sacred heart. Do not withhold the things that I intended you to share. Leadership in the church comes from preaching My word. Let all preachers focus on bringing the Good News to modern ears. The ancient biblical texts had a select audience of the time. So, the preacher of today must inject words from the past into contemporary life.

Blessed are the teachers who instruct on living a Christian lifestyle while following Me. The Bible is more than just a holy book; it is a blueprint for life. Listen to your teachers as they unfold the tutelage from the past in your life today. Worry less about your church position and focus more on what you can learn from one another.

Blessed are you when you are open to learning from your spiritual teachers.

The elders who direct the affairs of the **church** well are worthy of double honor, especially those whose work is preaching and teaching. (1 Timothy 5:17 NIV)

DECEMBER 24

*M*y church is the physical reality of your spiritual birth. Ever since the first person was born, there was a desire to worship Me. The desire to worship and commune with Me comes from the human spirit's yearning to be at one with Me. There is a natural inclination to gather as a band of spirits. The gathering forms the church, which is the nursery for the firstborn of heavenly places.

Be very aware of the purpose of My church. You are to encourage each other in a life of perfection. Perfection is never a place or a desired goal. Perfection is a moving target that follows My lead. You must learn to shift and scuffle with the changing times. Perfection comes when you are in the right spot at the right time to serve your children and Me. When your life is aligned with Me, then we will share the momentary taste of perfection.

Spiritual perfection comes in the moments we align our lives with serving and loving God.

To the **church** of the firstborn, whose names are written in heaven. You have come to God, the Judge of all, to the spirits of the righteous made perfect. (Hebrews 12:23 NIV)

December 25

*E*very one of My earthly churches has a guardian angel watching over it. You worship in a physical building, but you are guided and guarded by spiritual forces. Do not think that this is such a great thing, My child. You are a spiritual being as you have your human experience. Physical bodies gather in a temporal location to worship in body and spirit.

The blessed Savior was born in a physical location at this historical point in time to touch all of My children's spiritual lives. You celebrate his birth on a specific day because your spirit yearns to draw close. Just as angels watched over the birth of the Savior, so they tend over your life today.

Behold, I bring you good news to all the churches. Today your Savior is born.

"To the angel of the **church** in Ephesus write: These are the words of him who holds the seven stars in his right hand and walks among the seven golden lampstands. (Revelation. 2:1 NIV)

DECEMBER 26

*Y*our earthly life begins and ends in Me, oh sacred heart. Let the rays of the early morning light bring forth your hope for what lies beyond this life on earth. Your hope is this, what begins in Me, will end with Me, and will continue forever beside Me. This is the message that all of My churches must preach. The Good News was born, lived, died, and rose again in the life of the blessed Savior. He is the model for the passageway of eternal life.

I have placed an angel at the door of each of My churches. The angel whispers the Good News to everyone who enters for worship. Listen to the message of the angel every time you pass through the threshold of My church. Do not lose sight of the fact that we are not separated by death. Death is just a passageway to eternal life.

The church carries the message of the promise of life eternal; listen to it.

"To the angel of the **church** in Smyrna write: These are the words of him who is the First and the Last, who died and came to life again. (Revelation 2:8 NIV)

DECEMBER 27

*M*y holy words go directly to the point. My words can convince, confirm and even convict the hearer of My message. My words confirm the message of My everlasting love for you. Hearing and accepting My words are the foundation of your faith. As My message takes root and grows in you, become convinced that I am real, and your desire to be with Me grows stronger every day.
You must also realize that My words carry the power of conviction. You hear My message, and you realize your life needs to change. Confessions expose your conviction and invite My forgiveness from sin. Your faith exposes your sin, and you receive My healing forgiveness. Let the church be your healing pool of grace. My word is preached, and healing and health are received.

God's Word has the power to convict our sins and confirm our faith.

"To the angel of the **church** in Pergamum, write: My message convinces your faith that My words are trustworthy and true. These are the words of him who has the sharp, double-edged sword. (Revelation 2:12 NIV)

December 28

*F*ire has the power to remold and reshape lives. My church is the fiery furnace where lives are changed and souls receive refinement. I bring the same refining fire as I brought with the flaming tongues of fire when I gave my church life. The first disciples huddled in fear, but they rose in power as I refined their souls. Do not fear, for I bring you the fire of love and grace. My fire does not burn. It has the power to bless.

Stand in silent stillness and let the holy fire of My grace cleanse you and refine your soul. I will forge your corruptible body into a perfect incorruptible spirit. I will reform your dented and dark heart into a soul of brightly polished bronze. You will stand as a living statue of the power I bring to all of My children. Do not fear the fire of refinement; it glows with the power of My love.

God's love is the refining fire of God's grace.

To the angel of the **church** in Thyatira write: These are the words of the Son of God, whose eyes are like blazing fire and whose feet are like burnished bronze. (Revelation 2:18 NIV)

DECEMBER 29

Listen to the message of My angel divine. My angel has a message to all of my churches that are the heavenly portals for earthly gatherings. Do not slumber in your spiritual search for Me. Keep your eyes wide open to My movement among you. I am not a resting Spirit but a Spirit of action and dynamic movement. I go where My people need Me. Pay attention so you can follow Me. If you look back, you can quickly see My patterns of shifting and moving in new directions. I moved the disciples out on Pentecost. They could not remain in the upper room of safety; they had to go out and proclaim My name to the nations. My church is not just a resting place for the spiritually weary but a launching pad for those who will follow Me. Sing your hymns, say your prayers, and preach your sermons. When you conclude your worship, service, grab your coats and follow Me to serve My people.

The church is not the endpoint for spiritual rest but the starting point for Christian service.

"To the angel of the **church** in Sardis write: These are the words of him who holds the seven spirits of God and the seven stars. I know your deeds; you have a reputation of being alive, but you are dead. Revelation 3:1 NIV)

DECEMBER 30

I have given you the keys to My heavenly reign in your earthly church. Remember that you are only the keeper of the keys and not the guard to the gate. I called you to open the gates wide so that all of My children may have access to the blessings of My church. If you deny any of My beloved children, you also exclude Me. Remember, My blessed child, that none of you are worthy to enter the doors of My church, but by My loving grace, all are welcome. You hold the David Key which is only a one-way key. It will open doors, but it will not shut and lock them. When you shut the doors of your heart from My love, you also close the doors of your church. Do everything in your power to prevent this tragic event from taking place. You not only lock the world out, but you also seal yourself off from the people of My world. Closing your doors is your death sentence not easily reversed. Your future does not lie within you, but it stands on the outside, knocking you to enter. Open the door to your future, and follow Me.

The church's future is not contained in its walls but lies outside its' doors.

"To the angel of the **church** in Philadelphia write: These are the words of him who is holy and true, who holds the key of David. What he opens no one can shut, and what he shuts no one can open. (Revelation 3:7 NIV)

DECEMBER 31

*T*here is an order to all things under heaven and on this earth, My blessed sacred heart. My creation has no blemish or bruise. Everything I created is perfect in its own way. Learn to appreciate My creation first, and then you will enjoy it more. Your role is to be a living witness to what I have made. Let your life point to Me at all times. I am the true holy north for all that exists. Let your faith draw you to Me like a magnet.

Gather together as My beloved church and show the rest of the world the path to My divine presence. After all, all My children live in My creation's garden; they should also enjoy the comfort of My loving presence. Let your "Amen" end your worship of Me and begin your service to Me. Faith must never become a noun in the life of My church. Faith is the verb with which I send you into the world. Carry your faith with you as you follow Me.

Amen is not an ending but a new beginning.

To the angel of the **church** in Laodicea write: These are the words of the Amen, the faithful and true witness, the ruler of God's creation.   (Revelation 3:14 NIV)